WHEN AMERICA FIGHTS

WHEN AMERICA FIGHTS
THE USES OF U.S. MILITARY FORCE

Donald M. Snow

University of Alabama

CQ PRESS

A Division of Congressional Quarterly Inc.
Washington, D.C.

CQ Press
A Division of Congressional Quarterly Inc.
1414 22nd Street, N.W.
Washington, DC 20037

(202) 822-1475; (800) 638-1710

www.cqpress.com

When America Fights was typeset by Septima Design, Athens, Ohio.
Cover by: Ed Atkeson/Berg Design
Printed and bound in the United States of America

04 03 02 01 00   5 4 3 2 1

LIBRARY OF CONGRESS CATALOGING-IN-PUBLICATION DATA

Snow, Donald M., 1943–
    When America fights : the uses of U.S. military force / Donald M.
Snow.
        p. cm.
    Includes bibliographical references and index.
    ISBN 1-56802-521-1 (pbk.)
    1. National security—United States. 2. United States—Military
policy. 3. World politics—1989– 4. United States—Foreign
relations—1993– I. Title.
    UA23 .S52624 2000
    355'.033573—dc21
                                00-009486

Contents

Tables and Figures

Preface

When, where, how, and to what ends the United States will apply force in the new century are matters of intense debate and controversy in policy and academic circles. The collapse of Soviet communism in 1991 removed the clear opponent to which U.S. military policy and strategy had been tethered for the previous half-century. In its place are diverse and diffuse military contingencies that seem less compelling than those we confronted during the cold war.

The controversy has several aspects and anomalies. The United States has reduced its military capabilities dramatically since the end of the cold war, yet our military is proportionately more dominant on the world stage now than it was then, and the rate at which American troops deploy has increased. The deployments increasingly are in unglamorous peacekeeping operations in parts of the developing world where our interests are not at stake and with which our troops are unfamiliar and disinterested. The effects of these peacekeeping operations on the U.S. military establishment include sagging troop morale, diminished force retention, and budget strains.

A central contention of *When America Fights* is that the major occasions in which the United States might use force over the next five to ten years will be in peacekeeping operations similar to those in Kosovo, Bosnia, and Somalia. *When America Fights* extrapolates from those operations in an effort to analyze the future uses of military force: what types of forces will be needed, how and when will they be employed, and what can they reasonably be expected to achieve?

The debate about where and when the United States should fight is more than abstract; it has been a concrete, partisan issue for a long time. Most Republicans oppose U.S. involvement in places where American vital interests are not at stake, which would preclude U.S. participation in most peacekeeping operations. At the same time, the party calls for increased investment in defense, without specifying where that military capacity might be employed. The Democrats remain supportive, although not too loudly, of the so-called Clinton Doctrine, which permits American intervention in some of these conflicts. The issues play out in rancorous debates in Congress not only over the U.S. defense budget and force structure but also over payment of UN dues and UN assessments for specific peacekeeping operations. Regardless of the outcome of the 2000 presidential and congressional elections, these points of disagreement will continue to vex the U.S. government at the policy and implementation levels.

The purpose of *When America Fights* is to clarify the debate by placing the elements and concepts of the disagreement over American force in accessible, jargon-free language. It makes suggestions about the direction U.S. policy might or even should take, outlines the difficulties associated with the different objectives, and provides a checklist by which to assess when the United States should intervene in the developing world. The fundamental purpose is not to advocate one solution but to present the alternatives as an aid to framing discussions. It is my hope to add to the debate currently under way in policy circles. In courses on American foreign policy, defense policy, or international relations, I hope this book will serve as a useful instrument for framing the debate over the use of force in the future.

The book is arranged in a logical and cumulative manner. Chapter 1 assesses the policy debate and describes the current state of the international environment in which decisions to use force are made. An analysis of the current pattern of violence is included. Chapter 2 introduces the subject of strategy. It begins by discussing the strategy-making process and explaining how that process affects strategic decisions. It then uses the dichotomies of realism-idealism and internationalism-neoisolationism to describe the strategic orientations that individuals bring to the policy debate. The chapter concludes with my suggestion that the United States adopt a strategy of *realistic internationalism* as its approach to international conflict.

Chapter 3 provides an overview of the "menu of violence" that the United States may confront and to which it may respond with military force. The distinction between "deployments of necessity" and "deployments of choice" helps organize this discussion. It concludes that involvement in peacekeeping operations is the most likely form of U.S. force employment in the future.

Chapter 4 looks at the problems that the United States, or any other state, encounters when intervening in civil wars by means of peacekeeping operations. The deployment in Kosovo is a major example to which the chapter often returns, since the outcome of that experience will color Americans' attitudes toward future endeavors. The chapter examines the nature and purposes of such missions as well as the operational problems associated with them. Chapter 5, the conclusion, looks at contemporary influences on strategy, lays out the strategy of realistic internationalism, and provides guidelines for its implementation drawn largely from current policy.

I would like to thank those who have read and commented on the manuscript. Special thanks go to three good friends and colleagues: Phil Myers of Western Kentucky University, a talented military historian as well as one of my college roommates and fraternity brothers; and Cols. (ret.) Jim McCallum and Mark Walsh, colleagues at the U.S. Army War College and now analysts at the U.S. Army Peacekeeping Institute. All made generous and valuable suggestions. In addition, helpful comments were made by Lt. Col. Gwendolyn Hall, U.S. Air Force Academy; Witold Lukaszewski, Sam Houston State University; George Quester, University of Maryland; Sheldon Simon, Arizona State University; and Gen. Fred Woerner (USA, ret.), Boston University. All errors remaining, of course, are mine.

Donald M. Snow
Tuscaloosa, Alabama

WHEN AMERICA FIGHTS

Introduction: Military Force in the Post–Cold War Environment

THE USE OF AMERICAN AIR FORCES IN SUPPORT OF THE NATO operations directed at the Yugoslav province of Kosovo in early 1999 and the use of ground forces in the peacekeeping operation after the fighting had ended provide a convenient lightning rod for a discussion of the appropriate uses of American military force in the post–cold war environment. As the slaughter and displacement—mostly of ethnic Albanian, Muslim Kosovars by the Serb military and police—continued, the United States and its NATO allies debated how to end the carnage. Reflecting the American fascination with airpower, a bombing campaign was the first means suggested to bring the Serbs to heel. NATO hoped that a peace settlement would somehow appear, and in June, after tough negotiations in which the Russians played a major role, it did.

Allied leaders surmised that the Serbs (who dominate the legal government of Yugoslavia, of which Kosovo is a province) would withdraw rather than endure the relentless bombardment to which the country was subjected for eleven weeks. Keeping order would pass to an international peacekeeping force on the lines of the Stabilization Force (SFOR) in Bosnia. Because the United States is the predominant force in the world, naturally there would have to be an American contingent on the ground in Kosovo to stamp the enterprise with legitimacy after peace was restored.

To the surprise of most analysts, the air campaign worked. Although the bombing initially solidified public support for Yugoslav president Slobodan Milošević, it gradually eroded Serbian will and convinced Milošević to accept

1

a peace settlement largely on allied terms. However, the bombing also increased the flight of Kosovars out of the province, as the Yugoslav army and paramilitary forces engaged in ethnic cleansing with a vengeance while the bombs dropped. Most of the Kosovar population fled, creating an enormous refugee problem in Albania, Macedonia (technically the Former Yugoslav Republic of Macedonia), and Montenegro and later a massive relocation and repatriation problem.

Policy Disarray

The debate over the operation reflected the disarray of American policy toward the use of force in the post–cold war world. Despite the articulation of policy guidelines in documents like Presidential Decision Directive (PDD) 25 (which specified the conditions for U.S. participation in various ways, including using force, around the world) and PDD 56 (which authorized contingency planning for various scenarios), we yammered about what to do in Kosovo because there was no consensus on a coherent policy for determining when and when not to put American forces in harm's way. We appeared not even to know the proper questions to ask: What interests does the United States have at stake in this internal war? What would we seek to accomplish by being there? When would conditions be such that we could leave?

PDD 25 provides some guidance on these matters but never entered the public debate. When President Bill Clinton announced in February 1999 the prospect of inserting Americans into Kosovo as part of a multilateral effort, he insisted that a peace would have to be in place before the deployment occurred, that the prospects of the peace holding would have to be relatively sure, and that an "end game" for withdrawal would have to be defined. Apart from vague references to a U.S. stake in peace in Europe and the fear of "another" Balkan conflagration that could spread to NATO allies Greece and Turkey, however, the president hardly mentioned American interests or how military forces could achieve them. His first two conditions (peace and peace holding) were met when the "peacekeepers" began entering Kosovo in June 1999; if anyone knew when U.S. troops were going to be able to leave, they were being very quiet about it.

U.S. strategists had benchmarks, for we had been in similar situations before. The post–cold war deployments in Bosnia, Somalia, Iraq (notably the ongoing—and seemingly endless—Operations Northern and Southern

Watch), and even Haiti all share, at least to some degree, three characteristics with the proposed deployment in Kosovo.

First, they have occurred in places about which American understanding was deficient or, in the case of Haiti, where we chose to engage in self-delusion about a situation that we had reason to understand. What do we know about Kosovo that would encourage American involvement?

Second, all lack sizable American interests that would, under the realist paradigm that organized cold-war determinations, justify the insertion of American forces. The United States had some interest in Haiti, if it was no more than stanching the flow of boat people to the south Florida shoreline, but one would be hard pressed to find any geopolitical interests in the others. What concrete, direct American interests are affected by *any* outcome to the hostilities in Kosovo? That question underpins this book.

Third, in each instance, it has not been entirely clear what the United States sought to achieve, and hence, when we could proclaim "mission accomplished" and ride off into the sunset triumphant. We are still stuck in Bosnia and Iraq and cannot leave unless we are willing to throw those we have protected to the wolves. We limped out of Somalia with an empty feeling, muttering that we had saved a bunch of lives but were leaving the country in the same state of anarchy that had existed when we arrived. We left Somalia little better than we found it. After we "upheld democracy" to Haiti and left, it slowly slid backward, and today our wildest hopes are that the government of René Préval will not deteriorate to the point we feel the need to go back. In Kosovo we face a civil confrontation where only mutually exclusive outcomes are acceptable to the parties (independence to the Albanian Kosovars, continued union to the Serbs) and where animosities and passions go back at least as far as the battle fought in 1389 that ended Serbian independence until the twentieth century. What is the "end game" for "peace with honor" (to borrow Richard Nixon's ambition for Vietnam) in that situation?

These are all questions of grand policy and strategy, and they are not being asked or answered with any clarity. U.S. actions seem to demonstrate otherwise. A decade has elapsed since the cold war evaporated, and one of the victims was the structure of threats to American and other Western interests that dictated American national security policy and the military strategy and force structure flowing from that policy. The questions that we asked during the cold war have not changed; they are the same ones that we ask now. The difference between then and now is that we had answers on which most of us agreed then; it is not clear we *have* answers now, much less a consensus around them.

We need a structure, and consensus on that structure, to help us avoid making errors in military displacements and to add meaning and substance to our role at the negotiating table. The world has changed since 1989, and one of the obvious areas of change is in the structure of threats with military consequences. During the cold war the West confronted an overwhelming military threat that, if not met and blunted, could have had catastrophic consequences for the United States and its friends. That clear threat has disappeared and almost certainly will not reappear in the foreseeable future. As the Department of Defense's 1997 *Quadrennial Defense Review* rightfully concluded, the United States lacks a "peer competitor" (truly threatening enemy), and one is unlikely to emerge for another decade. The threats today are smaller and narrower, metaphorical flea bites on the elephant's hide: proliferation of weapons of mass destruction, terrorist attacks, chaotic bloodletting in what during the cold war was called the Third World. All of these issues are nasty and upsetting; they are also uniformly much less important or threatening than the cold war confrontation.

We *know* that the world has changed and that it is far less threatening than it used to be, but we do not *act* as if we realize the implication of this change. In 1996, for instance, the United States defense budget was reported at over $270 billion, a figure far smaller than projections from the cold war would have suggested had the cold war continued. Nonetheless, the U.S. defense budget is still enormous by current world standards. Russia, the country with the second largest budget (which it subsequently cut back), spent roughly $70 billion. If you add the Russian budget to the next five largest spenders, you still do not quite equal American spending. And those next five countries are Japan, Germany, France, Britain, and Italy—all American allies. Only when you add the $12.5 billion spent by China, the eighth largest spender, do you surpass the U.S. defense budget.

Are we stuck in some kind of conceptual time warp, trapped in the images of the past and unable to escape to the present or future? What *is* the basis of American national security policy? Clearly, it is not the military deterrence or physical frustration of communist advancement in the world (the military element of the foreign policy of containment). Communist expansionism around the world—and more clearly in some places than in others—posed basic threats to American interests that were important enough (vital, in other words) to demand a forceful response. Soviet nuclear-armed missiles hung like the shadow of death over American soil, and deterrence of their use was clearly necessary for American survival.

The American foreign policy of containment and its military backbone prevented the communist states from breaching the containment line by force. This forty-year effort brought clarity to American purpose. Indeed, knowing the nature of the threat and the physical shape of the military problem made countering it a relatively straightforward, if expensive and occasionally frustrating, process. Deducing battlefield tactics from American foreign policy was a nice, neat, logical exercise that began with clearly articulated principles that provided guidance in almost all instances. The rules and the signposts were there to be followed.

Admittedly, the deductive logic could be carried a bit too far, as it was in Vietnam. The first principle of containment there (as career diplomat George F. Kennan initially warned and consistently pointed out) led to a military involvement of a size and nature that far outstripped any possible U.S. interests. Instead of using existing policies for managing relations and operations, we let events drive policy, especially when the events did not seem to fit the policy very closely.

The conceptual clarity of the cold war vanished in the rubble of the Berlin Wall and the demise of Soviet communism. No first principle of the nature, clarity, and force of containment has emerged to be translated into defense policy, military strategy, forces, and the like. The Clinton foreign policy of "engagement and enlargement" is, in a national security sense, soft and flabby. It may be fine for guiding foreign economic policy and for organizing our stance toward the globalizing economy, but it does not provide clear guidance one can translate into the size and mission of the military. Where and how should force be used to promote and protect the expanding "circle of market democracies," which is the goal and centerpiece of engagement and enlargement?

Partly reflecting our altered environment, we are conceptually adrift. If we reask the question, "Why would we want to send American troops into Kosovo?" there is no first principle from which we can follow the logic train down to a dictate to save the Kosovars. We lack the principled base for making defense policy decisions. We cannot create scenarios because we cannot imagine how the landscape upon which we operate will look after we leave. We fail even to ask the question: What will we gain in the outcome? President Clinton's public justification for intervening in Bosnia ("It's the right thing to do") provides no guidance for forming strategy. One has to look beyond rhetoric to find helpful guidance, such as our interest in promoting Balkan stability.

Toward a New First Principle

Maybe the absence of a first principle is inevitable given the amorphous nature of the new world order. Although the idea of a lack of principles sounds bad (after all, it is not good, in a general sense, to be unprincipled), is it necessarily so? I think not, at least in the extreme. The ongoing world situation is so disorderly that the only effects that principles, especially rigid ones, could have would be to render much policy irrelevant to situations it does not fit. Moreover, principles might even be pernicious, when their application forces the country into positions with unfortunate consequences. The American analyst Edward Luttwak makes this point about U.S. policy toward China: were the United States to apply a rigid policy on human rights to China, it would force us either to condemn China or to look the other way at human rights and other violations. Neither is a pretty prospect, and the dichotomy leads Luttwak to favor an "incoherent" foreign policy, by which he means a pragmatic, case-by-case policy. Much of the world may display ambiguity, even ambivalence, making it difficult to hone and apply overarching principles. Maybe Americans (like everyone else) do not understand the new dynamics. Or maybe the world is so tranquil that the hard work of forming a coherent national security policy is unnecessary. If that is the case, maybe pragmatism is enough.

The problem with embracing pragmatism is that it can lead to "ad hocracy" (taking every situation as unique and starting from scratch in determining what the response will be). Once again, take Kosovo. Is there anything in the American experience that suggests the virtue or the undesirability of becoming involved there? The answer depends on whether Kosovo is a case of "ethnic cleansing" or something else entirely. What is U.S. policy in regard to humanitarian intervention (of which involvement in Kosovo would be an instance, at least as far as the ethnic Albanians are concerned)? Is it like Bosnia? Or is it *sui generis*? If the latter, do we have any idea what to do when we get there, how those already there will react to our presence, and when we can leave Kosovo a better place (minimal definition: a place we are unlikely to have to occupy again in the foreseeable future)?

As the reader can surmise, I am not entirely satisfied with the current state of intellectual affairs. We are not so much in disagreement over the nature and dictates of American forces and how and where and why they will be used as we are in disarray: no one has proposed anything resembling a comprehensive national security policy that can be translated into a grand military strategy and lower levels of strategy. No wonder we look confused to the rest of the world.

There is a certain amount of irony here. The cold war was organized around the so-called realist paradigm, which, among other things, legitimized the use of force as an instrument of policy (the Prussian dictum). The realists who ran policy applauded the construct as hardheaded and, well, realistic. Those who decried the use of force, who sought (and still seek) to diminish its influence, attacked the construct.

After the cold war ended, the proponents and opponents of the realist paradigm remained the same, but the consequences of their arguments changed. The old realists, sometimes referred to as "hawks," look at today's world and see few situations worth putting American lives at risk, because no serious interests are threatened. Their opponents, "doves," see a world of ideals, where those who suppress and kill others should be pilloried on the altar of universal human rights; the doves see many places where the employment of American forces is justified. And so the tables have turned. The security environment has been turned on its conceptual head.

I think that the level of confusion can be reduced and that we can find a policy, somewhere between rigid principle and no principle at all, that can answer the question raised in the subtitle about where American force can be used in this post–cold war world. The answers, or suggestions, will not be entirely pleasing to those who prefer a deductive world guided by universal principles or to those pragmatists who believe that every process is inductive.

The Structure of the Book and of the Argument

This book will follow a five-step (and five-chapter) progression. Chapter 1 will deal with the environment that now exists, emphasizing and explaining the realist paradigm, which dominated the cold war and at least implicitly continues to guide policy makers. Major questions to be asked are how much of that paradigm is still relevant and where is it relevant? The preliminary answer, shared by Max Singer and Aaron Wildavsky and more recently by Robert Keohane and Joseph S. Nye Jr., is that it is still applicable in some parts of the world and not so relevant in others. The locus of conflict today—and that part of the world where the paradigm is probably still most applicable—

is the old Second and Third Worlds (which I call the Second Tier). Although recourse to violence remains a policy option for many states and especially for internal movements (congruent with the paradigm), the application of the criterion of vital interests (also at the root of the realist paradigm) would suggest that most of these situations do not constitute grounds for U.S. involvement because of what I call an *interest-threat mismatch*. In addition to the paradigm's limited applicability in the Second Tier and its inapplicability in the First Tier (the most advanced countries, among whom military force is not an option), there may be a *paradigm-reality mismatch* that suggests the need to alter the paradigm.

Chapter 2 will turn to the process by which we think about the use of military force as an instrument of policy. Following from the framework developed by Donald M. Snow and Dennis Drew, it will emphasize the relationship between military force and the political purposes for which it is maintained. Although this analysis is firmly rooted in the realist paradigm, it is possible to exorcise those elements of the paradigm that do not apply. For instance, much of the accumulated wisdom about the use of force is based on two presumptions that are no longer evident. One is the "Napoleonic corollary" to the paradigm, which suggests that force should be used for clear and obviously worthy purposes—overthrowing dictators, protecting "good" regimes from communist insurgents, repelling invasions. Few of the contemporary conflicts rise to this level of worthiness. The other presumption is the clear distinction between war and peace. Our consistent (if implied) model is *peace-war-peace*, where peace is shattered by acts of war, where we fight to overcome evil-doers, and where the end state is the resurrection of the normal condition, which is peace. See how well that model applies in Kurdistan, Bosnia, or Kosovo.

The third chapter will turn to an assessment of the present and likely future pattern of violence in the world—the "menu" of opportunities the United States will have over the next decade or so to employ force. None of these opportunities is likely to be at the upper rungs of the spectrum of violence. Most likely, they will be at the lower ends: from paramilitary activities such as terrorism and proliferation to widespread, nasty internal wars (of which Kosovo is a current example).

The most prominent form of violence is the chaotic *new internal war*. One aspect of new internal wars is their unmilitary character: in most instances, there is very little "combat" in the conventional sense of the term. (With the exception of some Kosovo Liberation Army actions against the

Serbs, Kosovo fits the definition.) Rather, the method of "fighting" is for partisans on one side to attack and either kill or displace supporters of the other side. The purpose of this activity, to the extent it is articulated explicitly, is seldom to overthrow a government or restore a government's power (the traditional aims of civil war), and the pattern of action greatly increases hatreds that make postwar reconciliation all the more difficult, if not impossible. It is a very personal kind of violence. It is hard to imagine, for instance, how Bosnians or Kosovars will ever be capable of embracing their Serb brethren.

This description of the pattern of conflict is necessary as a preface and framework for looking at the problem of intervention, which is the topic of the fourth chapter. The nonmilitary nature of these conflicts renders military solutions inapplicable: the enemy to be subdued will not stand and fight. Foreign soldiers (including Americans) inserted in these circumstances are placed in a never-never land between being a fighting force and being a constabulary enforcing a peace that not everyone wants. The absence of political leaderships seeking control means there are no unambiguous internal groups to whom the mantle of government can be easily passed.

With the landscape of opportunity established, the fourth chapter will ask what we want to do in different circumstances, on the one hand, and what we realistically can do, on the other. This latter discussion in turn will come to center on the problem of successful intervention in the internal affairs of states, a prospect often advocated (once again, as in Kosovo) but with grossly inadequate analysis of two factors: the impact of intervention and the prospects and mechanics of moving toward desired end states (ours and, we hope, theirs).

Unraveling what can and should be done requires us to make a pair of determinations, the explication of which will dominate the chapter. First, policy makers need to assess the sort of politico-military situation they confront, since that determines the kinds of forces they will need and what the forces will have to do. Three basic situations will be described. The first is a state of *war*, in which case the basic task will be ending hostilities, what I call *peace imposition*, which requires combat forces. The second is *unstable peace*, where peace has been imposed but is dependent on the continued presence of outside forces. The task in this situation is *peace enforcement*—keeping the former combatants from resuming their mayhem—which requires a mixture of forces. Peace enforcement represents a midpoint on the continuum between the extremes of a peace that is barely holding and one that is embraced by almost all. The third, and simplest, situation is where peace has been reinstalled and all parties prefer it to war. The intervenor's task in this case is one form of *peacekeeping*, keeping the former combatants apart while a meaningful peace process grinds toward success. This role requires a lightly armed constabulary force that mostly observes and reports violations.

The other determination deals with the goal of the proposed mission. There are two distinctly different alternatives. The first, and simplest, is to stop the fighting and keep the combatants apart for some period of time (the length of the intervention), in the hope that some form of reconciliation will occur. *Conflict suppression*, as we will call it, consists of peace imposition (if necessary) and peace enforcement; the latter is necessary when some form of peace accord has been negotiated but its durability is in question (the Dayton Accords and Bosnia, the accords on Kosovo). This kind of task is "doable"; the question is whether it makes any long-term difference.

The second possible form a mission can undertake is *state building*, which is the conscious decision to help build a viable postintervention state in which peace holds after the outsiders leave (a condition of *stable peace*). By definition, new internal wars occur in states that are somehow "broken." State building involves identifying people (both criminals to be arrested and punished and potential leaders to be nurtured and promoted), building institutional bases for governance, repairing infrastructure, reviving or creating an economic base that will attract outside investment, and a host of other activities that are nonmilitary, even if they require a military shield behind which to develop. This form of mission is more arduous, long term, and problematical to achieve

The analysis of the politico-military situation and definition of goals lead to the last chapter. We know that the physical environment is violent, chaotic, and unsettling. The question is: How much effort are we willing to expend to try to bring that reality into conformity with the world we prefer? Is that vision attainable, and if so, at what price? To the extent that military effort is involved, what are those costs in blood and treasure, and are we willing to bear those costs? If not, are we willing to subsidize others to do those things for us? What does the role we choose portend for the size and shape of the military forces that we need to carry out the mandate? Or can we engage in a deductive exercise sufficient to get from grand policy to the muddy boot soldier on the ground.

Much of the discussion in Chapter 5 is on new and uncharted ground. There does not exist, to my knowledge, any reliable instruction book for state building in a place like Kosovo that, if studied and applied, would allow a policy maker to predict with confidence whether a particular mission would succeed and thus be a good path to follow. It is also not entirely clear how long a state under what amounts to a protectorate will acquiesce before it begins to wonder about the permanence of this new form of colonization. Where we may break some new ground is in the exploration of some of these kinds of questions.

Bibliography

Keohane, Robert O., and Joseph S. Nye Jr. "Power and Interdependence in the Information Age." *Foreign Affairs* 77 (September–October 1998): 81–94.

Luttwak, Edward. "Why We Need an Incoherent Foreign Policy." *Washington Quarterly* 21 (winter 1998): 21–31.

Singer, Max, and Aaron Wildavsky. *The Real World Order: Zones of Peace, Zones of Turmoil.* Rev. ed. Chatham, N.J.: Chatham House, 1996.

Snow, Donald M. *Distant Thunder: Patterns of Conflict in the Developing World.* 2d ed. Armonk, N.Y.: M. E. Sharpe, 1997.

————. *National Security: Defense Policy in a Changed International Order.* 4th ed. New York: St. Martin's Press, 1998.

————. *The Shape of the Future: World Politics in a New Century.* 3d ed. Armonk, N.Y.: M. E. Sharpe, 1999.

————. *UnCivil Wars: International Security and the New Internal Conflicts.* Boulder: Lynne Rienner Publishers, 1996.

Snow, Donald M., and Dennis M. Drew. *From Lexington to Desert Storm: War and Politics in the American Experience.* Armonk, N.Y.: M. E. Sharpe, 1994.

1 | Policy Adrift

IT IS FAIR TO SAY THAT AMERICAN NATIONAL SECURITY POLICY IS, and has been since the Soviet bloc and the rest of the communist world began to crumble ten years ago, rudderless and adrift in an international environment very different from that of the cold war. The cold war was concrete and highly structured, and it presented real dangers and challenges around which the policy of containment and its concomitant military strategies logically flowed. Most important, policy and strategy were logically connected, both intellectually and in terms of force structure and capabilities. We knew the problems and what to do about them. The cold war was part of our way of life.

All that has disappeared. As the dust settled from the crash of the Berlin Wall and communism disappeared, so too did the rationale for the way we viewed the international environment and attempted to manipulate it to our national advantage. The policy of containment makes no sense when there is nothing to contain. The Air-Land Battle strategy designed to blunt a mighty Soviet thrust into West Germany lacks coherence when there is no red menace. Huge stocks of antitank weapons are not so sensible when we have the only formidable tank army left in the world. The same could be said about hunter-killer submarines and a host of other systems and preparations for their employment.

Georgi Arbatov, then director of the USA and Canada Institute in Moscow, defined the U.S. national security dilemma best when he said in 1990, "We have done a terrible thing to you. We have deprived you of an enemy." To a policy driven by an enemy, it was close to a mortal blow.

But the forces and ways of looking at problems associated with the containment policy have refused to die. A decade later, there is little to suggest that American national security policy has changed very much. In documents such as the annual *National Security Strategy of the United States,* one sees hardly anything that looks like national *security* strategy. Certainly, the grand foreign policy of containment has gone by the boards, replaced by the policy of engagement and enlargement espoused by the administration of Bill Clinton, but that policy is about economics and how to encourage the emergence of market democracies in the globalizing economy. The security rationale has hardly changed at all. One of the tools that is absent from the implementation of engagement and enlargement is military force. We are left with the skeleton of a grand national strategy, with little military content to guide the development of a new national military strategy.

This is not to say there has been no intellectual activity within the military or the broader defense intellectual community. All of the services have tried to look into the future to figure out what the national security environment will look like and hence what kinds of challenges they may have to face. To cite the example of the U.S. Army, its Force XXI (twenty-first century) is advertised to have "knowledge-rich attributes" which will "be enhanced with the physical agility of Army After Next Era Battleforces" (U.S. Army War College, 1). What this means is the Army is trying to prepare for the kinds of exigencies it may face in the years ahead. The U.S. Army War College devoted its 1999 strategy conference (an annual affair) to the topic "Organizing for National Security in a New Century?" The emphasis was on *how* strategy should be made, *who* should make it, and whether the cold war organization was adequate, not on what national strategy should be.

The military's efforts to date are well and good and may be as much as the uniformed services can reasonably do within their mandates. The role of armed forces is not, after all, to decide national policy (although they may seek to influence those who do decide); their role is to implement national policy through appropriate military strategies.

This is a "bottom up" rather than "top down" approach to strategy formulation. A top-down approach would begin with the national political leadership saying, "Here is what we want to accomplish in the world, now you plan for the military contingencies that may apply." In a bottom-up approach, the political leadership says, "Here is what may go wrong in the world, and we want you to prepare for all of it, since we will not tell you in advance what you are supposed to do." Admittedly, any real planning will consist of both approaches, since the world is rarely so orderly that one overarching policy or strategy will cover everything.

What, then, is the guiding principle for national security policy and strategy? On the basis of what policy guidelines does the United States propose to apply and not apply military force in support of national goals? These are good questions; they do not have equally good answers.

Framers of national security policy and strategy have been remiss in answering these kinds of questions. Those in charge of the other instruments of national power have adapted to their new environment. Those in charge of diplomacy, for example, have recognized the implications of the U.S. stature as the sole remaining superpower, and they deal proactively with the world's problems. Progress in Northern Ireland and in the Arab-Israeli confrontation are but two results of this new activism. In the economic realm, President Bill Clinton created the National Economic Council as one of his first acts in 1993 and has sent it aggressively forward to promote globalization of the economy through its leadership in such initiatives as the Asia-Pacific Economic Cooperation (APEC) and the proposed Free Trade Area of the Americas (FTAA).

There has been nothing even vaguely reminiscent of this kind of activism in the area of American national security policy. Certainly, many political and military leaders have admitted that the world has changed, that the problems are different than they used to be, and that we must adapt to the new environment, which we hardly understand and is more uncertain and thus fraught with more unpredictable circumstances than before. Yet no one has enunciated a grand policy worthy of the name that answers the question: What are the uses of American military force in a new century?

Why not? There are as many answers to the question as there are respondents. Having said that, I think we can group the reasons into five categories that, individually and in combination, explain the inertia. Some answers are honest; others are less ingenuous.

The Causes of Inertia in National Security Policy

New Environment

The first explanation is the changed nature of the environment, the idea that we confront a new, more fluid, and more complex international environment than during the cold war. As a result, we need to adjust to the new environment, and we have not yet sorted it all out enough to form a clear and coherent picture of the national security problems we confront.

This argument, while self-evident on its face, is also misleading. With a decade of experience behind us, this excuse loses force. It should be clear by now that the principal way in which the national security problem has changed is that it has been dramatically reduced. All of the threats facing us today were there during the cold war: terrorists; weapons of mass destruction and their proliferation; Iraq and other rogue states; and violent, nasty internal wars in the developing world.

If the environment has changed, it has done so in subtle ways. Most notably, our national security problem has been reduced by the disappearance of the central threat posed by the confrontation between communism and anticommunism. The absence of that clear focus may make it harder to think about the world, but it also makes the contemplation of national security a lot less frightening. As George Bush put it in one of the debates during the 1992 presidential election campaign, our children no longer go to bed worrying about the prospect of nuclear war. With the threat of massive destruction peeled away, we are left with the smaller problems of terrorism, proliferation, and the like, which are different than before in that the superpowers can no longer constrain states that were clients. We have added (some would say made up) a few new problems, such as "cyberwar" (war against electronic information systems), but the environment is not all that different now that the threat of World War III (admittedly a very major change) is stripped away. The Department of Defense, through its 1997 *Quadrennial Defense Review*, admitted as much when it said we lack a "peer competitor" and will for quite awhile. This recognition has not found its way into central strategy.

Conservative Nature of Defense Planners

A second explanation is the conservative nature of the defense intellectual community. This community, which consists of civilian policy makers, the military itself, and academic and other defense analysts and observers, has a conservative bent that is the natural concomitant of the problems it confronts. In a policy environment where mistakes could result in serious injury to the country or worse, it is not surprising that the community embraces change cautiously and has a tendency to cling to old constructs, ideas, and even hardware that have worked in the past. We would not really want a wildly innovative defense community, which, when faced with new circumstances, adopted the attitude, "this policy may not work, but let's give it a try anyway." The stakes are too high for that. At the same time, dedication to old, tried-and-true prescriptions can lead to ossification, even sclerosis. Clinging to a force structure and definition of roles and missions strongly reminiscent of the cold war can result from such attitudes. When conservatism becomes reactionary, there is cause for concern.

Bureaucratic Resistance

A third source of resistance to change is a fear among some members of the defense intellectual community that adaptation may make them irrelevant. Most of the people now at high levels of decision making and implementation are products of the cold war and the cold war way of doing things. "Cold warriors" are prominent in the military services—today's generals and admirals entered the services in the 1970s or late 1960s. Observers who joined the "growth industry" of national security studies during the 1970s and 1980s are also products of the cold war.

The implications of change are especially threatening to those in senior positions in the services. By and large, they represent military specialties that were vital when facing the Soviet Union but are not clearly so today. Within the Navy, for instance, submariners and carrier-based aviators have been in the glamour areas and on the fast track. Carrier-based aviation, because it can bring firepower to bear on a target without getting permission to land somewhere, still has relevance in places like the Persian Gulf, where forays like Operation Desert Fox have become a way of life. However, the use of carriers has changed: in preparing for battle with the Soviet Union, carrier flotillas demanded a 750-mile wide swath of ocean and numerous support vessels to protect the carrier from predators. The idea of inserting one or more of these platforms into the Persian Gulf (which at its widest point is about 150 miles wide) would have created potentially fatal palpitations among naval planners. With no one to attack the carriers, the support cast that protects them—destroyers, guided missile cruisers, and anti–submarine warfare ships—loses some of its salience. As such, the changed environment threatens the careers and professional interests of those in carrier-support roles.

The situation facing submariners is worse. The captains and crews are the heart of the hunter-killer submarines, those underwater vessels designated to ferret out and destroy their counterparts in the briny depths. When the cold war ended, a new generation of these potent predators was about to come off the drawing boards and go into production. But after the demise of the Soviet Union and the disintegration of its navy, no hostile power in the world had submarines to be attacked by our submarines. Only Hollywood envisioned a submarine war, in movies like *The Hunt for Red October*, a story set in the cold war.

Change is similarly threatening to the Army. Promotion through the ranks of the Army went to the "heavy lifters," those military personnel who by virtue of their operating specialties would fight the Soviets. That meant principally the infantry, armor, and heavy field artillery. Having a formidable tank army made a lot of sense when the United States confronted an equally impressive counterpart with whom to slug it out in Germany, and those heavy elements had applicability in the Persian Gulf. It is not at all clear what application many of these elements would have in the contemporary environment.

The Air Force also has its problems. The bombers are still in business and will remain so as long as we remain committed to the idea—less than fully validated by experience—that bombardment can force our opponents into submission. The traditional darlings of the Air Force, the fighter pilots, do not have it so good. The fact is the United States has the only real fighter air force and possesses the finest fighter aircraft in the world. "Why would we need more?" is a reasonable question that the Air Force has difficulty answering. The desperation of the Air Force to justify a large purchase of F-22 fighters is demonstrated well by its argument that we may sell some of our most potent fighters to friends who could eventually become adversaries, in which case we would need the most advanced equipment available.

The Marines and the special forces, especially in the Army, have been the most adaptive and least resistant to change. The Marines, who have learned to be light on their intellectual feet to protect themselves from extinction, looked at the new world order and saw involvement in nasty internal wars as a top priority. They began preparing to fill that need through programs such as Emerald Express, annual week-long symposia on peacekeeping begun in 1991. Special forces are also well positioned for this kind of duty, which requires intense political as well as military activity and a more sophisticated grasp of political realities than the more traditional military specialties are credited with having.

The lack of concrete missions and the resulting strategic vacuum are particularly traumatic for those who have made careers in military specialties that may be less vital in the future. It is, after all, human nature for someone who has dedicated his or her life to submarines (or tanks or heavy bombers) to believe that if that capability was important then, it always will be. Admitting the obsolescence of what you have done is an implicit admission of your own obsolescence, which is not easy to accept.

Past Success

A fourth impediment is the legacy of the Persian Gulf War, which reinforces resistance to change by seeming to reinforce orthodox ways of doing things. Without going into the question of whether that encounter was the last gasp of the cold war or the first conflict of the new order (a case can be made for either belief), the ease with which the American-led coalition dispatched Iraq seemed to vindicate the cold-war military system. In the Kuwaiti desert —where strategies could be implemented without the nasty impediments to rapid maneuver that exist in Germany, such as varied topography and towns —the Army executed in essence the Air-Land Battle plan that it had devised for Europe, with great precision and effect. And it did so against the fourth-largest army in the world at the time, one equipped with front-line Soviet equipment and employing the Soviet ways of fighting for which we had prepared for so long. To make matters more daunting, the Iraqi army was a "war-tested," veteran army that had fought for eight years against Iran.

The result was an absolute walkover that seemed to put the seal of approval on the armed force we had equipped, trained, and prepared for combat in the European theater. In retrospect, we know that the Iraqi army that we met in Kuwait was composed mostly of first-term Kurdish and Shi'ite conscripts who were much more interested in surrendering than in fighting, and that most of the wartime veterans were sick of war. The victory was so thorough and so nearly effortless that a message seemed to come through loud and clear: the armed forces have finally shed the last vestiges of the Vietnam and post-Vietnam doldrums. Lost in the euphoria was the question, not thoroughly vetted to this day, of whether the Iraqi armed forces were an enemy of sufficient merit for the United States to deserve the accolades it received (and asserted for itself). This American armed force, the argument went, is now a formidable machine, the most powerful in the world. We have worked extraordinarily hard to effect this turnaround, and we are very proud of what we have done. *The system works; change it at your own peril!*

The other legacy of Desert Storm was to reinforce the American military's (and especially the Air Force's) fascination with airpower and technology. Airpower blinded the enemy by taking out his air defenses and ability to collect electronic intelligence, while improvements in precision-guided munitions (although less impressive than advertised at the time) allowed us to attack precisely; gadgets like the Global Positioning System allowed American units and individuals to know exactly where they were all the time, while the Iraqis wandered across a flat desert with no distinguishing features to tell them where they were. For better or worse, the effect of the war has been to reinforce the mavens of the twin gods: airpower and technology.

Lack of Urgency

The fifth and final impediment to change has been the lack of urgency attached to military reform. Since 1990 no significant American interests anywhere in the world would have been compromised regardless of how well we were equipped to defend them. Does it really matter if the current force structure and plans for its employment are out of touch with the threats we might have to encounter if these threats are not significant? Aircraft carrier flotillas may not have much to do with preventing Serbs from killing Kosovars and vice versa, but would the addition of a thirteenth carrier affect our ability to deal with those kinds of problems? And even if a thirteenth carrier does leave us with the wrong military force configuration for dealing with Kosovo-like situations, does an untoward outcome in a Kosovo really make all that much difference?

Defense planners have lots of reasons (or excuses) to resist change, and the reasons reinforce one another. The "natural" tendency to remain conservative and to stick with forces and concepts that have served well in the past was reinforced in the Kuwaiti desert. If the world is very different and we decide we do not need additional tanks to fight guerrillas in the tropics, might we not need them somewhere else at some time? And if we do not have them, we could be sorry. Besides, for the time being, keeping lots of tanks and other traditional "stuff" does no harm.

Is any of the above overstated? Certainly, and I am sure that different readers will take exception with different parts of the analysis. What is hard to deny, however, is that defense policy and strategy have not adapted to change to the extent that other parts of foreign policy have. The environment has indeed changed, and we have had a decade to take a comprehensive look at the problem and to adjust policy and strategy accordingly. But we have not.

The Contemporary Environment

The search for policy and strategy logically begins with an examination of the environment to which the policy responds and for which the strategy applies. The post–cold war world bears less resemblance to its predecessor in the field of national security than, arguably, in any other area of foreign policy. Certainly, the globalizing economy has become a more prominent part of the architecture of the millennium, and the United States has emerged as the dominant political power (which, in and of itself, has some security implications that have been only indirectly addressed). The central element of the traditional national security environment (the problem of systemic war) has collapsed. Arbatov understated the change the Soviet Union wrought as it declined and disappeared: not only was the United States deprived of an enemy, we (and the rest of the West) were deprived of a framework for looking at the world and responding to it.

That part of foreign policy that is uniquely national security in content and for which strategy is devised has traditionally dealt primarily with military threats to the national well-being or even existence. For most of American history, threats to the United States were blunted by wide oceans and friendly, manageable neighbors on our borders; until the need for exotic materials and cheap energy forced us to look overseas, the United States was basically self-sufficient and, for many purposes, aloof from the power politics of the world. Only when the United States ventured outward, as in acquiring a Pacific empire from Spain, was it exposed to the vagaries of potential predators. Our isolation was a luxury that few other countries through history have enjoyed.

The emergence of an ideologically alien Soviet superpower after World War II changed that by helping create an all-encompassing competition that contained real threats to American security; American fear of and aversion to "godless" communism added to the heat of the conflict. The cold war was an ideological competition to see if the world map would be painted more blue (anticommunist) or red (communist). Although the communist states never in fact (and especially in retrospect) posed much threat economically, it took awhile for us to determine the flaws of socialist economics. Our analysis of the motives behind Soviet foreign policy never truly reflected its defensive-expansionist thrust, which is central to the revisionist analysis of cold war history, or the extent to which it was driven by internal considerations, such as Soviet fear of the multiethnic diversity within its territory, with all its centrifugal possibilities.

The cold war was most distinctive in the area of national security. At the most obvious level, after 1957, when the Soviet Union successfully tested an intercontinental ballistic missile (ICBM) capable or raining nuclear destruction on the U.S. heartland, the physical existence of the United States was at risk. The United States's closest friends and allies in Europe and northeast Asia were similarly under the gun and needed American assistance to remain free and unfettered. The cold war competition even slopped over into the newly decolonizing states, where the Americans and Soviets sponsored opposing states, or factions within states, and even engaged in proxy conflicts through their "clients." As the United States became dependent on exotic minerals and cheap energy, the need to guarantee their flow naturally followed. That the Soviets profoundly threatened all of our values was a given rarely challenged by conservative, realist cold war strategists, whose views dominated serious discussions within the policy community and whose prosperity was guaranteed by their dominance.

The threat-driven environment, with real adversaries posing real challenges to us, was the kind of setting for which the conservative realist paradigm that dominated thinking was ideally suited. And that environment is almost totally gone. There is no military competition in Europe, and the developing world is no longer an attractive forum for competition or the sponsorship of governments or factions. The sea lanes of communication are still there, but they are hardly menaced by anyone. Russian nuclear-tipped missiles are the only part of the old realty that remains; by agreement, they are not aimed at us but could be with a little computer programming. What is missing there is any convincing reason for Russia even to contemplate attacking the United States.

Everyone realizes all of these changes have occurred; it is not revelatory to state them. What the changes cumulatively mean is that the threat has changed; it has diminished in size, and that has left us scrambling intellectually for new ways to think about the problem.

It became clear to defense planners in the mid-1990s that they were going to have a difficult time reformulating policy and strategy from a threat-based analysis, because such an approach would reveal relatively few threats worth confronting. Moreover, as one began to move down the strategy ladder from threat analysis to defining forces and missions, threat-based assessments could lead only to the conclusion that we needed fewer forces for lesser missions. In an environment where every one of the most important countries was cutting back on defense spending, the rationale for force modernization and the like suffered. We could not justify doing what we used to do in this new environment.

We have, of course, tried to justify carrying on as before. Force planners, realizing that threat-based assessments yielded gloomy results, suggested that we move from a threat-based to a capability-based force: the force should be configured not to meet current or foreseeable opposition but to meet all possible contingencies. This "be all you can be" approach, which has died away in the public debate, always floundered on the "capability against whom or what?" question, itself a measure of threat.

The second approach to force planning has been to make up a threat. The prototype is the "two major regional conflicts" capability, where the worst case the United States *might* face is the emergence of two more or less simultaneous wars to which we should have the capability of responding. The two chosen villains in this scenario have been Iraq and North Korea: Saddam Hussein's forces launching a new attack on Kuwait (or even Saudi Arabia) at the same time that Kim Jung Il unleashes the Korean People's Army into the south. When this scenario, originally a part of classified Pentagon planning documents, was first leaked to the press, it met with so much ridicule that embarrassed defense officials had to backpedal and admit that the likelihood of this happening was very low. However, thinking about this scenario challenged us to figure out what we needed to succeed in this perilous world.

In the remainder of this chapter, I will begin to answer two questions that will help frame the policy and strategy debate. The first question is: How is the contemporary international system similar and dissimilar to that of the cold war era? The new international system is what I call "a world of tiers." The second question is: How adequate are our cold war constructs, captured in the realist paradigm, for understanding this environment and responding to it?

The New Environment: A World of Tiers

One of the awkward aspects of confronting an international system that no longer contains a meaningful communist component is describing it in language that is not insulting. During the cold war, for instance, we often talked about the "developed" and "developing" (or "underdeveloped") worlds, but that was criticized as insulting to those deemed less developed and culturally biased for its implication that the West is the exemplar toward which everyone should aspire. In a somewhat less loaded sense, we talked about a First

World (the most developed states), a Second World (the communist or socialist states), a Third World (the developing states), and sometimes a Fourth World (the truly poor states).

The ordinal scheme is no longer adequate to describe the current situation. The Second World consists of four states (China, Cuba, North Korea, and Vietnam), and two of those (China and Vietnam) openly advocate nonsocialist economics, and a third (Cuba) has recently begun to sanction a private sector in its economy. Only North Korea—one of the world's true economic basket cases—continues fealty to the intellectual tradition of Engels, Marx, Lenin, and (especially) Stalin.

How, then, should we talk about the world today? Although there is no consensus on the subject, Eugene Brown and I have devised a scheme that divides the world into two tiers, a First Tier composed of the most economically advanced states (roughly the same as the First World), and a Second Tier composed of the rest of the world. The Second Tier is further divided into subtiers differentiated by levels of economic and political development. The scheme is similar to Max Singer and Aaron Wildavsky's "zones of peace and turmoil," described in *The Real World Order*.

The first premise and rationale for the notion of tiers begins from the observation that the two tiers are fundamentally different in a variety of economic, political, historical, cultural, and other ways that make it impossible to make meaningful generalizations about the behavior in both tiers.

Take an example. As Robert Keohane and Joseph S. Nye Jr. argued in "Power and Interdependence in the Information Age," the primary characteristic of the most advanced world (the First Tier) is economic and political interdependence, but that clearly is not the case in the Second Tier. As they put it, "Outside the zone of peace, the world of states is not a world of complex interdependence" (p. 84). If that is true, then what generalizations can be made about the dynamics of financial markets that are equally true in both parts of the world? The answer is few, and we more accurately describe economic reality by saying one set of dynamics describes the First Tier, and another the Second (although some states in the Second Tier are attempting to emulate the economies of the First Tier, thereby narrowing the differences).

The distinction between the First and Second Tiers is not an idle, academic one, because the differentiation applies with equal clarity to the security dimension and to the likely, appropriate, and relevant application of armed forces. To demonstrate why this is so, we begin by describing the two tiers and the interaction between them, with emphasis on the security implications of the observations we make.

First Tier

The First Tier corresponds roughly to the membership of the Organization for Economic Cooperation and Development. As such, its membership consists of Canada and the United States, the European Economic Area (the European Union and the old European Free Trade Area), Japan, and the Antipodes (Australia and New Zealand). A number of states are close to meeting the criteria for membership (South Korea, for instance), but do not quite qualify. (South Korean political and economic stability is still tentative, especially in the wake of the 1997 economic crisis and the continuing uncertainty of relations with North Korea.)

What characteristics do members of the First Tier have in common? And what does it take to enter the category? All of the members are *established* political democracies with *advanced* market-based economies, what President Clinton has described as the "circle of market democracies." The adjectives modifying each characteristic are key to differentiating First Tier members from the rest. The term *established* democracy means that members of the First Tier have political systems that have operated democratically (have held and enforced elections over a period of time, are able to collect and distribute tax revenues, have legitimate court systems, and so forth) for some time. The term *advanced* market-based economy means that members of the First Tier are not only part of the technology-driven global economy but are contributors to as well as consumers of the technology that underlies the system.

This unique combination of political and economic freedom leads Singer and Wildavsky to describe the countries as possessing "quality economies." By this they mean that the ability to shape one's destiny that economic capitalism provides and the political freedom that democracy brings with it combine to create a unique climate of entrepreneurship and incentives. The combination of economic freedom with political freedom drives the members of the First Tier to rising levels of attainment and innovation that advance them ahead of the Second Tier states. This notion is not universally accepted, of course: a few scholars argue that democracy and capitalism are incompatible (Jacque Attali, for instance), while a number of Asian apologists for one-party authoritarianism maintain that Western-style democracy is not necessary in—or is even incompatible with—their cultures. Still, the fact that the democratic countries are economically the most advanced in the world is hardly coincidental. The East Asian financial crisis of 1997 is testimony to the impact of cultural "values" such as secrecy and corruption on the financial sector of economies.

The states of the First Tier share several characteristics relevant to national security policy and strategy. The first is that they are the most consequential, core members of the international system in economic and political terms. Between them they have the preponderance of world power.

Their predominance extends to the military dimension as well. Although some countries of the Second Tier have larger military forces (China is the most obvious example), the countries of the First Tier have by far the most sophisticated, potent forces in the world. The only countries, for instance, with military capabilities that even conceivably could challenge those of the United States on a level playing field are the other First Tier states. As noted in the Introduction, for instance, the rank order of spending on military forces in the world in 1996 had only one Second Tier country (Russia) in the top seven.

Stating the distinction in this way does not mean there are no militarily or otherwise consequential states outside the First Tier. Russia, as the most powerful successor to the Soviet Union, remains militarily important because it retains the old Soviet Union's nuclear arsenal, even if it lacks any good reason to use it. At the same time, the recent performance of Russia's armed forces within its own borders (Chechnya) would lead one to doubt the ability of the Russians to project force outside their boundaries, and it is hard to imagine how their enfeebled economy could sustain a major force buildup.

China and India also matter. China has the world's largest population, its largest army, and nuclear weapons, and it is said by some to be developing a capability to project force (at least against Taiwan) for which it has not been noted. It is difficult to conceive of China as a threat to any First Tier state other possibly than Japan, with which it enjoys major economic relations, which a military menace would jeopardize. India has a large and growing population, very large conventional forces, and at least some nuclear weapons. These factors may affect the power balance on the subcontinent, but it would be a stretch to conceive of India projecting force far beyond its borders without some very questionable assumptions about escalation.

This assessment leads to a second characteristic common to every First Tier state: the absence of serious political or economic differences with the other members of the First Tier. Certainly, there are differences in policy between members: the United States and Japan disagree about terms of trade, the United States and France disagree over where and when to use military force against others, for instance. However, there are no serious differences in either economic or political ideology. All the states share a common commitment to political democracy and the market.

This broad ideological agreement has important implications for national security planning. Since the possibility of war between any two First Tier states is negligible, there is no chance, for the foreseeable future, that the United States will go to war with any of the other First Tier states. If these states are also the only ones with the military wherewithal to pose a threat to the United States, then planning and preparation for high-intensity, sophisticated warfare has to be justified in some way other than threat, because the members of the First Tier have no differences important enough to fight about.

Furthermore, the ideological agreement implies that military force plays no important role in the relations between First Tier members. When disagreements arise in the economic or political realm, economic and political threats and measures may be invoked to settle them. The use of military threats among First Tier states lacks relevance and credibility, although U.S. forces may protect other First Tier states (like Japan) from real or potential enemies (like North Korea). The United States, for instance, may be frustrated when France bans American movies from French markets on the grounds of cultural assault; threatening France with nuclear weapons to lift the ban would hardly be believable.

Some people will disagree with this notion of "democratic peace." Some argue, for instance, that democratic states are as likely to fight as undemocratic states but rarely fight one another. Admittedly, the only cross-border war since Desert Storm involved two putatively democratic states, Peru and Ecuador, but both states are embryonic democracies lacking a democratic tradition, and the border issue that activated them predated their democratization by a long time. The instances where true democracies have fought one another are so few as to be dismissed as aberrations.

This leads to a third characteristic common to all First Tier states: the growing interdependence among them. The notion of complex interdependence, first raised in the public eye by Keohane and Nye in 1977, is primarily economic in nature. It suggests that trade, increasing penetration of corporations by different nationals, and the like create a degree of dependence and similarity that reinforces the similarities among First Tier states. As the economy becomes more global and the application of the theory of comparative advantage spreads economic functions across borders, the inability to make war compounds the lack of motivation to do so.

The argument that economic interdependence leads to peace has been made before. It was certainly an important argument at the turn of the last century; many suggested that any war like World War I would be physically impossible. Extrapolating from 1900 to 2000 to the current situation is fatuous, however. If one were to look at those countries that are now the First Tier as they were in the 1910s, one would note deep ideological differences among and within the two coalitions that fought the "Great War."

A fourth characteristic extends from the democratic nature of the countries of the First Tier: the use of military force by First Tier states is limited primarily by public opinion, not military capability. Because the military forces of the First Tier are individually and collectively the most sophisticated and deadly in the world, no First Tier state need rule out military action on the basis of the likelihood of military defeat. If one assumes (as I do) that no First Tier democracy will declare an aggressive war in which it attacks a country (the NATO attack against Yugoslavia is a possible exception), then even those countries with militaries large enough to tax First Tier capabilities will be unlikely to find themselves at war. India has a large armed force, but it cannot attack the United States, and it is difficult to imagine why the United States would send an expeditionary force to the Indian subcontinent. The same is true of Russia and China. Any attacks on the United States or U.S. citizens are likely to be asymmetrical to our power—small terrorist attacks or cyberwar against our computers, for example.

Most of the opportunities for the United States and its fellow First Tier states to use force will be in relatively small and strategically insignificant states in the Second Tier. In almost all instances, there will be few if any clear and important interests at stake for the United States, with the possible exception of those places where petroleum is involved. Given that the stakes will be low, the United States will employ armed forces only where it chooses to do so, not because its existence or well-being requires it to do so. Ours will be discretionary employments of military force, not employments of necessity.

The discretionary nature of U.S. military action is where the role of public opinion comes in. If the United States does not have to involve itself in particular conflicts, then how will it decide into which to thrust itself? The answer to this question is, it will go when the public allows it to (political leadership, or its absence, of course has a strong impact on public opinion and, within boundaries, can move it). The ability of political leaders to shape public opinion, in turn, will be conditioned by the most recent experience the United States has had in a similar situation. Critical in this determination will often be the level of casualties the United States has endured compared to the gains won; once again, political leaders influence how the public views costs and gains. After intervening in Somalia from 1992 to 1994, where the United States had little at stake, achieved only transitory results (saving some lives from starvation), and suffered some casualties, the lesson learned was to avoid similar instances or at least to modify how we conduct such missions. While arguably a bad lesson to learn, it was clearly the lesson learned by a relatively inexperienced Clinton administration, for a time. The lesson of Somalia did not, however, prevent the deployment of U.S. troops in Haiti in 1994, where little was accomplished but no one was killed by hostile fire. Nor did it inhibit the Clinton administration from sending U.S. troops to Bosnia in 1995. (A majority of Americans initially opposed our sending troops to Bosnia, but not so strongly as to stop deployment. The longer we stay without casualties, the weaker the opposition to deployment becomes.) The Bosnian "success," in turn, made it easier to "sell" the public on sending forces to Kosovo in 1999.

The fifth and final characteristic common to all First Tier states is a preference for collective action. Although there will be times when a First Tier state will act unilaterally because of some special interest not shared by the others (Haiti, for instance), most of the time First Tier states will seek to spread the commitment by acting in concert. Authorizing a joint peacekeeping effort through NATO in the Bosnian Implementation Force/Stabilization Force is probably the prototype for actions in and around the European theater, and the ongoing no-fly zones over Iraq (Operations Southern and Northern Watch) suggest that NATO partners will act together in other parts of the world, as their interests dictate.

Collective action helps make the use of force acceptable. Collective action adds legitimacy to a mission within the international community, especially if it is sanctioned by some multilateral organization such the United Nations or NATO. It also reduces the physical commitment and expense that any single state has to bear, thereby avoiding the "free rider" problem of some members not taking part in the group's activity. In addition, the fact that one's friends and allies are willing to commit to a particular action makes it easier to convince the public at home that involvement is worthwhile.

What can we conclude from this analysis of the First Tier? For the moment, let me draw three implications on which we will elaborate as we go along. One implication is that the First Tier states can conduct military operations to order the pattern of violence and instability in the Second Tier unfettered by limits on their military capability. Although their superior military capabilities may not be effective in certain circumstances, and although their threats of military involvement will vary in credibility in different situations, the First Tier states will decide where they want to act. Their involvement will be consensual, not dictated. The public will go a long way toward determining where states of the First Tier employ armed forces. Clearly there is no consensus on this subject today, which is part of the reason why a new and clear national security policy and strategy are so desperately needed.

Finally, action will be collective almost all the time. In most instances, the United States will be thrust into a leadership role because of its position as the sole remaining superpower. This does not mean the United States will necessarily have to take the leading *military* role all the time, but it will be expected to participate and to provide leadership. As Bosnia and Kosovo demonstrated, an American presence is a sine qua non for the former combatants to accept a multilateral force to monitor their situations.

Second Tier

The homogeneity of the First Tier is in sharp contrast to the heterogeneity of the Second. In fact, the rest of the world cannot be thought of as a unit at all. Rather, it is more useful to think of the Second Tier as divided in two ways: by developmental subtier and by participation or nonparticipation in the global economy. Both of these distinctions help explain those parts of the Second Tier that are the most and least violence-prone.

Developmental Subtiers The states of the Second Tier can be divided into four subtiers. Three of these subtiers are distinguished by level of development, and the fourth by the anomaly of possession of large amounts of energy resources, which makes the states advanced financially if not otherwise.

The three developmentally defined subtiers are differentiated by level and quality of economic development and, secondarily, political development. At the bottom of the hierarchy is the *developable* subtier. States in this category range from the extremely destitute countries that live almost exclusively on subsistence agriculture, fishing and hunting, and some above-ground resource harvesting (cutting down trees, for instance) to the countries that have begun the process of harvesting below-ground resources (energy or mineral) and are on the verge of entering the first economic revolution of primitive manufacture. Most are politically underdeveloped, although a few

Table 1.1   Second Tier Subtiers by Geographic Location

Region	Developed	Partially developed	Developable	Resource-rich
Asia and Pacific	4	8	18	1
Middle East	2	6	2	7
Latin America and Caribbean	5	19	8	1
Former Soviet Union and Eastern Europe	1	8	19	0
Africa	1	11	37	4
Total	13	52	84	13

(Mali, for instance) have functioning democracies. The greatest concentration of countries in the developable subtier is in Africa, although they are found elsewhere as well *(see Table 1.1)*.

The second category is the *partially developed* subtier. As the name suggests, countries with this designation have developed at least some segments of their economy (manufactures that are labor-intensive but do not require high skill levels to produce, for instance). A number of countries in this category can lay some claim to entrance into the global economy, either because they have made themselves attractive targets for foreign direct investment or have enticed multinational corporations to locate parts of their manufacturing operations in them on the basis of comparative advantage due to low wages. Typically, countries in this category vary greatly in terms of development across the society; India, a prime example, has a middle class estimated at more than 100 million people and a burgeoning electronics industry, but it also has large areas where subsistence agriculture remains the norm. (The contrast between China's special economic zones and the rest of the country is similar.) As the world learned in 1997, when Indonesia and several other Asian nations experienced severe financial problems, many states in this category have insufficiently developed financial and other economic sectors to rise through the developmental ranks.

The third category is the *developed* subtier. The smallest subtier in terms of size (with thirteen members), it contains the countries closest to membership in the First Tier. Most are important players in the globalizing economy and have large and growing economic sectors in advanced areas of technology and production (although they are distinguished from First Tier states by being primarily consumers, rather than producers, of technology). A number of these states have at least fragile democracies, although in countries like South Korea, they may not have repeated the electoral process often enough for there to be great confidence in the stability of democratic institutions.

The final category, effectively outside the developmental hierarchy, is the *resource-rich* subtier. It is also small, consisting of thirteen states concentrated, but not located exclusively, in the Middle East. What distinguishes these states is their wealth, which is a result of world dependence on petroleum. They tend to redistribute wealth to their populations as a way to ensure loyalty, but they generally are underdeveloped in other ways: the financial sector is usually the only part of the economy that is well developed or regulated, and only one country (Trinidad and Tobago) is a political democracy. It is fair to say that most of these states, if oil revenue were to disappear, would revert to the developable subtier. This is a point to note because the states of the developable subtier and resource-rich subtier are statistically the most likely to engage in violence in the contemporary system.

The distribution of states by subtier is by no means uniform geographically. As one would expect, there are more African and Asian states in the lowest developmental subtier than there are states from elsewhere in the world. The distribution of Second Tier states by geographical area is captured in Table 1.1. A number of observations can be made from Table 1.1. First and foremost is the predominance of developable countries (84 of 162, or 52 percent). If the likelihood of violence is tied inversely to the level of economic development (as I argue it is), the task of reducing the likelihood of violence is formidable. Second is the distribution of misery: Africa accounts for 44 percent of the states in the developable category, and fully 70 percent of African states are developable. The other concentrations of developable states are in south and southeastern Asia, in central Asia (the former republics of the Soviet Union), and in the Balkans. (Azerbaijan will move from developable to resource-rich if the Caspian Sea oil and gas fields are fully exploited, a development that would affect the status of the other states on the Caspian littoral as well.)

Participation and Nonparticipation in the Global Economy The other point distinguishing the Second Tier states from First Tier states is their differential participation in the global economy. No exact geographic definition of the global economy exists to my knowledge, but I have devised what I view as a useful one. The globalizing economy can be thought of as incorporating the countries of the First Tier, the Asia-Pacific Economic Cooperation (APEC), and the proposed Free Trade Area of the Americas. This grouping includes all of western Europe, all of the Western Hemisphere except Cuba, and nearly all of the Pacific Rim, including Russia and China as members of APEC. Some states fall into more than one category: Canada and the United States are members of all three, and Japan is First Tier and a member of APEC, for instance.

The reason for aggregating these states and designating them as the core of the global economy is that they, through treaty and other commitments, have embraced free trade as the core value of international economics. Although some of these associations are more developed than others (the Free Trade Area of the Americas is no more than an agreement among heads of state to negotiate a set of trade-barrier-removing measures), they all share this commitment.

Two things stand out when dividing the world into those places that are and are not part of the global economy. The first is the omission of all of Africa and a good bit of central and south Asia, the same places where a preponderance of the developable states reside. This correlation of geography and prosperity is almost certainly not coincidental. The second thing is that the omitted areas are where the violence and instability are concentrated.

Policy toward a Heterogeneous, Peripheral, and Violence-Prone Tier

On this basis, we move to a more detailed discussion of the characteristics of the Second Tier, since they are relevant to the use of force in the system. The first characteristic is the tremendous diversity of the states of the Second Tier. In sharp contrast to the homogeneity of the countries of the First Tier, nothing unifies the states of the Second, other possibly than a desire to share in the greater prosperity of the First Tier. It is possible to make some distinctions about regions, but even these are of limited value and assistance. The impact of Islam in the Middle East is an example of a regional trait, but it does not necessarily help explain much of the politics within or among Islamic states. Similarly, politics in most African countries is tribal in its orientation, but that does not explain, for instance, why some African states evolve stable political systems and many do not.

Diversity has important consequences for our understanding of and dealings with the Second Tier. It is difficult to make meaningful generalizations about the countries of the Second Tier. Rather, observations must be narrow and specific to regions or countries. This diversity has a major consequence for making policy toward the Second Tier and helps explain the paralysis of policy toward violence in Second Tier countries: there is almost no universal standard to dictate whether the United States should intervene in a Second Tier country's wars, essentially all of which are internal. Some people have attempted to define such a standard, but none seem to work. When the United States reached the decision to send troops to Bosnia, for instance, national leaders and commentators offered vague (and mostly unconvincing) arguments about how the American interest in a tranquil Europe was somehow threatened (and these arguments begged the question of why Europe itself showed little enthusiasm for the enterprise). The same arguments have echoed over Kosovo, with about the same impact. President Clinton was reduced to the rather lame explanation that the Bosnian deployment "was the right thing to do." That is hardly a strategic principle, but it is arguably as much as we can do in a fragmented world where no single principle covers all contingencies. It is difficult to find first principles that are worth defending with American blood and that can be applied with any uniformity across the Second Tier, and much of the difficulty derives from the heterogeneity of the Second Tier.

A second characteristic of the Second Tier is its peripheral status within the international system. Once again, this is not to say that there are no consequential states within the Second Tier who could not produce major systemic trauma. An Indo-Pakistani nuclear exchange over Kashmir would certainly qualify as traumatic, if for no other reason than the unknown possibilities for escalation beyond the subcontinent. Russia may lack the incentive to launch a massive nuclear attack against the United States, but it certainly could do so, and making sure the Russians continue to lack incentive is an important matter. Force modernization may allow China to threaten Taiwan soon and others, including the United States and Japan, later, although it is not clear why China would become aggressive. With a little inventiveness, other scenarios can be constructed as well.

These exceptions notwithstanding, most of the Second Tier, and especially that part outside the globalizing economy, remains of only peripheral concern to the overall system. Since these peripheral areas are the locus of most contemporary violence, a reasonable question to ask in forming U.S. grand or military strategy is the extent to which we care about the outcomes of their conflicts. If caring is equated with the structure of American interests and how those interests may be affected by outcomes of conflicts, the peripheral status of those parts of the world will simply reinforce our disinclination to get involved. How, for instance, is the United States worse off because, several years after our withdrawal, Somalia remains in a state of anarchy, the alleviation of which might have been an American objective in intervening in the first place? Given where Somalia is in the world order, it is hard to say the outcome makes a difference.

The third characteristic of the Second Tier is that it is the locus of almost all of the violence and instability in the post–cold war world. This observation could also have been made in the cold-war era, but the pattern appears more stark in the absence of conflicts with military potential in the core of the system (the First Tier). During the cold war, conflicts between and within Second Tier countries were often proxy affairs extending the cold war, with the Soviets backing one country or faction and the United States the other. That overlay has disappeared with the demise of one sponsoring state and the realization by the United States that countering Soviet mischief was about the only interest we had in many instances. One beneficial effect of our withdrawal is that we have unloaded some unsavory characters like Mobutu Sese Seku of Zaire (now the Democratic Republic of Congo) and Jonas Savimbi of Angola; the flip side is that both of those countries have since plunged back into chaos.

Two things should be said about the pattern of violence in the contemporary world. The first is that conflict is almost exclusively internal, what I have called *new internal war,* a term that distinguishes these wars from the Vietnam- or Salvadorean-style civil wars of the cold-war period. Most of these conflicts occur in the so-called *failed states,* a term devised to describe Somalia that suggests countries so unstable as to be almost ungovernable. The new internal wars that occur in these countries tend to be vicious (typically 90 percent or more of the casualties are civilians), unmilitary (rarely do battles occur between organized armed units), and often politically pointless (in some cases, it is not clear that either side has as its goal gaining control of the country and governing).

These qualities produce two problems. The first is the legality of intervention. International law sanctions interfering in civil wars only for limited purposes (for example, rescuing and evacuating your own nationals, as the U.S. Marines did in Liberia in 1996). The invitation of a government (or other group) for outside assistance is generally not considered an adequate legal basis, although when anarchy rules, a legal basis may be moot. Who in Somalia, for instance, could have asked for American intervention? The imprimatur of a United Nations Security Council resolution adds some legal weight to involvement (Article 39 gives it the authority to counter threats or breaches of the peace), but the framers of the charter were looking more at interstate than intrastate violence.

Within this legal ambiguity, some people have asserted a right of "humanitarian intervention" when large-scale atrocities are occurring. When atrocities approach the status of genocide, the provisions of the Convention on Genocide would seem to allow some form of action, if only after the fact. Moreover, the question of whether humanitarian concerns justify action has never been fully raised and answered in the crucible of public opinion in these First Tier states that are the candidates for enforcement. Kosovo may provide the test.

The second observation is that the pattern of conflict has been geographically and developmentally specific. According to data collected by Project Ploughshares, there were thirty-seven violent conflicts involving thirty-two countries in 1997, the most recent year for which data are available. The pattern is summarized in Table 1.2. All of the conflicts were occurring in the Second Tier (India, Indonesia, Iran, Iraq, and the Philippines had multiple conflicts).

The pattern of conflict is striking: nineteen of the thirty-two conflicts (almost 60 percent) are occurring in developable-subtier countries, and seventeen of those nineteen are in Africa and Asia. The African conflicts involved every part of the continent, including such places as Algeria, Angola, Burundi, Chad, Congo, the Democratic Republic of Congo, Egypt, Kenya, Rwanda, Sierra Leone, Somalia, Sudan, Uganda, and South Africa. The Asian conflicts (including those of the Middle East), covered a swath of south central Asia anchored in the west by Turkey and extending to Papua New Guinea. If one adds violence in the partially developed subtier, the total soars to twenty-seven of thirty-two, or 85 percent. The only other places where conflicts are occurring (other than South Africa) are Israel/Lebanon, Algeria, Iran, and Iraq.

The same impressive statistic results when the conflicts are divided according to where the global economy has penetrated, as defined earlier. Of the thirty-two conflicts, only five are occurring in countries that are a part of the global economy: three in APEC countries (Indonesia, Papua New Guinea, and the Philippines) and two in the FTAA (Colombia and Peru).

The concentration of conflict in countries that are outside of the global

Table 1.2 Conflicts by Subtier and Continent

Region	Developed	Partially developed	Developable	Resource-rich	Total
Africa	1	2	9	1	13
Asia	0	2	8	0	10
Europe	0	0	1	0	1
Latin America	0	1	1	0	2
Middle East	1	3	0	2	6
Totals	2	8	19	3	32

economy has implications for strategy and policy. The fact that almost all of the violence is happening far from the mainstream of the international system means that ignoring these problems will, in most cases, not be systemically traumatic. The correlation of nonviolence with the more developed members of the globalizing economy and violence with the poorer countries outside the economy points toward both the solution and the difficulty of achieving it. The failed states tend to be not only politically unstable but also very poor (the two characteristics not being coincidental). Certainly, the relationship is not perfect: there are stable poor countries (Mali, for instance) and unstable yet fairly wealthy countries (South Africa). Still, the correlation of stability with prosperity suggests that long-term amelioration of the conditions that cause violence entails economic development and creating a stake for people to support peace. Promoting economic investment was the premise of Secretary of Commerce Ron Brown's mission to Bosnia with American businessmen, which ended in disaster when his plane plowed into the side of a Croatian mountain. The fact that most of the countries are in the developable subtier suggests the size and complexity of the developmental task and raises the question of whether anyone cares enough to undertake it.

The fourth and final characteristic is that in most of the Second Tier, physical capability is the major constraint on using force. Although many Second Tier countries have large, sometimes even sophisticated armed forces, in those parts of the Second Tier where most of the violence is occurring, the central government (where there is one) lacks sufficient armed forces to enforce political order. The forces that are available are often too weak or ineffectual to quell regional differences. The United States, for instance, has proposed an all-African force to intervene in and pacify civil conflicts, but the proposal has foundered on the question of availability of sufficient forces (some people have also questioned the acceptability of some national forces based on their tribal and ethnic composition).

Relations between the Tiers

Given that almost all of the United States's opportunities to employ force will be in the Second Tier (which is also true for other First Tier states), *the* critical question for U.S. policy is where we will and will not employ it. The question is not as new as it may seem. Since World War II the United States has put troops in harm's way on numerous occasions, and always in the Third World. Without attempting to be exhaustive, the list of places American troops have been deployed includes Panama, Grenada, Haiti, and El Salvador in the Western hemisphere; the Persian Gulf (Kuwait/Iraq and Iran) and Lebanon in the Middle East; Korea and Southeast Asia; and Somalia and Bosnia.

How the United States chooses to employ its armed forces in Second Tier internal (and other) conflicts is one aspect of the broader foreign policy of the United States. During the cold war, American national security policy toward the Third World was a reasonably straightforward extension of the military confrontation in Europe. The author of containment, George F. Kennan, consistently opposed its extension beyond the Sino-Soviet periphery, but it was a mainstay nonetheless. Since America (or, for that matter, the Soviet Union) had few direct interests in most of the Third World, we instead derived an indirect interest in gaining some influence in different places or, at least, denying influence to the other side. The U.S. *modus operandi* was the equipping and training of favored forces and, in extreme cases, supporting them with troops in the face of their enemies.

That rationale died when the Soviet Union imploded and the Russians did not fill the void. As the Russians retreated from their Third World commitments and perceived interests, the Americans were left alone in far-off places, suddenly lacking a rationale for being there. Containment has given way to engagement and enlargement, but it is unclear how that translates into military policy or strategy. Figuring out how to translate it is the burden of most of what follows.

The Paradigm Problem

One impediment to developing a coherent national security strategy for the new century is the conceptual burden of the past. During the cold war, a consensus evolved within the American national security community on how to look at the national security problem, the so-called realist paradigm. It was a comprehensive and enduring way of dealing intellectually with an environment and opponent whose way of looking at things was very similar to our own.

Is the realist paradigm an adequate device for organizing our thinking about the post–cold war world? To answer that question, we must first describe the paradigm's basic premises and their consequences. That analysis will allow us to "layer" the paradigm onto the current situation to see where it does and does not fit and to determine the consequences of applying the paradigm to the current situation.

Structure of the Realist Paradigm

Realism was the dominant operational philosophy throughout the cold war. Arguably, its ascendance can be dated to the series of treaties that produced the Peace of Westphalia in 1648, which created the modern state system as we know it. Some scholars date the realist way of thinking about international relations to Thucydides's *The History of the Peloponnesian War* (fifth century B.C.) or Niccolò Machiavelli's *The Prince* (sixteenth century). Both of these works defined deliberate politics behind strategy. Military power maintained the strength of the political heads. Alliances were tools to be used for the same purpose—to maintain "golden ages" of power enhanced by an ascendant security. The generally accepted twentieth-century "father" of realism is Edward Hallett Carr, whose scathing critique of the idealist approach to the interwar period was published as *The Twenty Years' Crisis, 1919–1939* in 1939.

Policy makers employ realist theory for two purposes, one of which is germane to our discussion: realism provides them with an operating code that derives from the assumptions and dynamics underlying realism. It is the use of realism as a guide to action that flows from Machiavelli's guide to the ruling family of Florence, the Medicis. Because the appropriate uses of military force are a central part of realism (and the part we will emphasize), it is highly relevant to assessing the present and future. The other use of realism is as a framework for studying international relations and reaching scientific knowledge about the international system. Were this a book on international relations theory, that use would be relevant; since that is not our purpose, we will deal with *operational* rather than *theoretical* realism.

The heart of realism is *sovereignty,* the supreme authority over the territorial state that defines political jurisdictions. Sovereignty is a property possessed by states, and it is a property that they jealously guard. Within the boundaries of states, sovereignty is sometimes the basis for legitimacy and usually the basis for authority.

The consequences of sovereignty are fundamentally different for international relations (the relations between states) than for domestic politics. In an international system where state sovereignty is the highest authority and where its protection is the highest purpose of states, there is no mechanism to regulate the relations among them; international relations thus are conducted in a state of anarchy (the absence of government). In this circumstance, there is no authoritative institution to settle differences between states, and the result is that states resolve conflicts however they can, and if they can. Conflict resolution becomes a matter of *self-help.* Since prevailing in a dispute generally comes at the expense of an opponent, international politics inevitably is power politics (power being defined as the ability to get a state to do something it would not otherwise do). Among the so-called instruments of power that a state has available to persuade or coerce an opponent is military force; the military becomes part of a state's "arsenal" to compete in the international environment.

States also have *interests,* which, under the realist paradigm, are superior to those of any other entity (international body or individual, for instance). The interplay of various states' interests (conditions of importance to them) defines both international relations and the appropriate recourse to force. Under the realist paradigm, states have hierarchically arranged interests, ranging from those that are of relatively little importance to those that affect the integrity and even survival of the state.

This hierarchy defines when national leaders feel compelled to use force to achieve national interests. Within the realist paradigm, the operative term is *vital national interests,* conditions deemed so important to the state that it will not willingly compromise them. The term "willingly" is important, because it suggests that states sometimes can be coerced into compromising their interests; indeed, when the vital interests of two or more states come into conflict, one or more of the parties must compromise their vital interests. Given that one state realizing its interests is an exercise in asserting power over the others, the use of force is justified when the interests at stake are vital. (Indeed, vital interests are sometimes defined as interests worth going to war over. This definition, however, is circular and leads to the conclusion that whenever force is used, vital interests must be involved, which is not necessarily true.) Two inescapable conclusions of the paradigm are that military force is a "natural" part of international relations and the threat or recourse to force to achieve national ends is legitimate. Those people with an interest in reducing or eliminating force from international politics find this consequence especially repulsive.

There is one more piece that must be added to the realist paradigm, at least to its American variant: what I call the *Clausewitzian-Napoleonic corollary*. This construct adds two requirements to the paradigm that the United States, and probably any other democracy, must meet when resorting to force. The first is that the use of force must be subjugated to political purposes and that force has meaning only in terms of the political purposes for which it is invoked. This is the influence of Carl von Clausewitz, an early nineteenth-century Prussian officer. The Napoleonic contribution is that force is justifiable only in the service of noble, lofty purposes, like those of the French Revolution and its aftermath. Certainly, in the early days of the Revolution, the French citizens who became the basis of the *levée en masse* that swept across Europe were so motivated, even if their leaders may have had more traditional geopolitical ideas in mind. The legacy of the noble cause remains.

The paradigm fit the cold war like a glove. The two major combatants were locked in a mortal competition where the most important, most vital interests of both were clearly at stake. The political goal of thwarting "godless" communism certainly met the Napoleonic standard of loftiness, and military force was clearly a tool of policy with a legitimate mission of protecting our most vital interests. Even the extension of the competition to the Third World, where it otherwise made little sense, met the conditions of the Clausewitzian-Napoleonic corollary. (The conflict on the Asian subcontinent was about many things—religion, ethnicity, even water—but it was never inherently about communism and anticommunism except by extension).

Realist Paradigm and the Post–Cold War World

If the realist paradigm made sense out of the cold war, does it extend as well to the international relations of the twenty-first century? More to the point, does the imposition of the paradigm to the current situation clarify or muddy when and where force should be employed? And, does it help clarify the quest for principles in which to ground national security policy?

The answer rests in part on the distinction between the tiers. Keohane and Nye, in their 1998 extrapolation of their theory of interdependence to the information age, argue that one of the ways in which the new international order differs from the old is that there are now two subsystems with two different sets of dynamics and rules. Their observation is similar to my description of tiers and Singer and Wildavsky's zones of peace and turmoil. According to Keohane and Nye the overwhelming dynamic in what we have called the First Tier is economic and political interdependence, since, as we have already noted, the members share political and economic ideas that include their gradual merger into the global economy. In the Second Tier, they suggest that conflict and force remain viable options.

What Keohane and Nye are implying is that, in contemporary international relations, the realist paradigm remains a viable way of describing and operating in part of the world (the Second Tier, or at least those parts of it that are violence-prone), whereas in the other subsystem (the First Tier), the realist paradigm, and especially its emphasis on the use of force, is irrelevant.

This makes a good deal of sense, since one of the salient characteristics of the First Tier is the near impossibility of any two member states going to war with one another. It flows from that observation that even the *threat* of force by one First Tier state toward another is so incredible as to be dismissed. Certainly, states have disagreements and apply power to resolve them, but the military instrument of power is not one of the tools. Thus, to the extent that the realist paradigm legitimizes the use of force as a "normal" part of international relations, it does not contribute to our understanding of the relations among the states of the First Tier.

The paradigm's legitimation of force remains relevant, however, in parts of the Second Tier, and especially in the internal politics of countries undergoing bloody internal wars. Military force retains its cogency, but with a twist. In a great number of these conflicts, the warring factions are not pursuing traditional political goals, and they are certainly not pursuing anything as ennobling as to gain power and rule on the basis of a set of political principles. Often, as in the criminal insurgencies in Africa, the political goals are simply to create political anarchy so that no authority can interfere with the "insurgents'" criminal behavior. Edward Luttwak refers to this kind of warfare as "post-heroic," and the British historian John Keegan argues that we are leaving an era where Clausewitz was relevant and are returning to an era of warfare that does not conform to Clausewitzian dictates. At any rate, the standards of the Clausewitzian-Napoleonic corollary do not help explain most of the conflicts now raging in central Africa.

The basis of using military force in the pursuit of important interests is also jeopardized when the realist paradigm is applied to the contemporary scene. The problem here is something I call the *interest-threat mismatch*. That concept implies that if one were to apply the criterion of vital interest to the use of American force in the current environment, its use would almost always be rejected.

Interest-Threat Mismatch and the Critique of the Realist Paradigm

The interest-threat mismatch is a commentary about the post–cold war world. It consists of two parts, as it affects the United States. The first part says, "where there are significant (read *vital* within the realist paradigm) American interests, there are hardly any meaningful threats." The parts of the world where the United States has important interests are, after all, the same places where it had important interests during the cold war: western Europe, northeast Asia, and North America (more or less the First Tier) and the Western Hemisphere (a part of the globalizing economy, by our definition). During the cold war, nearly all of the First Tier was threatened physically by the prospect of Soviet aggression, and the extension of that threat through Cuban mischief in Central America and the Caribbean created some problems there for which military force might arguably have been appropriate. The structure of animosity that aligned interest and threat so neatly during the cold war has evaporated. The resulting lack of immediacy in the threat environment means that we have the luxury of sitting back and thinking about what strategies we prefer rather than having strategies thrust upon us by necessity.

The other part of the mismatch says, "where there are threats to the peace, there are hardly any American interests." This observation reflects the pattern of violence discussed in the last section, and it suggests that where there are situations, even "opportunities," for the application of American armed force, American interests are insufficient to justify it. The Kosovar crisis fit this observation and exemplifies the ambiguity of strategy. American policy makers knew the crisis was coming and had plenty of time to develop and implement an approach to avert it. They did not; instead, they waited until it happened, then devised strategies on the fly.

The reasons to justify the application of American force are insufficient if the realist paradigm is the standard for employment. If the *vital interest* standard—that certain outcomes of conflicts would be intolerable to the national interest or to large numbers of Americans—is applied, where will we use force in the world? In the First Tier, the interests are adequate, but the use of force is unthinkable. There are plenty of opportunities in the Second Tier, but where would we be so grievously injured by untoward outcomes? Apart from those places where the hypodermic needle of petroleum addiction is apparent, the list is very short indeed.

So, the realist paradigm suffers when applied to the current situation. In the Zone of Peace, where interdependence is arguably the major dynamic, disagreements continue to arise and power is still exerted to exact outcomes, as the paradigm suggests, but the military instrument of power is irrelevant. In parts of the Second Tier, where, as Keohane and Nye point out, "realist assumptions about the dominance of military force and security issues remain valid," the calculus of interests that underpins realism effectively paralyzes U.S. military power because a hard-headed analysis of the calculus would conclude that virtually nothing that goes on in those circumstances is worth the expenditure of American blood and treasure.

Conclusion

At first blush, the analysis presented to this point could be construed as nearly neoisolationist, suggesting that the conditions of the world render the application of American power unnecessary and that we can retreat from the world, at least in military terms.

Such a conclusion would be premature and contradictory to my intent. The global system in which we now operate is one where American leadership is indispensable; the notion of retreat into some new form of isolation is impossible. The questions are how much American leadership, how soon, and in what form? The world expects American political leadership, and we try to supply it, even if we are wrong or some people do not like the form our leadership takes. The global economy, which we took the leadership role in creating, has in turn created a structure of interdependence and interpenetration from which extrication is impossible, and if it were possible would be overwhelmingly misguided.

We have faced these changes and have, by and large, adjusted to them rather well. Where we are having trouble is in determining how and where we will use force in this new order and hence for what kinds of situations we need to prepare. Do we continue, as we have for a half-century, to exert effort and expend resources on preparing for a big war that would provide the greatest, worst-case stress for our military assets when there is no "peer competitor" on the horizon to challenge us? Do we concentrate on the pin pricks of countless deployments in what are sometimes euphemistically called "peacekeeping operations," which undermine troop morale in places about which, to paraphrase Rhett Butler, we "scarcely give a damn?"

The problem is that we have not determined where in the world we will use force. It has been the burden of much of this chapter to suggest that the older rationales and strategies are inadequate in the contemporary situation. We face the equivalent of an interest-threat mismatch in what might be thought of as a *paradigm-reality mismatch,* a situation where theory does not match well the reality. We act as if we were still processing the cold war. The place where the paradigm is weakest is in the area of interests as a guide to action. To repeat, a traditional application of interests would paralyze American use of force in most real-world situations. For instance, policy makers trying to determine how any outcome to the conflict in Kosovo would grievously affect the United States or many Americans would inevitably conclude that American application of force was unwarranted, unless the paradigm is somehow changed.

The realist paradigm thus emasculates the application of American force, other than the most specialized forms of force (counterterrorist capabilities, for instance), most of the time. Maybe that is all right, and maybe not. Whether we should continue to decide on a case-by-case basis when to become involved is a matter of policy and strategy. The quest for policy and strategy is closely related to our choice of paradigms.

Bibliography

Attali, Jacques. "The Case of Western Civilization: The Limits of Markets and Democracy." *Foreign Policy* 107 (summer 1997): 54–64.

Carr, E. H. *The Twenty Years' Crisis, 1919–1939: An Introduction to the Study of International Relations.* London: Macmillan, 1940.

Clausewitz, Carl von. *On War.* Princeton: Princeton University Press, 1976.

Huntington, Samuel P. *The Clash of Civilizations: The Debate.* New York: Foreign Affairs Press, 1993.

Keegan, John. *A History of Warfare.* London: Hutchison, 1993.

Keohane, Robert O., and Joseph S. Nye Jr. *Power and Interdependence.* 2d ed. Glenview, Ill.: Scott Foresman, Little Brown, 1989.

————. "Power and Interdependence in the Information Age." *Foreign Affairs* 77 (September–October 1998): 81–94.

Luttwak, Edward. "Toward Post-Heroic Warfare." *Foreign Affairs* 74 (May–June 1995): 109–122.

Machiavelli, Niccolò. *The Prince.* Irving: University of Dallas Press, 1984.

Project Ploughshares. *Armed Conflicts Report, 1998: Causes, Conflicting Parties, Negotiations.* Waterloo, Ontario: Institute of Peace and Conflict Studies, 1998.

Singer, Max, and Aaron Wildavsky. *The Real World Order: Zones of Peace, Zones of Turmoil.* Rev. ed. Chatham, N.J.: Chatham House, 1996.

Snow, Donald M. *The Shape of the Future: World Politics in a New Century.* 3d ed. Armonk, N.Y.: M. E. Sharpe, 1999.

————. *UnCivil Wars: International Security and the New Internal Conflicts.* Boulder: Lynne Rienner Publishers, 1996.

Snow, Donald M., and Eugene Brown. *International Relations: The Changing Contours of Power.* New York: Longman, 2000.

————. *United States Foreign Policy: Politics Beyond the Water's Edge.* 2d ed. New York: Bedford, St. Martin's, 2000.

Thucydides. *The History of the Peloponnesian War.* New York: Penguin Books, 1954.

U.S. Army War College. *America's Army: Preparing for Tomorrow's Security Challenges.* Army Issue Paper no. 2. Carlisle Barracks, Penn.: Strategic Studies Institute, 1998.

2 | Thinking about Strategy in a New Environment

THE GIST OF CHAPTER 1 WAS THAT THE UNITED STATES ENTERS the millennium lacking an overall strategic concept, an overarching principle around which to develop a coherent set of policies and strategies to help policy makers answer the questions when and under what circumstances will the United States contemplate using force. The cold war consensus on traditional realism has been shattered by the collapse of the threat that enlivened its application. A decade of relative tranquillity, during which Americans have gotten used to the idea that any use of force will likely be discretionary on our part, has not made the hard work of redefining strategy seem compelling.

The experience in Kosovo has the potential to focus our attention on those situations where we will contemplate using force and thus on the question of how proactive we wish to be in ordering those parts of the world. The Kosovo experience did not sneak up on anyone, after all; there were clear warnings that it would explode as early as 1991, when Slobodan Milošević rescinded Kosovar autonomy and brought down the Serb yoke on Albanian necks. Although some in the policy community heaved a sigh of relief at the 1995 Bosnian cease-fire, many others pointed to the east and Kosovo.

Yet when Kosovo began to unravel, the United States seemed almost totally unprepared. Although various quarters offered advice touting or condemning the efficacy of airpower to induce Serb contrition and the need for inserting ground forces, few people were asking the serious questions: *why* and *for what ends* would Western, including American, force be brought to bear. We even wondered if Kosovo was another Vietnam. The disarray in the West could only bring solace to the Yugoslav leadership that holding out would eventually shatter what little consensus there was behind any Western action.

Need it have been so? I think not. We had had a full decade to think about policy and strategy toward the kinds of contingencies discussed in the first chapter, and, by and large, we squandered the opportunity. The Vietnam analogy held only in part: the early reliance on airpower in Kosovo to bring the enemy to heel, followed by the realization that ground force might be the only means to achieve a decisive end, certainly suggested a parallel, but it pretty much ended there. Kosovo was a civil war of secession, it was in the heart of Europe, and all the United States's principal allies were committed to ending it. Vietnam was an American enterprise; Kosovo was a First Tier adventure.

There is no sense bemoaning the absence of an exact analogy. Instead, the Kosovo experience can serve a useful function if it does no more than motivate us to take seriously the task of crafting a new national strategy.

The Factors Conditioning Strategy

Strategy does not arise in a vacuum. It is conditioned by several factors, two of which are worth noting. One is past experience: present and future strategy are affected by past strategy, which influences the intellectual outlook of those in the process; also, its success or failure suggests the extent to which change seems necessary. A second influence on strategy is its place in the overall political process that produces the policies with which military strategy must cope. The shape of that process and its outcomes are influenced by what I call *strategic orientations*, or how the country views its place in the international milieu. The concept of strategic orientations in turn leads to some notions about how orientations intersect with perceptions about the new environment and our national place in it.

Influence of the Strategic Past

We can identify two legacies of the cold war, traditional realist paradigm that contribute to our confusion in thinking about the present and future and which form an inertial drag against change. The first is the *conservative influence of the realist paradigm*. As noted in Chapter 1, the paradigm's intellectual roots go far back into human history, so far back that we can argue that some form of realism has always been around and is an inevitable part of thinking about strategy. The structure of realism imparts a belief that military force is the bedrock of national security and that the country is obligated to prepare itself for as many threats, mostly military, as might be mounted against it.

The result is the *national security state*, to which the structure of decision making toward the world evolved during the cold war. Prior to World War II, the United States's orientation toward the world was narrow and focused: foreign policy was the domain of the diplomats of the State Department, not something with which the average citizen needed to worry. Politics, as they said, ended "at the water's edge." Although this phrase refers to bipartisanship in foreign policy, its sense can be extended to beliefs about national security.

The cold war confrontation, regardless of who started it or how it started, changed the traditional American view of international relations. After World War II ended in 1945, and most certainly after 1957, when the Soviet Union successfully tested its first intercontinental ballistic missile and put U.S. territory under the Soviet nuclear gun, policy makers could not avoid emphasizing the military nature of international relations and thinking about the state's affairs primarily in military terms. Those who decried the militarized view of the world that the national security state implied were dismissed as dreamers; the "realists" would save the country, sometimes from itself.

The second legacy of the cold war paradigm is *a traditional view of warfare*, which has deep roots in the American experience and which is highly questionable in the contemporary environment.

The first element of the traditional view of warfare is the model of war on which it is built, what might be called the *peace-war-peace model*. According to this formulation, war is an interruption of peace, which is the normal and preferable condition. The function of military force is to repair a broken peace by going to war, subduing those who had breached the peace, and then returning to the more normal condition, which is peace. Americans generally view these breaches as being forced upon the United States rather than being of our own initiative (an assertion with which a number of American Indians might disagree, as, for that matter, might the Serbs). The implication is that we have a desire to restore normalcy to the world.

The peace-war-peace pattern dominated the American military experience through World War II. Typically, the United States (apart from the U.S.

Navy) disarmed during periods of peace, mobilized for war once it was forced upon us, and, after defeating the foe, disarmed and returned to the normalcy of peace as fast as possible.

The pattern also influenced how we thought about military force. Force is an aberration, not a normal part of the national existence. Certainly, it is needed some of the time, but not always. The sudden outbreak of the Korean War in 1950, which caught us off guard and largely unprepared, moderated the traditional American aversion to keeping large numbers under arms. The Korean experience gave rise to the so-called force-in-being, which would have fought World War III against the Soviet Union, against whom there would have been no time to mobilize. Despite a general acceptance of the force-in-being concept, the idea remained that we would use force only under duress and for the proud purposes of reinstating peace and promoting our ideals. Americans also continue to believe that war is a bounded activity; once it is over, it is over.

The second element of the traditional American view of warfare is the *way* that Americans fight. The American way of war, which probably dates to the final campaigns of the American Civil War fought by Gen. Ulysses S. Grant, who ground down the Confederate Army as it circled around Richmond, is hard and brutal. In the grinding and pounding of two armed forces against one another, victory goes to the biggest and strongest opponent. In the twentieth century, that has generally been the approach of the United States, which has been able to put more weight, often measured in firepower, into a fray.

There were signs that these traditional influences on the American perception of warfare were weakening even before the end of the cold war. Firepower-intensive war did not work in Vietnam: "bombing them back into the Stone Age" was indecisive against the North Vietnamese, and on the ground, masses of firepower were not enough to break an enemy who refused to stand in front of the rain of lead. As the cold war has melted away and it has become increasingly apparent that these traditions do not apply well to current realities, their relevance has come under increased questioning.

Once again, Kosovo mirrors our agony with the past. Constrained by presidential guidance that casualties were to be avoided, policy advisers proposed a Bosnia-style bombing campaign. The analogy was strained, because in Bosnia there had been a concomitant ground war; in Kosovo, there was no equivalent. Bombs raining from the sky were expected to bring yet another tyrant to heel, as apparently Milošević had been in Bosnia, but when that did not quickly and easily occur, our response was not to question the strategic premise but to up the ante with more airplanes and more bombs, despite military advice that this alone might not work (a view shared by the Army and Air Force). And our view of how to win changed in another way. No longer would the United States put its armies into the meat grinder against an opponent on the ground. Rather, the first premise of the "war" was that nobody (other, of course, than the Serbs, who do not vote in American elections) was to get hurt. Why not use ground troops? Because they would incur casualties, came back the answer, and casualties in war are no longer acceptable. General Grant could not have contemplated such an answer. Retired general Colin Powell, author of the so-called Powell Doctrine (which says you enter war with overwhelming force that overpowers and quickly subdues the enemy while minimizing—but not completely eliminating—casualties) must have been rolling his eyes.

Influence of the Political Process

Making strategy involves both those who are charged with devising it and those inside and outside the formal process who seek to influence it. Beyond their idiosyncratic personal characteristics, those people who make strategy tend to be influenced by two major factors: the way in which military force is considered and the institutional network in which they operate. Both of these factors are conditioned by the context of the international environment, a grounding in reality that makes strategy credible and acceptable. Each has a somewhat different impact on the shape and content of the strategic product.

In the American experience during the cold war, these influences emerged gradually and congealed. Particularly after the perceived debacle of Vietnam, the U.S. armed forces—and especially the Army—consciously adopted a Clausewitzian view of military force and the role it plays. Prominent among the Clausewitzian values the Army adopted and refined were those imbedded in the so-called Prussian dictum and the Clausewitzian trinity, both described below. Institutionally, the National Security Council system, the top of which was structured by the National Security Act of 1947 (as amended several times later), blossomed into an interagency policy formulation mechanism beginning under Dwight D. Eisenhower (1953–1961) and continued as such through the administration of Bill Clinton. Among the more powerful influences on the process are the military services, each of which brings its own distinct orientation. Each continues to affect strategic thinking; each will have to modify its views if strategy is to change.

Clausewitzian Legacy. As a demoralized and humiliated military began to collect postmortems on what had gone wrong in Vietnam, two themes dominated its concern. One was viewed as the politicization of the conflict, and it had two subthemes. One subtheme was what the professional military in particular viewed as excessive control of the military conflict by civilian politicians, captured by the term *micromanagement*. The other was the general confusion about what we were trying to accomplish. The second theme, especially severe from the Army perspective, was the loss of public support for the war effort. The net result was a sense of confusion about the whole Vietnam experience, which had to be clarified for the armed forces to become well. Carl von Clausewitz's *On War* provided the curative.

The problem of politicization of the war was particularly troubling and confusing. The U.S. military had a tradition of being apolitical that dates to the American Revolution and the fear among many colonial leaders and citizens that the military might become a Cromwellian monster, as it had in England. As an institution, the American military had, throughout its history, adopted an attitude about politics that bordered on disdain. Its attitude was manifested not only in a lack of political activism but also in a large degree of ignorance about politics and the political process, and especially about the relationship between political objectives and military activities. In this regard, the U.S. military was decidedly Jominian in its orientation (the French strategist Antoine Henri Jomini [1779–1869] believed in a very strict separation between the military and political authorities). This apoliticism began to break down under Secretary of Defense Robert McNamara during the 1960s, as the services began to compete more aggressively in the highly political competition for resources.

In Vietnam, political concerns placed considerable limitations on the way that the military conducted the fighting. The most obvious concerns arose out of the fear that some military action might cause the Soviet Union or the People's Republic of China to honor its defense commitments to the Democratic Republic of Vietnam (North Vietnam), thereby broadening the war and possibly escalating it to a general war between the communist and noncommunist worlds. The most famous constraint was the prohibition, until December 1972, on bombing Haiphong Harbor (through which most of the north's war-making supplies arrived on Soviet bottoms) for fear of sinking a Soviet ship. Effectively declaring the Ho Chi Minh Trail in Laos and parts of Cambodia a sanctuary until 1970 was another instance.

The military greatly resented this interference, which many officers and enlisted alike believed had the effect of making the military fight "with one arm tied behind its back" and contributed to the lack of military success we experienced. Even some years after the war ended, uniformed officers continued to grumble about Vietnam being a "political war," which is an obvious redundancy.

Another part of the backlash was questioning what we had sought politically to accomplish in Vietnam. Once again, many within the military (and outside it) questioned not only the worthiness of the enterprise (were any American vital interests at stake?) but also the apparent vacillation about what we sought to do. Within this charge were imbedded the idea that we had misunderstood the nature of the political situation in South Vietnam (was the war a popular insurgency rather than a cross-state invasion, as was officially argued?) and the notion that the military should have been given its marching orders and allowed to do its job unfettered by civilian authority.

The backlash also included the loss of popular support the military suffered in "the first war America lost." This was especially galling to the U.S. Army, which bore the brunt of the fighting and thus the criticism for the outcome. The Army, as RAND Corporation analyst Carl Builder has so eloquently argued, views its unity with the public as its most basic value. That knot was severed during the war, and into the 1980s the professional military was a disoriented institution that wanted desperately to reestablish its prestige with the American people.

Clausewitz provided a framework for rehabilitation. The Prussian dictum ("war is the continuation of politics by other means") and its elaboration in *On War* helped put Vietnam in perspective and helped establish the basis for a more politically sophisticated, activist military. The relationships embedded in the Clausewitzian trinity (the necessary coalition between the army, the people, and the government) provided the guidance necessary to reestablish the army's bond with the population and to assure that it would not be fractured in the future. The landmark study by the late Harry Summers (Lt. Col., USA), *On Strategy*, published in 1982, was a major turning point in adopting Clausewitz.

Clausewitz's admonitions about the relationship between war and the political purposes for which it is fought were simple and straightforward:

war (the use of force) has as its only meaning the attainment of the political objectives for which it is waged. To the extent that those political objectives are articulated, they translate into military objectives and campaign strategies to attain those political ends. Any attempt to conduct military operations outside this framework is a perversion of military force, which, Clausewitz argued, civilian authorities must be constantly vigilant to avoid. In his view, war has its own language (how you fight) but not its own logic (reason for fighting).

Accepting the Clausewitzian logic, the U.S. military began to put politics into perspective. The idea of "political war" disappeared from the lexicon, and at military schools (the war colleges, for instance) the curriculum moved beyond military history and strategy to the broader political milieu into which the military might be thrown. Officers added international relations to their credentials and became sophisticated in the process. Among the things they learned was their crucial role in advising political authorities about what kinds of political objectives can and cannot be attained by military means. One of the legacies of the Vietnam postmortem was the recognition not so much that the objectives in Vietnam were vague and vacillatory but that we could never devise adequate military means to attain them. In the process of accepting Clausewitz, the military became a major player in trying to influence policy, including counseling caution in military operations, as it did in Kosovo. The views of retired general Colin Powell are the quintessential example of this change in the military.

The Army, and especially Gen. Creighton Abrams, concluded that the rupture between it and the people was crucial to failure in Vietnam and would be an intolerable condition in the future. Following from the Clausewitzian trinity of army, people, and government, Abrams and others concluded that the rupture was caused by the fact that the American people had not been asked to support the war at the beginning and hence had little personal stake in its outcome. Abrams reasoned that in the future this problem had to be addressed up front; his solution was to put major responsibilities for waging war in the reserves. If the American people's friends and neighbors were going to be forced into military action from the beginning, their acquiescence could be assured by their reaction to activation of the reserves. This proposition was first successfully tested in the Persian Gulf War, and reserve call-ups have become a routine part of military deployments.

The Clausewitzian influence remains within much of the strategy-making process, and it is clung to tenaciously by many who see the rejuvenation of the military as the result of adopting Clausewitzian logic. At the same time, Clausewitz is closely associated with the realist paradigm, and as that paradigm comes under scrutiny, so too must the relevance of the Clausewitzian formulation.

Some have argued that it is no longer relevant. John Keegan, the British military authority, has been a leading critic. He argues that the period between the French Revolution and Napoleonic Wars (on which Clausewitz reported) and the end of World War II was an interlude in military history where the Clausewitzian formula worked, but that the relationship between war and politics that Clausewitz described and prescribed did not exist before and no longer does. Evidence supporting this assertion in the post–cold war world is the fact that many modern internal wars cannot be understood in Clausewitzian terms.

Does the fact that some actors on the contemporary stage eschew Clausewitzianism mean that it is no longer relevant to American strategy or the strategy process? Not necessarily. Clearly, the subjugation of military force to political authority remains a pillar of the American political system, and the relationship between clear political objectives and attainable military objectives and strategies is something that needs strengthening, not abandoning. If anything, military *and* civilian authorities should redouble their effort to understand this relationship. In the early days of Kosovo, for instance, many in the professional military said that bombing Yugoslavia was a military strategy that could not attain the political objective of ending Serbian repression of the Kosovars, advice ignored or countermanded by the White House.

"Pay attention to the Clausewitzian trinity" is equally good advice. One of the most striking characteristics of the post–cold war world is the lack of consensus on strategic goals and the application of military force in particular situations. During the cold war, such a consensus existed around the mission of containing communism (even if there was disagreement on individual applications of the doctrine), and hence the public did not need to be consulted with quite the same frequency as it needs to be now. If there is an aspect of the trinity that needs attention, it is the emergence of the idea that the application of military force is tolerable in the public eye only when there is near certainty that it will not result in any, or at least significant, American casualties. If the decision to rely on airpower rather than ground forces in Kosovo was dictated by the desire to avoid significant casualties rather than strategic reality, then some public education (and some would argue presidential leadership) would appear appropriate.

Those elements of the Clausewitzian influence discussed above remain relevant when planning strategy. Although the Clausewitzian approach has been tied historically with traditional realism and its emphasis on vital interests as the guiding criterion for deciding when or whether to use force, it need not be so tied. The Napoleonic aspect of the corollary may have to be altered, but not necessarily the dictum or trinity. If its alteration is necessary, it may be that we will have to alter our thinking to recognize that the opponents we contemplate facing do not begin from the same assumptions that we do. That, in turn, may affect the calculation of attainability of goals within the Clausewitzian framework.

Interagency Process. Over the years following passage of the National Security Act of 1947, foreign and national security policy came to be made through what is known as the interagency process. At the heart of this process is the National Security Council (NSC), whose statutory members include the president, vice president, and the secretaries of state and defense. The director of central intelligence (DCI) and the chair of the joint chiefs of staff (CJCS) are the statutory advisers, and the president may add others at his or her discretion. Typically, the White House chief of staff, the national security adviser, and the director of the Office of Management and Budget are also included.

The process has been enlarged over time by adding subordinate bodies. When the NSC meets without the president (either because the topic under discussion is not important enough to engage the president or the president feels discussions will be more candid in his or her absence), it is designated as the Principals Committee. Below the Principals Committee is a body comprising the chief assistants of the members, known as the Deputies Committee. At the bottom of the formal structure is a series of functional (for example, economics) and geographical policy coordinating committees, staffed at the assistant secretary level from the various agencies.

The interagency process as it currently exists is a cold war artifact, and with the cold war over, some have come to wonder if more relevant policy would not result through its reform. The NSC itself reflects the cold war milieu by placing the secretaries of state and defense as coequal advisers to the president, which in effect says that a major component of American policy toward the world is military. Designating the DCI and CJCS as principal advisers further reinforces the importance of what has become known as the national security state.

Such a distribution of expertise was at least arguably appropriate to the cold war (although some would argue that the military was *too* prominent), which was a confrontation with a heavily military flair and included a large amount of clandestine activity directed at the other superpower. From this process, the strategies and policies for containing communism were developed and implemented. The disappearance of communism as a major force in the world is, at least indirectly, a testimony to the success of the process. Admittedly, four communist states remain, but two are authoritarian regimes controlled by communist parties that eschew Marxist economics—China and Vietnam—leaving only minor powers Cuba and North Korea as believing tributes to Marxism-Leninism.

With operational communism consigned to the dustbin of history, the guiding principle of containment is irrelevant for the organization of American policy toward the world, including where and under what circumstances we will employ force. It has been over a decade since the cold war began to crumble, and yet there has not been a successor principle from which to derive strategy.

Some have begun to question whether the interagency process itself may be partly to blame for our conceptual sluggishness. At the Army War College strategy conference of 1999, for instance, a number of speakers raised this concern, primarily from the perspective that the interagency process as constituted is top heavy with governmental institutions with a national security emphasis. The conference speakers were concerned that this organization thus may not reflect the less militarized international environment, wherein other dynamics, such as the globalizing economy, are more prominent but not broadly represented in the NSC system. Suggestions for reform included statutory amendment to designate a broader array of statutory members (the secretary of commerce, for instance), closer coordination between of the NSC and the National Economic Council, and even tearing down the process and starting over.

There is another, subtler reason to think that the interagency process is part of the problem rather than the solution. That process was designed and refined to manage a single, large, and encompassing problem, and that is what those who staff it learned to do. This emphasis on a single problem led the military to emphasize preparations to deter and if necessary fight large wars against large, similarly configured opponents (the Soviets and their allies). Blunting this "worst case" was the standard, and it largely still is. Implicit in this mindset is the idea of the "lesser included case." What this means is that if you have prepared adequately for the worst that can happen, by definition you also have prepared for smaller problems that may arise. This predisposition is reflected in high-level military pronouncements that, for instance, any good soldier can "do" low-intensity warfare: if you can stop the Red Army, you can also defeat guerrillas or engage in peacekeeping operations. In reality, military capability is a question both of the size of forces one needs and what kinds of things those forces should be prepared to do, which is a training question.

The assumption that the worst case encompasses lesser cases is questionable at best. At the philosophical level, it implies that lesser scenarios are microcosms of the worst case. That presumption underlay early American conduct of the Vietnam conflict, when heavy armor units swept into the field on "search and destroy" missions only to discover that the enemy simply melted into the countryside rather than stand in front of the tanks to be mowed down. One way to look at the lack of military success in Vietnam is to view the mindset of preparing for European-style heavy warfare as precluding the development of strategies and tactics for successfully confronting the style of warfare the North Vietnamese and their South Vietnamese allies presented us.

Not only is the assumption that the worst case includes lesser cases empirically shaky, but the whole idea of the worst case is weakened in a world where there really is no worst case. Continuing to prepare to fight at the Fulda Gap when there is no enemy to come through it is silly, although one would scarcely realize the silliness by looking at the configuration of the army. Instead, the old worst case is replaced by smaller versions, such as the simultaneous North Korean invasion of the South and a repeat of Iraq's invasion of Kuwait (and possibly beyond). In the abstract, such a scenario presents a worst case that, if successfully countered, would result in the capability to surmount lesser scenarios, or so the reasoning goes.

This kind of thinking is fundamentally flawed in at least two ways. First, although the Iraq-North Korea scenario is conceivable (it has been said, after all, that anything anyone can think of is by definition conceivable), it is also highly unlikely. True, it would be serious if it did occur, but is preparing for this unlikely scenario a good use of scarce material and intellectual resources? Second, the real threats to international security for the next decade or so are internal wars of the Kosovo-Rwanda variety, which do not resemble at all the Iraq-North Korea plan, meaning there is no lesser inclusion. Planning based on these two contingencies boils down to incredulous planning for which there are no realistic applications. Other potential problems (Taiwan and China, Russia and some of the other Soviet successor states, for instance) cannot be ignored. Planning for them militarily, however, is problematical.

Why then would the people in the process adopt and implicitly sanction this form of planning and thinking? One reason is that preparing only for the small, if likely, contingencies could leave us with armed forces incapable of fighting the North Koreans or the Iraqis again in the closest facsimile to conventional, European-style warfare that one can conjure. It is thus "comfortable" planning, employing ways of looking at things that evolved from the cold war environment. Yet it runs the risk of operational irrelevance in dealing with the real world.

Can the interagency process be reformed adequately to deal with real uses of force in the future? Although one should never say never, the track record over the past decade or so is not very encouraging. Part of the problem comes from the top of the system, where possibly too narrow a range of institutional perspectives is represented. Certainly that is true lower down the ladder, where specific strategies for dealing with military contingencies are made.

The structure of military opportunities is the subject of Chapter 3. That chapter's emphasis is weighted away from the traditional contingencies and toward Kosovo-type situations. I am uncertain whether the people currently guiding the interagency process either can or, more appropriately, want to undertake fundamental change. For that reason, I will propose, in Chapter 5, some alterations to the process to make it more responsive to current and foreseeable reality.

Strategic Orientations: The U.S. Self-Perception

Fundamental to answering questions about the future use of force by the United States is how the United States sees itself and its role in the world. During the cold war, there was essential agreement on the threat of communism and the need to contain its spread and to deter Soviet (and Chinese) military advances. The realist paradigm neatly described the orientation that the United States adopted toward a hostile international environment dominated by a concrete Soviet opponent and dictated an activist, internationalist posture that seemed so clear that only the fringes of the political spectrum could take issue with.

The end of the cold war deprived the United States not only of an enemy but of an intellectual focus and consensus. With the largest and most compelling threat removed, the environment was both simplified and confused at the same time. The world is simpler (and arguably a much better place) because the danger of a system-threatening war that could escalate to nuclear war has all but been removed. Granted, Russia still maintains the thermonuclear arsenal that it inherited from an imploded Soviet Union (indeed, the United States helped make sure the Russians, rather than any of the other successor states, got the strategic inventory), at a level of about six thousand warheads. Early in the post–cold war era, Russia and the United States took the symbolic step of aiming the arsenals away from one another, although Russia threatened to re-aim them (a process that takes only a couple of minutes) over NATO's bombardment of Yugoslavia in 1999. Still, it is difficult to imagine why Russia might start a nuclear war.

The world has seemed more confusing because of the lack of focus. Most of the problems in the world today were also there before 1989, if in sometimes different mutations; except in Cambodia, Sri Lanka, and a few countries in Latin America, there was less of the systemic savagery and atrocity that have become almost commonplace in internal wars. Proliferation was a problem then and remains one now, and terrorism had begun to raise its ugly face to the world. So what is different now?

There are two major and related differences, each of which contributes to the lack of consensus from which we currently suffer. The first is America's role in the world has changed. It is commonplace to describe the United States as the only superpower in a world where we do not have significant opponents. The disagreements that we have with people in other countries (and that people in other countries have with us) are exactly what American predominance means in terms of American responsibilities and levels of activism. The second difference has to do with which conditions in the world are so important as to impel us to undertake decisive action to make conditions conform to our preferences.

The situation is different in another way as well. During the cold war, U.S. actions, including the use of force, appeared to be dictated by the force of events. Expansionist communism was a force to be stopped, but it took the initiative, to which we reacted. When we used force, it was of necessity, or at least that is how we viewed it. Occasionally, we miscalculated, using force when some different form of action was arguably more appropriate; Vietnam was a case in point. In the contemporary environment, few situations compel our action, and especially the extreme action represented by military force. Our uses of force in the contemporary milieu are of choice, not absolute necessity.

The absence of consensus reopens old debates, which fill the pages of journals like *Foreign Affairs* and the op-ed pages of leading newspapers. We can think of the debates on two axes: realism versus idealism and internationalism versus neoisolationism. Each axis represents a continuum between the extremes of, for instance, total isolation from the world and total involvement. After briefly describing each axis, we can combine them to describe strategic choices.

Realism versus Idealism

We have already discussed the realist paradigm in sufficient detail, so it need not be described again. What may be important is to highlight those elements of realism that are most affected by the changes that have occurred since the end of the cold war.

The bedrock of realism, as a philosophy and guide to action, lies in two basic concepts and their dynamics, which were introduced in Chapter 1: sovereignty and state interests. In combination, they create the justification for armed force and the rationale for its use. Sovereignty describes the basis of a state's authority over its territory and, conversely, the absence of its authority over the events in other sovereign jurisdictions. Absolute sovereignty (total and complete control devoid of any outside influence) has probably never been possible and is certainly not possible in the twenty-first century. Although states routinely cede parts of their sovereignty as matters of convenience and choice, at the heart of the Westphalian system is the political principle of a state's control of its territory and the absence of any superior authority in the relations among states.

Realists and idealists agree on the role of sovereignty as a descriptor of system dynamics, although idealists will point more readily to exceptions—or dilutions—of sovereign control than will those who believe in the philosophy of realism. Their differences are around the center of the continuum: how much authority the state has versus how much its authority has been diluted.

Where there is fundamental disagreement between the two sides is over the *desirability* of state sovereignty as the guiding principle, and the answer has both theoretical and practical implications for how one views the world and what is to be done in it. Within realism, state sovereignty leads to a state-centric system, which in its most extreme rending results in the "billiard ball" analogy of international relations: states are like impenetrable billiard balls, and international politics consists of the balls bouncing off one another. Because the balls are impenetrable, the relations between them do not affect their insides (authority of the state within the state).

No one takes the billiard ball analogy literally, of course, since things that happen within one state affect others, as do the relations among them. The philosophical question is the desirability of maximizing or minimizing the extent of state sovereignty.

Within the United States, the realist interpretation has always been dominant, particularly with regard to protecting American prerogative within the territorial boundaries of the state. Evidence of this predominance has come in a number of ways, but especially in American resistance to the extension of international norms (even when they are similar to our own) to cover Americans. Sometimes the results are quite anomalous: the United States failed to ratify both the United Nations Declaration on Human Rights (most of which is lifted from the U.S. Constitution) and the Convention on Genocide for more than forty years after they were framed on the grounds that the imposition of these standards would violate American sovereignty. More recently, the United States took the lead in opposing international, and particularly internationally enforceable, war crimes conventions. Lining up with some of the true thugs and villains of the international system, which had truly to fear the application of these norms to *them*, the United States took the position that since numerous American soldiers are stationed overseas who might be accused of some war crime, having such laws in place would put Americans under the jurisdiction of others—a clear violation of the American sovereign right to control the treatment of its nationals.

Idealists find such claims ludicrous. Basing their own position in individual sovereignty (the idea that ultimate authority resides with individual humans, who may forfeit some of their authority to the state), they argue that a major consequence of state sovereignty is to provide a shield behind which states can regularly violate the rights of their citizens. If the right of state sovereignty is taken to its extreme, for instance, the international system had no right to interfere in the "ethnic cleansing" that the Milošević regime of Yugoslavia inflicted on Albanian Kosovars in 1999, because Kosovo is a part of sovereign Yugoslavia.

Starting from the idealist position yields different results. The term "idealism" suggests a belief in the existence of certain rights to which all people are entitled and the promotion and defense of which should be the key to international politics. Most idealists do not argue that their philosophy guides international relations, and except for those at the extreme who argue for world government (a position not seriously put forth in a generation), they do not expect state sovereignty to disappear any time soon. What they do see are operational flaws in the state system for which they believe aspects of sovereignty must be sacrificed in the service of the rights of humans.

One perceived flaw is that the system normalizes interstate violence (war). Sovereign states, after all, engage in self-help to achieve their ends, and in a world where there is no authority higher than the state to adjudicate conflicts, the use of military force will be a normal recourse in some instances. Many idealists believe that the normalcy of war is a *structural flaw* in the system, and since sovereignty is the building block of the system, it is central to the idealist agenda to lessen the extent of state sovereignty.

Another flaw is that sovereignty becomes the curtain behind which the tyrants and thugs suppress their populations with impunity, knowing that other states would have to break the established rules to interfere in their internal affairs. The United States, like most states that advocate strict state sovereignty, does not do so in order to condone internal atrocity, but the result can often be to put the United States in bed with a strange set of characters and to advocate policies that on their face seem ludicrous. U.S. advocacy of the direct violation of Yugoslav sovereignty through the bombing campaign and the placement of foreign troops into Kosovo was anomalous given our position on sovereignty.

Idealists, with their conceptual grounding in individual sovereignty and the concomitant protection of individual rights and security, take exception to the notion that the international community is prohibited from taking actions when human rights are violated—especially in atrocious ways such as ethnic cleansing. They advocate a loosening of sovereign barriers to effective international actions when crimes against humanity are involved. The actions against Yugoslavia over Kosovo represent an almost perfect mirror of this disagreement. The NATO allies in effect argued the idealist position by punishing Yugoslavia through the air (thereby violating sovereign Yugoslav airspace) and by insisting that NATO troops be stationed on Yugoslav territory after the conflict ended. Yugoslavia, in contrast, argued (quite correctly) that everything NATO did and proposed was a direct violation of their sovereignty and therefore illegal—the realist position. The United States took the schizoid position of arguing that force was appropriate to end Yugoslav atrocity (the idealist position) while arguing for state sovereignty in other venues over other issues (the realist position).

The other dynamic of realism is the primacy of *national (or state) interests* as the guide to policy implementation, including (and specifically) the use of force. Once again, the positions of the realists and their opponents are often caricatured by describing the extremes.

There are two basic disagreements about interests. The first is over what entities have interests. In the classic state-centric realist formulation, it is the state that has primary interests, and the interests of others (individuals, groups within states, international organizations) are subsidiary to those of states; whenever state interests clash with those of others, it is the others' interests that must suffer. Most idealists would not deny that states have interests and that most of the time they are ascendant; what the idealists question is the exclusivity of state interests within the international realm; they would argue that there are times when the interests of individuals and even of the state system as a whole transcend the interests of states. The current idealist emphasis on humanitarian interests is an example of this assertion.

The other disagreement is about what levels and whose interests justify the application of force. In the classic realist formulation, the question revolves around *vital* interests. Although there is no consensus on what constitutes a vital interest, I have always defined it as a *condition or situation over which the state (or whatever entity) will not willingly compromise and which it will defend with all available means, including the use of force.* The litmus test for whether an interest is vital is the answer to the question, "To what extent will I (the average American, or the state) be adversely affected by the outcome of a situation?" If the effect of the worst outcome is negligible or tolerable, then the interest is less than vital and the use of force to achieve some desired outcome is unjustified. If, on the other hand, the worst possible outcome would be intolerable, then presumably vital interests are engaged and force is justified. Different observers will view these distinctions differently; the location of the line between vital and nonvital interests is the basis of much of the national security debate.

Three points should be made about this definition. The first has to do with the word "willingly." There are occasions when states are forced to compromise on situations of considerable import to themselves because they lack the ability (or power) to avoid compromise. This is a malady of the weak. Second, some people (including myself) have reservations about including the authorization of force as part of the definition because it makes the definition circular. Force is justified when vital interests are endangered; therefore, whenever force is used, vital interests must have been involved.

Third, determining when an interest is vital appears to be a lot simpler than it is in fact. At the extremes, the determinations are easy. For instance, the most important interests of the United States since the end of World War II have been the sanctity of American territory; a free, democratic, and accessible western Europe; and the security of northeast Asia (Japan and Korea). Those interests were worth fighting to protect during the cold war, and they remain so; the difference between the cold war and post–cold war eras is that those interests are not meaningfully threatened, with the possible exception of the Republic of Korea. At the other end of the spectrum, nothing that could happen in the Sahel region of Africa would adversely affect many Americans very much.

People disagree over situations that are more ambiguous in their effects. The boundary between interests that are vital and those that are less than vital is not a line but a confidence interval (a band of opinion on either side of the issue). In other words, there are a number of situations the vital nature of which is viewed differently by different actors, and much of the policy debate, including the current one on when to use force, is about where the line should be drawn. Where it should be drawn is a matter of philosophical and practical importance.

In the cold war context, the situation in Central America, and specifically Nicaragua, during the 1980s illustrates the difficulty of fixing the boundary between vital and nonvital interests. The question was how damaging to U.S. security was the Marxist regime of Daniel Ortega in that country? On which side of the line was the worst possible outcome: Cuban-sponsored mischief in the region that flanks the Panama Canal, which, should it spread, would butt against the southern border of Mexico?

Some people in the administration of Ronald Reagan (1981–1989) believed that a Marxist regime in Nicaragua was intolerable and hence launched the series of illegal events known as Iran-contra to organize, equip, and sustain Nicaraguan *contra* guerrillas to combat the regime and, hopefully, bring about its downfall. A number of Democrats in Congress disagreed about the tolerability of Ortega and his Sandinista regime and passed legislation (the Boland amendments, named after their sponsor, Rep. Edward P. Boland of Massachusetts) to prevent military aid to help overthrow the regime.

During the cold war the United States employed military force on a number of occasions when, arguably, less than vital interests were at stake.

The only unambiguous cases of vital interests being endangered were Korea (and we did not declare that to be vital until after the North Korean invasion began) and the Persian Gulf (which was added to the list of vital interests by the Carter Doctrine of 1980). In other cases (including Vietnam), our interests were not unambiguously vital.

So what is new about the post–cold war era? The most obvious difference is the lack of an overarching threat to which one can pin vital interests. The United States could not, in 1965, have made much of a case for invading and occupying the Dominican Republic except as an extension of the global contest between communism and anticommunism. We used force for small reasons, but we had a larger justification.

And that is what is currently missing. The realists of the cold war could pin militarization to the bugbear of communism, and there is no equivalent rationale to justify small applications of force. Thus, the debate about future uses of force comes down to a contention about where the line between vital and less than vital interests are and whether that line should move in different contexts. That, in turn, boils down to a matter of what conditions and situations in the world we find tolerable and intolerable.

Realists and idealists disagree on this matter, and the practical result is to invert the two groups' traditional positions on the use of force. From the vantage point of the traditional realists, there are few circumstances where American interests are sufficiently jeopardized to justify the dispatch of American forces into harm's way. Of the post–cold war deployments by the United States to date, the only one that realists can justify is Haiti, as a way to staunch the flow of boat people to south Florida, and even that is something of a stretch. The cold war's "hawks" are thus effectively turned to "doves" by their assessment of what is to be done in the world.

The cold war doves, on the other hand, are sharpening their talons. From the idealist concept that entities other than states possess sovereignty and thus have interests, there are plenty of situations for which force can be justified. These are generally linked to the concept of *humanitarian interests* or even, in the formulation of former United Nations secretary general Boutros Boutros-Ghali, humanitarian *vital* interests: conditions of individuals and groups that are so wretched the entire community has an obligation to alleviate them. From this vantage point, there are plenty of opportunities to employ force: the doves are now the hawks.

This disagreement could be seen in the debate that occurred about sending American forces to Kosovo. The question of using American force (and different forms of force) in the Kosovar tragedy was really a question about what side of the vital interest line the situation lay on, which in turn is a question about whether humanitarian interests (and which humanitarian interests) are on the vital or less than vital side and whether, given that it would be a NATO operation, supporting NATO was itself a sufficient interest. Although the public debate was rarely explicit in these terms, it is down to these terms that the debate can be boiled. In particular, the question was whether any outcome was worth the expenditure of American blood.

During the bombing campaign, discussions rarely focused on vital interests. Many realists couched their opposition in terms of vital interests (while acknowledging that whatever interests we had probably could be defended only by sending in ground forces). The administration and some analysts attempted to frame the issue in terms of U.S. interest in a tranquil Europe and a healthy NATO, but that effort tended to founder on the Europeans' initial lack of enthusiasm for ground action. In turn, the Europeans gradually came to accept implicitly a humanitarian interest and an analogy between Kosovo and the Holocaust.

The key unresolved question is whether the American public agrees with Presidents Bush and Clinton that some humanitarian interests have now entered the category of actions for which the United States will use force—and more to the point, actions that potentially involve American casualties. Kosovo is a test in this regard. The situation is unlikely ever to convince hardcore realists to favor intervention; even the prospects of renewed Balkan instability do not meet the definition of vital interest. Intervention must thus be justified otherwise, in this case on the grounds of human suffering. Given that Kosovo is located in Europe, if the case cannot be made there, it is not clear that the case can be made anywhere.

Internationalism versus Neoisolationism

Although the distinction between internationalism and neoisolationism is less clear now than it was a generation ago, there is still a debate within the United States about how active this country should be in the world system. During the cold war, there was no question that the United States be internationalist; since the United States was the necessary bulwark against Soviet communism, there could be no meaningful advocacy of a return to the isolationism that many blamed for the rise of Adolf Hitler and World War II. Is the situation different now that there is no meaningful opponent to force

American participation as a world leader? In other words, is American leadership more or less necessary now than it was then?

The answer is ambiguous, which is why the debate over the extent of American exposure to the world has reemerged. One can argue, as observers like Patrick Buchanan do, that we have done our part in the world and now it is time to retreat and take case of ourselves. But would doing so create a vacuum in the world that would be worse than what some critics consider to be America's overbearing presence in the world?

There are two dynamics in the contemporary international environment that make an American retreat from the world stage either impossible or foolish. The two factors are the growing economic interdependence of the countries of the globalizing economy and the fact that the United States, whether it wants to be or not, *is* the world's remaining superpower.

Economic interdependence replaced East-West confrontation as the principal dynamic of international relations in the 1990s, a point made forcefully by *New York Times* foreign correspondent Thomas L. Friedman (see *The Lexus and the Olive Tree* for his most complete argument). Despite setbacks like the 1997 East Asian financial crisis, interdependence is likely to continue into the foreseeable future. Granted, interdependence is more characteristic of the countries of the First Tier than the Second, but through economic associations like APEC and the North American Free Trade Agreement, it is spreading to select parts of the Second Tier as well. Where it has not penetrated, it is the overwhelming aspiration of most people in most countries.

The symbol and leader of the globalizing economy is the United States. Much to the surprise of the doomsayers of the 1980s, the American economy retooled itself from manufacturing to the knowledge industry during the late 1980s and early 1990s. Whereas analysts like Paul Kennedy and his fellow "declinists" were loudly announcing the deflation of the United States from the status of dominant player to struggling competitor, the 1990s reinforced American leadership. The U.S. system has become the symbol for economic organization, having swept aside the cronyism, opacity, and corruption of its chief rival, the Asian (or more specifically, Japanese) approach to economic organization.

The icon of the U.S. system is free trade, and its global apostle is Bill Clinton. British prime minister Margaret Thatcher and Ronald Reagan laid the groundwork for capitalist growth in the 1980s by emphasizing deregulation and privatization of economic activity to create the free capitalism of Adam Smith. The legacy of Bill Clinton and his chief economic adviser,

Robert Rubin, will be to have added the Ricardian principle of comparative advantage to the internationalization of economic activity—free trade.

This uniquely American creation is the envy of the world, detractors notwithstanding. Do some foreigners believe that the success of the U.S. economy has created a certain level of arrogance among Americans? Of course. Do many fear that the assault of Americanization erodes their social and cultural forms, that "American culture" is an oxymoron, that U.S. influence works like a computer virus, erasing what was there and not replacing it with much? Probably. Is it not also true that the elites (and especially the young and well educated) aspire to be as much like the United States as they can be? Overwhelmingly yes. They may love us and they may love to hate us, but they also want the prosperity that we exude.

Having been largely responsible for creating this situation, can the United States decline leadership or, more fundamentally, back away from the system it has created? Certainly there are some domestic pressures to do so, most coming from segments of the economy that cannot pass the test of global comparative advantage (textiles, rust-bucket union enclaves, and the like) and segments that have not yet seen trade barriers drop for them (citrus growers, for instance). Having said that, the overwhelming majority of Americans and many foreigners benefited from the conditions of the 1990s and would not like to see them reversed or derailed. The only way to reverse these effects would be to renege on the principles we have espoused and to erect new barriers to replace those we have knocked down. That is not practical.

The other reality is that the United States is the only remaining power that possesses the full range of realist instruments of power: the United States is the world's preeminent military power *and* economic power *and* democracy. When NATO appointed itself to represent the world and launch an air offensive in Yugoslavia, most of the airplanes and ordnance were American because the United States has the largest and most powerful air force. It is said that when the U.S. economy sneezes, the whole world gets a cold; the financial crises of 1997 and 1998 in Asia and Russia prove the reverse is not true. Joseph S. Nye Jr.'s "soft power" (the appeal of the principles of the American system) is an indication of the strength of the American dream.

U.S. preeminence has limits, however. Being the world's superpower does not endow the United States with hegemonic power: we cannot force the rest of the world to do much (although through the U.S. "deputy," the International Monetary Fund, many feel we effectively do so in the economic realm).

The pervasiveness of American influence comes from the fact that, alone among the powers, the United States has both global interests and global reach. That means when problems arise nearly anywhere, what the United States thinks and is willing to do have to be factored into the equation. U.S. influence is not always decisive, and the U.S. position does not always prevail; it is, nonetheless, always a consideration.

The effect of American superpower status is to make us the big kids on the block, and that has negative consequences regardless of whether one emphasizes the "big" or the "kid" part of the metaphor. To many, and especially to many Europeans, the United States lacks the leadership experience of, say, France. Whenever the United States ignores the lead of its more experienced colleagues, they accuse the United States of having the arrogance of youth. No recent series of events better illustrates this attitude than the tragic farce over what to do about Bosnia in the years leading up to the Dayton Accords in 1995. The Europeans (especially the British and French) vacillated on what kind of action to take. At times they said only decisive military action would break the impasse; at others they said such actions would put their peacekeepers on the ground in jeopardy. The United States took the lead in proposing action at some points and opposing it at others; whichever course we proposed triggered the opposite inclination from our allies. We were blamed for both action and inaction.

The biggest guy on the block is seldom the most popular and is usually, rightly or wrongly, viewed as the neighborhood bully. The biggest kid on the block gets what he wants because he is stronger than the rest; the most powerful country in the world can exert inordinate power in many circumstances and force issues to its liking. The responses when the United States acts as the superpower have become familiar enough: we are called "arrogant" or "imperialistic" and we are increasingly resented by a world that would like to clip our wings a little.

This new form of "America bashing" has even found its way onto the pages of generally internationalist journals like *Foreign Affairs*. The March–April 1999 edition, for instance, featured a predictably dour tract by Samuel P. Huntington ("The Lonely Superpower") that suggested our allies and the rest of the world are turning against us and a finger-wagging piece by Garry Willis (titled "Bully of the Free World") saying we must become less overbearing if we want to lead the world.

The notion that the United States is a menace to the system and must mend its ways falls short in addressing four salient factors about the contemporary system and the United States's place in it. First, it fails to address one of the most important reasons for American leadership: most of the world does not fear the United States. We may be a bumbling leader (a different issue), but few countries need fear the United States unless they are engaged in egregious behavior, such as slaughtering their own population (the Serbs in Kosovo), or in behavior that the United States deems offensive, such as drug running (Manuel Noriega in Panama). Could the same be said if any other country were the remaining superpower? Would the world fear superpower Russia? China? For that matter, Germany?

Second, the critics of American leadership fail to account for the fact that most of the world wants to emulate the American system, or at least the material quality of life associated with it. Sometimes envy is involved, which does not always lead to friendly relations, but the influence of American "soft power" is still there even when others disagree with us. The May 1999 flap with China over NATO's accidental bombing of the Chinese embassy in Belgrade comes to mind. Chinese citizens were indignant (probably rightly) over this incident and voiced their opposition vociferously with apparent government approval for several days. In less than a week, the worst of the propaganda barrage subsided, and the Chinese got back to the more normal routine of consuming Western luxuries and making things to sell to the Americans.

Third, whether foreigners like to admit it or not, they expect American leadership in most situations even if they may not always like the quality or content of American leadership. They often view U.S. attempts to be neutral as an abrogation of our responsibility. In some sense, we are damned if we provide leadership and damned if we don't.

The fourth factor is that no coalition has formed to oppose the United States. History demonstrates that whenever one state emerges as overwhelmingly powerful, a rival coalition will assemble to balance it. But that has not happened, nor is it likely to. For one thing, the United States is part of all of the structures and is aligned with all of the members of any potential coalition. For another, the fact that we are not feared means the traditional reason for a counter coalition—the fear of military threat or action—is almost entirely missing. France may resent having to listen to the bumpkin Americans and grouse that it wants to be taken into account—what one writer has referred to as wanting to be a "virtual" power (having the veil but not the responsibility of leadership)—but that does not translate into a serious and sustained challenge to U.S. leadership.

The fact that America's status extends to the military level is the major concern of this book. And the question has to be, is there an alternative to a vigorous exertion of American leadership in the military area? Put another way, is some form of neoisolationism possible or desirable?

The answer is no. Those who argue for a diminished level of American activism are, in effect, suggesting a dilute form of isolationism. If one starts from the assumption that the global economy has so entangled us (or that we have entangled the rest of the world) that it is impossible to engage in economic isolationism without bringing the global economy down around our ears, then what forms can a retreat take? The obvious candidates are the political and military areas, around which most of the complaints over American leadership tend to cluster.

Would a retreat from leadership in either the political or military arenas really be welcomed by the world at large? In some isolated instances and by some actors, the answer is undoubtedly yes. Certainly Saddam Hussein would prefer a less proactive American policy toward the Persian Gulf, and Slobodan Milošević would be happier if the United States faded into the background regarding the Balkans. Without American political leadership and the threat or use of American force in either area, the world's stance would be different than it is. Without the United States in both Kosovo and the Persian Gulf, the range of possible international responses would have been circumscribed. In Kosovo, for instance, an effective bombardment campaign would not have been politically or militarily possible, leaving the European NATO allies with the options of rhetorical bluster or a large-scale land invasion. Is that what the French really wanted? I do not think so.

Political and military retreat—the only two forms that neoisolationism can take—are probably impossible. To argue that the United States can be an active participant in the global economy while becoming politically and militarily aloof is to make the same error as was made in the interwar period and even earlier, in the nineteenth century. Politics, including the military instrument of power, and economics are not separable; you cannot be part of one game and not the other. The isolationists thought we could be after World War I, and so the option of applying American power to managing the system became unavailable, to the system's detriment and ultimately to our own.

Moreover, there is no alternate candidate for the global leadership role should the United States elect to retreat. For better or worse, the United States is the only country in the world with global interests and the resources (admittedly not unlimited) to pursue a global agenda. Others countries may grumble that there is no counterweight to the Americans and even suggest a coalition might be assembled to balance power once again. But no such coalition has arisen, nor is one likely to. A European Union-based military force, as has recently been proposed, might be of some use in dealing with small-scale contingencies on the continent and give the Europeans the feeling of being able to act without the United States. But such a force would have few teeth and probably little directed resolve, and it is difficult to imagine in what kinds of situations it could be employed while excluding the United States. About the only part of Europe that needs pacifying from time to time is the Balkans, a situation unlikely to change in the near or medium term. Would the proposed EU force, excluding the United States, have been of much use in Bosnia, or for that matter Kosovo? In the absence of a political unity of purpose that is not evident right now, the EU force package is a feel-good but toothless apparition suitable for only minor contingencies.

A geopolitical system from which the United States retreats would be largely leaderless and impotent in the event challengers to the system should arise. Some countries have the pretension of leadership but not the wherewithal. At worst, the system could deteriorate to something like that of the early 1930s, when the Western powers lacked the resolve or ability to stem the rising tide of fascism. Would the 1930s have been different had the United States been internationalist? We can never know. But a contemporary international system without its largest, most powerful member out front is a recipe for disaster, as it was before. To draw an admittedly shaky analogy, having the United States direct the rudder of the ship in a twisting, occasionally mistaken direction is almost certainly better than having no one or several others trying but failing to control the rudder.

The case for rejecting neoisolationism is not entirely idealistic or based on some abstract notion of international good. Rather, the third reason for rejecting an American retreat from realism is that it is not in America's best interests to do so. America's well-being, by whatever measure, is best served by a tranquil international environment. At the most elemental level, it is good business to have strong and stable markets and economic partners who will help spread the global economy and increase our own prosperity. When we tried between the world wars to separate our concern for international tranquillity from our interest in doing business with the world, we found it did not work. Political instability contributed to the depression and to the rise of economic nationalism, which in turn led to the erection of high barriers to trade and was one of the causes of the Second World War. Right now, a downward spiraling such as occurred in the 1930s is fanciful as long as the United States remains engaged.

Combining Perspectives

The two contrasting views of the world—realism versus idealism, internationalism versus neoisolationism—can be combined to create alternative perspectives on the American role in the new international system and the use of American force in the new system. From the combinations and my analysis to this point it should be clear that I am prejudiced toward certain positions and combinations. Those who believe in the neoisolationist position will be discontented by the way I characterize the two neoisolationist combinations. I make no pretense about being fair in my characterizations; I hope, however, that my observations pass the test of realism.

The two perspectives are combined in matrix form in Figure 2.1. The neoisolationist positions (Cells 3 and 4) can be explicated fairly easily, as each represents an historic American view of the world. The realist-neoisolationist position (Cell 3) is, in the current debate, most associated with Patrick Buchanan. His basic argument, shared by H. Ross Perot and others, is that America's intrusion on the world is largely unwanted and, more important, diverts our attention from more important domestic priorities, such as the health of the economy. Inherent in this argument is that most of the violence and instability in the world is none of our business, because American vital interests are so infrequently affected. Buchanan's position also includes an antigovernment strand, since foreign and national security policy are the province of governments. Buchanan and others like him would prefer to see more of U.S. dealings with the world directed through nongovernmental organizations. But as I suggested earlier, the major question is whether his position is realistic. For instance, can the health of the American economy and the well-being of American workers really be enhanced or guaranteed by isolating ourselves from other forces? Similarly, does turning our backs on difficult global situations like Kosovo or the Sudan really serve American interests in the long run?

The idealist-neoisolationist combination depicted in Cell 4 has a longer historical record. The idea behind it dates to the waves of immigration in the nineteenth century, when people fled tyrannies at home for a chance at a better life in the United States. To our forefathers from the seventeenth century

Figure 2.1   Realist-Idealist and Internationalist-Neoisolationist Perspectives

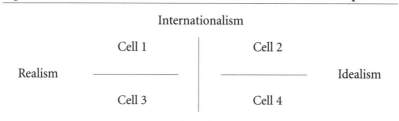

forward, the power politics of Europe, and later of Asia and elsewhere, was tainted and impure. The United States, to borrow a phrase often issued by Ronald Reagan, was the "shining house on the hill," a beacon of idealism in sharp contrast to the rest of the world. Opening the country's doors to the oppressed but slamming them shut against an impure world is an American tradition.

The tradition continues today. Although immigration policy has sought to put some controls on this process, fulfilling the Statue of Liberty's promise to the downtrodden remains a part of America.

Not only does isolationism run counter to the American tradition, it is also a questionable guide to policy. The desire to remain aloof, for instance, delayed the United States's entrance into World War I and contributed to our lack of preparedness for World War II. To the contrary, some of the anti-Vietnam sentiment arose from the tainting nature of the experience rather than an isolationist strand. It is illusory to think that the United States can live in a glass bubble, aloof from the rest of the world. American borders, after all, are almost completely out of control, in that we can no longer effectively regulate who comes into this country, especially along the Mexican border.

The other pair of possibilities reflects internationalist orientations attached either to realism (Cell 1) or idealism (Cell 2). In the real-world policy debate, the differences between the two are not so great.

Whether one likes it or not, some form of internationalist orientation seems dictated by the structure of the contemporary world. Involvement is unavoidable; the questions are the extent and content of that participation. If the arguments put forth to this point make any sense, the content and extent are pretty well dictated in the economic sphere. It would also be difficult for the United States not to take the leadership in most political concerns as well.

The question that remains the source of contention is that raised by this book: when, where, and for what purposes will the United States be willing to employ force in the future?

As already noted, the principal operational differences between realism and idealism boil down to two points: state sovereignty as the sacrosanct first principle of international relations, and the circumstances in which interests are sufficiently great to justify the use of force. There is considerable confusion and schizophrenia about these questions because only some fusion of the realist and idealist positions suffices as a philosophical underpinning for national security policy.

The American policy on sovereignty illustrates both the confusion and the schizophrenia involved. On one hand, the United States is the most fervent champion of national sovereignty among the major powers and demonstrates its commitment to *American* sovereignty in such diverse actions as refusing to ratify the Convention on Genocide and the Universal Declaration on Human Rights for more than forty years and, more recently, standing as the sole democratic power refusing to sign the treaty to create a permanent war crimes tribunal on the grounds that the United States would never relinquish control of its own citizens. Presumably, this claim to sovereignty would save a future Lt. William Calley from being tried for his crimes. In 1969, when Lt. Calley commanded the American infantry unit that committed the My Lai massacre, there was no authority to press war crimes charges against him and his subordinates; today there is—except against Americans, since we are not signatories to the treaty. *American* national sovereignty is inviolable. Other countries' sovereignty, depending on how they exercise it, is not so secure. There is considerable historical evidence to suggest that the sovereignty of countries that disagree with us is not sacrosanct, and we will violate it when we see the need. The multiple U.S. interventions in Central America and the Caribbean states during the first half of the twentieth century showed relatively little regard for the sovereignty of those we conquered. More recently, U.S. unilateral and multilateral military actions taken in direct violation of the sovereignty of other states include the invasions of Grenada, Panama, Somalia, and Haiti, and actions such as Operations Northern and Southern Watch against Iraq and Operation Allied Force against Yugoslavia. That some of these actions were sanctioned by international bodies (the UN Security Council, for instance) makes them no less violations of sovereignty and endow them with no more international moral or legal force than a unilateral action.

Are the positions contradictory? Absolutely! Are they an embarrassment to the United States, and are they a source of international accusations about American arrogance? Yes, they are. Then, why do we hold these positions?

At the most flippant level, we hold them because the United States is a big, powerful country that can get away with making up the rules as it goes. But there is another explanation that has to do with who proposes one position or the other. Those who argue most strenuously for the protection of American sovereignty are, by and large, lawyers and legislators (not mutually exclusive categories), who are more concerned with the United States than with the international system. Their job is to guard the United States from a hostile outside world (which, in a sense, makes them isolationist realists). Those who propose the violation of sovereignty in the name of redressing international ills—many analysts of international relations, for instance—are much more concerned with the international than the domestic ramifications of the positions they advocate (they are essentially internationalist idealists). The two groups do not interact with one another.

The idea that countries cannot interfere in one another's affairs because doing so violates national sovereignty is a dead letter. If anyone doubted this assertion before NATO launched Operation Allied Force against Yugoslavia, the absolute extent to which Yugoslav sovereignty was ignored indicates what the international system thinks about those who would hide behind sovereignty. The precedent of Allied Force is: abuse your citizenry and we *might* punish you.

Two rejoinders are necessary here. Although a country's sovereignty no longer precludes outside action, that does not mean the international community will react every time a government acts atrociously toward some part of its population. If the principle of intervention were universal, there would have been a sizable international commitment to the Sudan some years ago. The question, with which we continue to grapple, is what circumstances lead to international sovereignty-ignoring actions.

The second rejoinder is more cynical: actions are likely to be confined to countries that are too weak to deal with their internal problems (Somalia, for instance) or to resist the intrusion. President Clinton put a positive spin on this rejoinder in his May 23, 1999, op-ed piece in the *New York Times,* in which he enunciated the criterion for involvement: "Where we can make a difference." This criterion is an extension of the Weinberger Doctrine—named for Ronald Reagan's secretary of defense, Caspar Weinberger—which stated that we should become involved only where we can win, which is a legacy of

Vietnam. At a more cynical level, the Weinberger Doctrine means U.S. violation of sovereignty is limited to the weak; the United States can maintain its self-contradictory position with no danger that the new principle—that sovereignty is not inviolable—will be applied to us.

The second operational difference between the realists and the idealists is over what kinds of interests activate the use of force. As noted earlier, these positions have gone topsy-turvy in the post–cold war world, where idealists counsel the use of force in the name of humanitarian interests and the realists counsel restraint whenever vital interests are not engaged. Here the problem is not so much a matter of schizophrenia as it is a philosophical difference about the direction of the international system and America's role in it.

The near unanimity with which the international community embraced the cause of alleviating Kosovar suffering (quite apart from its tactical differences over how to alleviate it) suggests that the strict realist criterion of vital interests is no longer embraced by much of the world's political elite. Reducing the probability of taking military action because vital interests are not at stake is no more disqualifying than arguing that the violation of sovereignty precludes involvement. The failure to act in situations similar to Kosovo—in places like the Great Lake region of Africa—suggests that the international community has not universally embraced as its standard for intervention the humanitarian banner either. What is safe to say is that the standard has moved away from the strict criterion of vital interests to embrace some humanitarian interests and situations as well.

But which ones? The answer to that question is not yet clear but will be conditioned by at least two observations from the recent past, which will be mentioned here and explored more fully in subsequent chapters. Each observation suggests a limitation that will influence the development of standards.

The first has to do with costs and outcomes. If it is true that most humanitarian efforts will be undertaken by First Tier, democratic states against Second Tier states, costs and outcomes will be salient concerns. The bottom line in terms of costs is casualties: it is becoming apparent that the willingness of Western powers (certainly the United States) to become involved is inversely related to the number of body bags that come home. It is much easier to explain to the American people why we are involved in a place like Kosovo, which on its face does not much matter to the United States, if we are not making the ultimate sacrifice of young people killed. How many downed aircrews would have turned us against the Kosovar conflict? In terms of outcome, the bottom line in Kosovo was whether we would have needed to send in ground troops to affect a peace. Doing so would have upped the ante and brought casualties. Fortunately, it did not come to that.

The second observation has to do with achieving positive end states. Conflicts like Kosovo do not end when the last shot is fired and the cease-fire is signed. They are long-term commitments where outside forces are going to have to be on the ground for extended periods to keep the former combatants from one another's throats while their leaders work out an enduring peace arrangement and to aid in the recovery, in the repair of a physical and social environment broken by war.

Neither of these goals is easily achievable. Bosnia shows that we can keep the former combatants apart as long as we are there, but few people believe that peace would hold were SFOR suddenly to leave. SFOR is now over four years old: how much longer will it have to be in Bosnia? Operations Northern and Southern Watch have been protecting the Iraqi Kurds and Shi'ites since 1991 and 1992, respectively; when can we abandon them to Saddam Hussein? No one wants to guess.

I reach two conclusions from this discussion. The first is that the neoisolationist position is untenable in the present and foreseeable future, and any American grand policy will necessarily be internationalist and include provision for American political and military leadership. The second is that the idealist and realist positions need to be meshed. The old boundary between them, based in traditional vital national interests, has moved toward the idealists; the question is how far. If a grand policy is to emerge, it will have to meld these two observations into an approach that I call *realistic internationalism*.

I make no pretense to this being a revolutionary concept that will alter fundamentally the way we talk and think about the use of force. Instead, I put it forward as a synthesizing idea that, I hope, can become the basis for more common discussions of the force question. At heart, the idea behind realistic internationalism is that the standard for when force will be used has indeed moved. In the absence of traditional uses of force (such as in large wars of the Desert Storm variety or larger), force will now be used for smaller purposes, in more measured applications, and with lower costs but also lower expectations of what it can and will accomplish. This concept will be elaborated upon in Chapters 4 and 5, where its possible applications will be discussed. The traditional uses of force have expanded (although possibly toward a reversion to the "small wars" of the colonial period); exactly how and where is the major thrust of the analysis that follows.

Conclusion

The major purpose of this chapter has been to review how we think about the role of the United States in a changed international environment and, more specifically, how we think about employing force for national and international ends. The major thrust of the argument has been that the questions and orientations that were evident in the cold war period are pretty much the same now; it is the context—the kinds and qualities of problems extant—that is different. The realist paradigm ruled the conceptual universe for forty years, but it is too restrictive as a means to gauge where and when to use force. The idea of realistic internationalism pushes the envelope of the realist paradigm outward, in the process reshaping it to capture more adequately the international landscape of the twenty-first century.

The environment is different in one other way that has been implied but not explicitly stated: the very reduced prospect that the United States will be forced into a large war by an enemy that attacks the United States with major armed force. This is a two-part proposition. First, the likelihood of a big war (Korean War-sized or bigger) in the next decade or so is very slight. This is hardly revelatory; it is the same assessment of the environment that the Pentagon made in the 1997 *Quadrennial Defense Review* and that Harvard professor and former Clinton administration official Ashton Carter and former defense secretary William Perry made in *Preventive Defense* (they talk about the absence of Class I threats).

Second, the proposition speaks to *why* the United States may use force. On the one hand, although the United States is unlikely to be the victim of a major military attack, it will almost certainly be the victim of small attacks—the terrorist bombing at the Khobar Tower apartments in Saudi Arabia in 1997 and the bombings of American embassies in Dar es Salaam, Tanzania, and Nairobi, Kenya, in 1998—to which we may wish to respond with some force. On the other hand, the United States may *choose* to interpose itself with force into other circumstances, as it has in places like Kosovo.

What I am saying is that the United States will use force when it *wants* to, not when it *has* to for the foreseeable future. We will not be involved in what have been called wars of interest or necessity, which are the kinds prescribed by the realist paradigm. Rather, we will be involved in so-called wars of choice, discretion, or even conscience, where moral and political judgments, about which reasonable people can disagree, will be the deciding factors.

Going to war after being attacked by a perfidious enemy is not a difficult decision to reach; deciding whether intervention is, in President Clinton's justification of Bosnia and Kosovo, "the right thing to do" is much harder.

Bibliography

Boutros-Ghali, Boutros. *An Agenda for Peace: Preventive Diplomacy, Peacemaking, and Peacekeeping.* New York: United Nations, 1992 (supplemented in 1995).

Builder, Carl. *The Masks of War: American Military Styles in Strategy and Analysis.* Santa Monica: RAND Corporation, 1989.

Carter, Ashton B., and William J. Perry. *Preventive Defense: A New Security Strategy for America.* Washington, D.C.: Brookings Institution, 1999.

Clausewitz, Carl von. *On War.* Princeton: Princeton University Press, 1976.

Clinton, William Jefferson. "A Just and Necessary War." *New York Times,* May 23, 1999.

Friedman, Thomas L. *The Lexus and the Olive Tree.* New York: Farrar, Straus, Giroux, 1999.

Huntington, Samuel P. "The Lonely Superpower." *Foreign Affairs* 78 (March–April 1999): 35–49.

Jomini, Antoine Henri. *The Art of War.* London: Greenhill Press, 1996.

Keegan, John. *A History of Warfare.* London: Hutchison, 1993.

Kennedy, Paul. *The Rise and Fall of the Great Powers: Economic Change and Military Conflict from 1500 to 2000.* New York: Random House, 1987.

Luttwak, Edward. "Toward Post-Heroic Warfare." *Foreign Affairs* 74 (May–June 1995): 109–122.

Snow, Donald M. *National Security: Defense Policy in a Changed International Order.* 4th ed. New York: St. Martin's Press, 1998.

Snow, Donald M., and Dennis M. Drew. *From Lexington to Desert Storm: War and Politics in the American Experience.* Armonk, N.Y.: M. E. Sharpe, 1994.

Snow, Donald M., and Eugene Brown. *United States Foreign Policy: Politics Beyond the Water's Edge.* 2d ed. New York: Bedford, St. Martin's, 2000.

Summers, Harry. *On Strategy: A Critical View of the Vietnam War.* Novato, Calif.: Presidio Press, 1982.

Weigley, Russell F. *The American Way of War.* New York: Macmillan, 1973.

Willis, Garry. "Bully of the Free World." *Foreign Affairs* 78 (March–April 1999), 50–59.

3 | The Menu of Violence

To THIS POINT, THE DISCUSSION HAS FOCUSED ON THE USE OF
American force as if that were a singular exercise. The foregoing analysis implied that all uses of force are pretty much the same and that all applications
rise from a common set of calculations about threats to the United States and
the consequences of employing force. Such assumptions are false and misleading.

Force can be configured (or packaged) in a variety of ways for a variety
of purposes. The *military instrument of power*, as force is often referred to in
discussions of applying its various forms to the country's international problems, is not *an* instrument at all but a series of instruments of various sizes
and natures that can be applied to a panoply of situations. Each kind of problem requires different capabilities. The use of these instruments carries different consequences (costs and risks, on the one hand, and outcomes on the
other, for instance). A tank battalion would have been an ineffective instrument for attacking the alleged terrorist camps in Afghanistan associated with
Osama bin Laden, in response to his supposed involvement in the U.S. embassy bombings in east Africa in 1998. A Delta Force team would have been of
limited utility in the face of the Iraqi army in 1990 as it sat in Kuwait City.
Different situations create different needs.

Not all threats to American interests have military force as their solution,
or even part of their solution. To some extent, the limited utility of military
force is the result of the new post–cold war environment, where national survival is not threatened in the way it was before and where the security agenda

has been expanded to fill the void of current problems. Thus, people now commonly refer to "economic security" or "environmental security," concerns that are legitimate but for which the security label seems strained to most realists (nonrealists embrace this expansion). Moreover, they are uses of the security concept with no military aspect. For example, cyberwar, the idea that a potential enemy might try to infiltrate and disrupt the computer networks on which modern communication—including military communication—is based, is unconventional. Concern for computer security and integrity is reasonable; the reference to "war" seems a bit of a stretch from conventional usage.

The sharp distinction between military and nonmilitary solutions to the country's problems has dissipated. This change is symptomatic of the breakdown of the peace-war-peace model. Just as the idea that peace is interrupted by war (in which military force takes precedence over the more normal condition of peace), which is followed by the return to peace, has largely gone by the boards, so too the sharp distinction between military force and nonmilitary options has been overcome by a new reality.

In many instances, military and nonmilitary actions have been combined in nontraditional ways. Take the problem of embassy security, which can be extrapolated to the security of all American forces overseas. Is embassy security a problem for which the military should have the primary or sole responsibility, or is it a nonmilitary problem? Although one can make the case that protecting embassies is a responsibility of the military, the solution has both military and nonmilitary aspects.

The basic threat to embassies is from terrorist bombings, and that adds at least two elements to the problem that are not military in any direct sense. One prime method of securing against bombings is by taking antiterrorist measures, in this case making embassies more bombproof: making access to the grounds more difficult by putting them far from streets, installing "dragon's teeth" so that a bomber cannot rapidly approach, shielding them with structures that absorb a bomb's effect, and the like (measures recommended by the Inman commission in 1985, which Congress refused to fund at the time). Physical protection is the military's task, but authorizing and facilitating it have diplomatic and political aspects. Moving embassy sites away from streets or closing streets in front of embassies (as Pennsylvania Avenue in front of the White House was closed) require political action before they can be instituted. Some of the redesigning for protection is an engineering concern for which military expertise may be relevant but not critical (civilian engineers can erect barriers too), but implementation is military. In addition to physical protection, acquiring improved intelligence about the activities of potential terrorist organizations and the plans they make is a paramilitary task at best.

The "menu of violence" for which force may be used is not exclusively or always military. Not all force is military, and not all attacks merit a military response. We learned this lesson in the mission to Somalia, relearned it in Bosnia, and are relearning it yet a third time in the massive effort to rebuild Kosovo, so as to leave that troubled territory a more stable and peaceful place. We are also learning (or relearning) just how difficult such an enterprise can be.

The remainder of this chapter will focus on the broad range of situations in which the United States could conceivably decide to use armed force over the next decade or so. To organize the examination, I will borrow a distinction from the conclusion of the last chapter: employments of necessity, when the United States *must* use force because of the nature of the situation; and employments of choice, when the United States *voluntarily decides* to use force. As the preceding discussions suggest, the necessary applications are the least likely, because they encompass traditional uses of force. Nuclear war, the first example, is extremely unlikely, but it is possible and thus must be considered as a menu "choice." The vast majority of opportunities are of choice, but the interest-threat mismatch suggests that the choices will be hard, since traditional interests are not clearly or often entailed.

Employments of Necessity

Is it possible, in the contemporary environment, for the United States to be forced into military action? Could someone attack the United States, or attack reliable American allies with whom the United States has vital interests, or surprise the United States with some kind of military action to which we might feel obliged to respond? The answer to each question is yes.

Each scenario is one that the United States could face. The U.S. homeland remains *physically* at almost as much risk now from Russian nuclear weapons as it was during the cold war from Soviet nuclear weapons, although almost everyone would agree that the likelihood (or risk) of such an attack has decreased dramatically. A country could attack an important U.S. friend or ally, as has been done periodically in the past. And strategic surprises can still occur and necessitate action.

These problems have considerably different likelihoods of occurring and differing consequences. Deterring nuclear war with the Soviet Union was always the highest priority during the cold war because of the consequences of such a conflict. Nuclear war was also always the least likely scenario to arise, because the consequences extended to and were known by both sides. There was always a greater likelihood of someone attacking a friend, although among our friends, those of great importance to the United States (for example, western Europe) were probably less likely to be attacked than were those of lesser importance (for example, Vietnam). Crises such as the need to evacuate embassies (in Monrovia, Liberia, to cite one example) can occur at any time.

Each of these contingencies, all of which are familiar to the experienced observer, are different in structure and thus different in response, including the military nature of the response. Our possession of nuclear weapons presumably deters a nuclear attack against the United States but is probably of limited utility in deterring a conventional attack against an American friend. Similarly, American nuclear might is unlikely to dissuade an angry mob from attacking the U.S. embassy in some Second Tier country. Conventional forces, in one configuration or another, are most useful for defending friends but are probably not very effective in deterring nuclear war, and they are unlikely to be rapid and flexible enough to secure a besieged embassy. The worst case, in other words, does not encompass lesser cases.

Although historically less frequent, engagements of necessity fit the traditional image of American force and thus are the kinds of future conflicts that the realist paradigm would appear to fit the best. The reason is tautological: if wars of necessity are conflicts that one has no choice but to fight, then the most important interests of state, namely vital interests, must be involved. Since vital interests are the activating condition for employing military force within the realist paradigm, there is no reality-paradigm mismatch, since threats and interests are in alignment rather than in opposition. In other words, both the paradigm and the concrete threat counsel the same action.

Since employments of necessity, especially large and consequential ones, are the least likely in the foreseeable future, the realist paradigm provides an adequate framework only for those things that we are unlikely to do. It is less suitable for limited crisis uses of force.

We will look at each contingency, beginning with the most consequential and least likely (nuclear war), continuing through the somewhat less consequential and relatively unlikely (conventional war), and ending with the least consequential but most likely (crisis situations).

Nuclear War

During one of the televised presidential debates of the 1992 election campaign, President George Bush said that one of the accomplishments of his administration was that the American people no longer went to bed at night worrying about the threat of nuclear war. After the election he rued that the remark—and the accomplishment—did not seem to resonate with the American people. The reason it did not is largely that the nuclear threat was a matter of perspective. For older voters—who had grown up during the 1950s and 1960s, when the threat of World War III seemed real, and who had participated in drills of what to do if nuclear war started—the end of the cold war brought relief from worrying about the ghoulish prospect of nuclear incineration; but they did not want to be reminded of the past. Younger voters, who had grown up in the 1970s and 1980s, had *never* worried much about nuclear war and wondered what the president was talking about.

Nuclear war is still a possibility, in that both Russia and the United States retain nuclear arsenals of sufficient size and destructive capability to inflict on one another so much devastation that a U.S.-Russian exchange would not differ greatly in destructive effect from a Soviet-American exchange. Admittedly, arsenal sizes are down, so there would be somewhat less damage; however, to use an old Churchillian phrase, although the rubble would not bounce quite as often, it would still surely bounce. What most people would argue is vitally different now is that the motivation to begin an exchange has been greatly decreased: godless, authoritarian communists might have wanted to attack the West; nascent democratic Russians lack the ideological justification.

In large measure as a byproduct of improved Russian-American relations, the nuclear situation has changed for the better in many ways. Formerly Soviet weapons have been consolidated under Russian control. When the Soviet Union broke up, Soviet strategic nuclear weapons (those aimed at the United States) were located in four of the successor republics: Belarus, Kazakhstan, Russia, and Ukraine. Their dispersal was a problem, because it meant the potential for multiple fingers on the former Soviet launch buttons. With the assistance of the United States, negotiators succeeded in convincing the other three to turn over their weapons to Russia in return for assurances the weapons would not be used against them and for economic assistance.

Another improvement has come in the area of targeting and readiness. During the cold war, the United States aimed more than ten thousand nuclear warheads at targets in the Soviet Union, and vice versa. Under an agreement between former president Boris Yeltsin and President Bill Clinton, the arsenals have been retargeted away from one another, at remote areas of the world's oceans. The readiness levels have been reduced as well. During the cold war, for instance, 30 percent of American strategic bombers (B-52s) were constantly airborne, to guard against being caught in a sneak attack; today, the fleet is routinely on the ground.

Each of these improvements is arguably more symbolic than real. Although the United States and Russia no longer target one another, the warheads could be reaimed at their old targets in a matter of minutes, and no one has torn up the cold war target lists. Alert status also could be upgraded quickly. The point of retargeting and readiness reductions is to create a less charged environment; they improve the "atmospherics" of nuclear balance.

Russia and America have also improved their cooperation in the area of weapons. For a Russia desperately in need of hard currency and with little else to offer (other than minerals and energy that the state produces inefficiently), the temptation to trade in weapons and weapons expertise has been considerable. Unfortunately, those countries that want such contraband (Iran, for instance) are among those that the United States least wants to gain nuclear secrets. The Russian government has been very cooperative in attempting to avoid these perils and has worked with the United States in foiling criminal attempts by the Russian mafia, allegedly in cahoots with elements of the Russian military, to export plutonium.

Arms control is another area of Russian-American cooperation, although the record also displays some of the limits on cooperation and remaining frustrations in the relationship. On the positive side, the process of limiting the size of the two sides' arsenals that was begun during the cold war (the Strategic Arms Limitation Talks, or SALT) has continued under the umbrella of the Strategic Arms Reduction Talks (or START). START I was the first agreement that produced sizable cuts in nuclear arsenals, limiting nuclear warheads to 6,000–7,000 apiece (as opposed to more than 12,000 apiece at the height of the competition). The treaty, signed on July 31, 1991, in Moscow, was ratified by the U.S. Senate on October 1, 1992, and by the Russian Supreme Soviet on November 4, 1992.

START I spawned further efforts. Since the countries share an interest in the nonproliferation of nuclear weapons, and since none of the countries likely to gain the capability would have faith in their weapons without testing, Russia and the United States became leaders in promoting the Comprehensive Test Ban Treaty, which bans *all* nuclear explosions. Russia and the United States signed the treaty on September 24, 1996, and it had 154 signatories as of October 1999. Only 26 countries, however, had ratified the treaty by that time; Russia and the United States were among those that had not. The Senate voted against ratification on October 14, 1999.

START II, the purpose of which was the reduction of strategic arsenals to a level of about three thousand apiece, was signed in Moscow on January 3, 1993, and was ratified by the U.S. Senate on January 26, 1996. The Russian Duma (parliament) did not ratify it until newly elected president Vladimir Putin managed to push it through in April 2000. The United States delayed the long-planned commencement of START III while awaiting the Duma's ratification.

The plight of START II is symbolic of the volatility of Russian politics and the frailty of the Russian-American relationship, which makes the retention of a robust nuclear capability a prudent hedge against the small possibility of a revitalized nuclear confrontation. The main reason why the Duma had not ratified START II was that it became a symbol of the rancorous relationship between Boris Yeltsin and the very conservative, and in many cases procommunist, membership of the Duma. It was also an indirect symbol of the pro-Western, pro-American stance of Yeltsin and the latent anti-Americanism of those segments in the Duma that oppose the accord. Since Yeltsin had only tenuous control of the Russian political system during his last years in office, the United States did not feel that it could pressure him to force ratification, because the effect might have been to force a climactic confrontation between the president and the Duma that we were not sure who would win. Circumstantial evidence of the shakiness of Yeltsin's control over the body politic would include the deployment of Russian troops to the Pristina, Kosovo, airport on June 12, 1999, in contravention of agreements to which the Yeltsin government had agreed.

Although the cold war is over, not all of its artifacts have disappeared. The two principal antagonists still have large arsenals pointed at one another, and deterrence could still fail. Moreover, my assertion that the principal difference between then and now is the lack of motivation on Russia's part to initiate war needs qualifying. I meant that the pro-Western elite in Moscow, who are prodemocratic and procapitalist, have no motivation to revive the old confrontation. But there are people in Russia who resent the humiliation their state has undergone over the last decade, who harbor resentments against what history has taught them is a hostile West (and who see NATO's eastward expansion as evidence of their suspicions), who wish for a return of Soviet grandeur as a feared superpower, and who blame the West for their current predicament. There are ultranationalists and communists in Russia who feel all of these things. Although the likelihood of their gaining power may be small, it still cannot be ruled out altogether. As long as that is true, keeping our powder dry is probably good advice.

For the United States, it is prudent not to insist on further reductions while there is so much turmoil in Russia. Over the past decade, the once-mighty Soviet Union has been reduced to a tattered band of struggling states, and the embarrassment and humiliation of the fall from superpower status is felt no more strongly than in Russia, where there are deep grumblings about somehow restoring Russian glory and power. It was commonplace to refer to the Soviet Union as a "Third World country with nuclear weapons." The description is even more apt and embarrassing now to the Russians. To reduce the one measure by which the Russians can lay claim to great power status—nuclear weapons—is to strengthen the arguments of the superna-tionalists. Western security would not be served by heaping additional fuel on the supernationalist fire by insisting on further deep nuclear weapons cuts.

Furthermore, nuclear weapons have a stabilizing effect on the Russian-American relationship, especially given the political instability within Russia. One of the legacies of the cold war is a phenomenon I call *necessary peace,* which exists between the holders of large nuclear arsenals capable of inflict-ing massive societal devastation on one another. Since both sides know that the consequence of an all-out nuclear war is the annihilation of both soci-eties, they will avoid such a war at all costs. Moreover, since any military conflict between the two could escalate to nuclear war, all military conflict must be avoided.

The nuclear arsenals, therefore, place a lower limit on Russian-American relations. Even if the worst were to happen in Russian politics and a stri-dently anti-American regime came to power, that regime could not allow Russian-American relations to deteriorate to the point that war became pos-sible (assuming rationality on the part of such a regime). On the brighter side, a gradually strengthening Russian economy and democracy could clear the way for closer nuclear cooperation and greater arsenal reductions.

Russia is not the only nuclear or potential nuclear opponent with which the United States must concern itself. The revelations in mid-1999 that China had stolen U.S. nuclear secrets and China's public commitment to modernizing its forces remind us that at some time in the future China could become a formidable thermonuclear foe. Further proliferation in places like North Korea could put Americans under the nuclear gun. However, given that most of the candidates for proliferation are Eurasian, proliferation is a more immediate problem for Russia than for the United States. Moreover, nuclear saber-rattling by India and Pakistan raises the possibility (however unlikely) of American participation in a nuclear conflict in which it was not an initial combatant.

Conventional War

Cross-border wars between sovereign states have become, at least for the time being, almost an anachronism in the post–cold war world. Unless you count the NATO attack on Yugoslavia in 1999, there has been only one classic attack by one country against another since the Iraqis annexed and were subsequently driven from Kuwait during the Persian Gulf War. That conflict was a border war between Peru and Ecuador over an uninhabited area of the upper Amazon basin that has been in dispute for a century. The "war" consisted of some border probings that lasted about two weeks and resulted in a couple dozen casualties. Otherwise, since the end of the cold war international violence has been limited to skirmishing over disputed boundaries (Pakistani "irregulars" and Indian troops over Kashmir), flare-ups between long-time foes (periodic military interactions by the Koreas), or continuations of old wars of independence (Ethiopia and Eritrea). In some ways, this is not so new; there were relatively few cross-border wars during the 1970s and 1980s either. What may be somewhat different is our detachment from them; there are no longer any cold-war ramifications to pique our concern.

This changing state of military affairs has been traumatic for Western, and especially American, military establishments. Cross-border wars pitting national forces against one another in a military style reminiscent of World War II are the American way of war. Conventional war is what we have planned for and executed. Desert Storm validated the experience, as our armed forces executed against the overmatched Iraqis the strategy and tactics that had been designed for Europe, with enormous success.

Conventional warfare continues to guide our thinking and our planning. Although the military has been ridiculed for it, the basic planning paradigm remains the *two regional wars* problem: how to prosecute successfully two more or less simultaneous wars resulting from a renewed Iraqi invasion of Kuwait and a North Korean attack on South Korea. Neither is particularly likely, the chances of their occurring simultaneously are minuscule, and our forces would be hard put to do both at the same time, given their current size.

Why do defense planners place great emphasis on this problem? The partial answer is that the problem lends itself to comfortable thinking. Conventional cross-border wars, where armies mass on and cross borders, are the kind of warfare with which we are familiar, the kind we know best how to fight, and the kind for which our obsession with firepower and technology are the most clearly applicable. This last point is important: the evolving model of warfare is information war, where our advantages in intelligence, firepower, and strategy against massed opponents make us virtually unbeatable. One of the lessons of the Persian Gulf War is that a Second Tier country fighting in a European style does not stand a chance of victory against the world's most advanced militaries. A lot of planning will allow us to maximize this advantage.

Contemporary experience, most recently in Kosovo, suggests another dimension of modern conventional warfare: its bloodlessness. After the humiliating pictures of the corpse of an American Ranger being dragged through the streets of Mogadishu, Somalia, in late 1993 were broadcast on television, the Clinton administration became almost obsessed with "war without death" (at least of Americans). Significant elements in the military and elsewhere, however, disagree with the idea that casualties can always be avoided. Regardless, a principal measure of our success in Haiti and Bosnia has been that no American combat fatalities occurred in either place. Although I lack the data to prove it, my suspicion is that were you to ask Americans to name the most important outcome of Operation Allied Force in Yugoslavia, many would name the avoidance of American deaths in combat.

If "avoid casualties at all costs" is becoming a credo of the American way of war, then advanced technology is the key to waging conventional war. If military operations can be reduced to a confrontation between European-organized, combat-ready armies and the second-rate militaries of Second Tier states, then the armies of the First Tier, and especially that of the United States, will have an automatic and overwhelming advantage. Warfare then would become an extension of the Persian Gulf, where technologically superior forces armed with vastly more lethal weapons stood out of the effective firing range of the enemy and destroyed his forces in detail while being essentially safe from retaliation. Add newer technological wizardry like high-definition imagery of wide swaths of the battlefield, which can be generated by satellites in space, and the inferior enemy whose knowledge of the battlefield is limited to line-of-sight with binoculars (Iraq's predicament after the initial air attacks in January 1991 took out its radar capabilities) will never know what hit him. It is possible to destroy him physically and psychologically because he is at an absolute disadvantage.

Airpower is the epitome of this approach to war, and the campaign over Kosovo is its most recent application. Airpower, after all, is the ultimate combination of technology and firepower: a country's air forces, after achieving air dominance by destroying the other country's forces and suppressing its electronic surveillance capacity, can rain unrelenting destruction on the helpless enemy. Whether that rain of fire can defeat an enemy and cripple its ability to rebuild and reorganize without the insertion of ground forces was not answered positively (it may have been answered negatively) in Kosovo; just as strategists argued over the results of the Strategic Bombing Survey that was conducted after World War II, we may argue about the Kosovo outcome for years. Regardless of the outcome of the debate, that application of airpower in Allied Force is a quintessential expression of basic American values about how to use force.

In Kosovo and elsewhere we are attempting to use conventional means, such as aerial bombardment, for very unconventional purposes (in this case, to end the suppression and displacement of part of the population). The Yugoslav armed forces looked and fought like a conventional force, and so the war in Kosovo appeared rather conventional. In terms of why it was being fought and the possible political outcomes, of course, there was nothing conventional about it at all: it was an internal war over which ethnic group, Serb or Albanian, would control that province of Yugoslavia.

Three questions arise from the Kosovo experience that might influence our thinking about conventional war in the future. The first is whether waging a conventional campaign inverts the Clausewitzian relationship between war and its purposes by allowing the available means (airpower) to dictate the purposes we could successfully pursue (punishing Yugoslav forces rather than protecting Albanian Kosovars). The second is how future foes might adapt in light of the Kosovo experience and whether future besieged friends will turn to the U.S. Air Force for succor. The third is what has the campaign done to the nature and dynamics of the NATO alliance. Each deserves separate consideration.

Did Kosovo Stand Clausewitz on His Head? From its beginning, the NATO campaign to force the Serbian-dominated government of Yugoslavia to cease forcing ethnic Albanian Kosovars out of their homes and, ultimately, out of Kosovo itself was framed in largely conventional terms. The Serbs were conceptualized as foreign invaders imposing their will on the Kosovars, and hence the fighting was directed at Yugoslav/Serb forces in Kosovo and later in metropolitan Yugoslavia. The idea was to exceed Serb *cost-tolerance*, that is, to exceed their will to endure hardship and thus convince them to discontinue the policy of ethnic cleansing.

Was this the right way to think about the problem? It was if one started from the assumption that the introduction of allied ground forces into the province would produce unacceptable casualties (which apparently meant any casualties at all). Strategists and policy advisers, thinking about Kosovo not as a new internal war (which it was) but instead in conventional terms, produced a conventional response in the form of the air campaign. It is possible that a more accurate assessment of the nature of the conflict would not have changed the means. But was it necessarily the best way to frame the problem and the response?

Future assessments will answer that question definitively, but Clausewitzian language and logic may have gotten tangled in the application. It is a fact that the pace of the refugee exodus greatly increased after the bombing began, and that the Milošević regime used bombardment as an excuse to accelerate the ethnic cleansing of Operation Horseshoe. It is also a fact that the liberated Kosovo endured an enormous amount of damage, as did metropolitan Yugoslavia. At least a portion of that damage was inflicted by allied pilots, and one is left to ponder whether in a future Kosovo-like situation, the victims will enthusiastically embrace NATO bombardiers as their saviors. Finally, when allied forces entered Kosovo as part of the peace settlement with Belgrade, they were met by a well-armed Kosovo Liberation Army (whose actions during the air campaign had forced the Yugoslavs to expose themselves to allied attacks) bent on retribution and reluctant to put down their arms. Whether conceptualizing the conflict in other terms would have produced a different result is speculative. Clausewitzian language would have argued that only landpower could have achieved our strategic goals or was at least a necessary adjunct to airpower. The tangling effect may have been the reassignment of the critical role to airpower.

Adaptation of Future Opponents to the Western Way of War As Maj. Gen. Robert H. Scales Jr. (USA) has eloquently argued in a collection of articles, our fine tuning of conventional warfare techniques so clearly evident in the (sometimes errant) precision bombing campaign will almost certainly spawn adaptive strategies by future opponents to negate the effectiveness of high-technology firepower. As he points out, adaptation was evident to some extent in Vietnam, where the opponent blunted much of the effectiveness of massed firepower by techniques as simple as dispersing troops and using false targets. The Yugoslav armed forces used the same techniques to absorb, blunt, and minimize the effects of bombardment upon them.

How effective was Operation Allied Force? I suspect that once the breast beating by the bombardiers and their supporters has subsided, the answer will be mixed. The campaign appears to have been very effective against fixed, exposed targets, of which there were many, particularly in metropolitan Yugoslavia. Bridges were a favorite target and are a good example: you can neither move, hide, nor effectively fortify them. We were effective at attacking the Yugoslav infrastructure, which, conveniently enough, was pretty well developed. Arguably, the Milošević regime's unwillingness to see that infrastructure further demolished helped push it toward accommodation with NATO.

An assessment of the effectiveness of the air campaign against the Yugoslav military will, I suspect, be much more restrained. From their World War II resistance against Nazi occupying forces, the Yugoslavs learned to fight guerrilla style and had a large network of caves and tunnels where they could, and did, hide their troops and equipment from NATO bombers. As it retreated back into Serbia as the peace accords were implemented, the Yugoslav Liberation Army did not look like a defeated force. Maybe we really did need an army to defeat their army, assuming that was our purpose.

What does the Yugoslav military's experience against NATO tell future foes? Certainly it tells them not to stand toe-to-toe with Western conventional forces and submit to their firepower. A country that has fewer inviting, fixed infrastructure targets than Yugoslavia might reasonably conclude that a NATO bombing campaign unaccompanied by a coordinated land element is tolerable and should not be a deterrent. That was the case in Vietnam until the United States directly attacked those same kinds of targets (notably Haiphong Harbor); our enthusiasm for the "miraculous" efficacy of airpower acting alone in Allied Force may diminish on further evaluation. We may have to conclude that we will have to be willing to shed the blood of some of our soldiers to win future wars.

The Impact of the Campaign on NATO Did NATO, an alliance built for the mutual defense of its members from outside attack, transform itself fundamentally when it went on the attack to force the Serbs to end their persecution of the Kosovars? This question is part of a larger question about intervention in internal wars and the impact such actions have on the notion of sovereignty, which in turn is part of the still broader discussion of the kinds of situations in which we will use force in the future. That is examined in detail in the final chapter. At this point, it is sufficient to note that this was not the kind of operation for which NATO was designed. Arguably, what NATO did was engage in an aggressive war against a sovereign state in the name of humanity, and one can easily argue that this action represents at least a partial refutation of the *democratic peace* notion that democracies do not start wars. These are also important concerns, because Kosovo is about as close to a conventional campaign as we are likely to come for awhile.

Limited Crisis Uses of Force

A third, and less compelling, set of situations where the application of force may be necessary in order to secure American interests is the "limited crisis use of force." This concept covers a range of possible military and nonmilitary (or paramilitary) actions that might be taken in response to an equally broad range of problems and provocations.

Limited crisis uses of force are responses to small hostile actions or threatened actions that either could not be or were not anticipated and that put a small number of Americans or few American assets at risk. In some cases, they are responses to events that could have been precluded had action been taken before their occurrence. Conceptually, the three types of employments of necessity are not mutually exclusive: a nuclear or conventional war might evolve out of an unanticipated crisis, for instance. It is the smaller scale that sets the limited crisis use of force apart from nuclear or conventional war.

What kinds of crisis responses are we talking about, where are they most likely to occur, and what kinds of Americans are likely to be most vulnerable? No list of acts or places or victims could be comprehensive, so the best we can do is describe by example.

One example is a U.S. response to attacks on U.S. citizens or American property located in foreign countries. Rioting or civil war may spread to a capital city and endanger the American embassy to a greater extent than the normal Marine guard contingent can contain. In some cases, the only way to make Americans safe may be to remove them from the country until the crisis subsides. In such instances, the appropriate response may be to insert Marines or other highly mobile forces, such as a Delta Force team. In such instances, the purpose will not be to alter the military situation on the ground by combating the forces creating the problem; rather, it will be to provide a shield by which to protect the citizens. Contact with hostile forces is considered incidental. Freeing hostages is another example of this kind of action.

These kinds of actions are most likely to occur in unstable countries or in places where there is some anti-Americanism (or both). Most of the time, they will occur in the Second Tier. The most obvious candidates are in Africa and the Middle East, where elements other than the government commit acts against Americans. The need to evacuate Americans from Liberia is one example; the spate of kidnappings of Americans in Lebanon during the 1970s and 1980s is another.

Most of these uses of force are unconventional in content. They involve highly mobile, adaptable forces whose purpose is to accomplish their mission very quickly and leave. The use of a battleship's cannons off the Lebanese coast in 1983 may have driven terrorists out of a particular area, but it is not very good at rescuing hostages.

In most cases, the best form of action against these problems is preemption—anticipating instability and getting Americans out of harm's way before violence begins, and infiltrating groups wanting to take hostages and foiling their plans. However, the necessary intelligence is often not available to do so, because the United States has not invested heavily enough in a particular country to know what all the problems are or to notice warning signs. Gaining such knowledge is only marginally a military task.

Other examples of limited crises uses of force are occasions when the United States takes retaliatory action against a state or other actor that has done something harmful to the United States or Americans. Two examples are the 1986 attack on Libya's Mu'ammar Qadhafi in retaliation for the bombing of a bar in Berlin in which several Americans were killed, or the attack against the camps in Afghanistan (originally built by the CIA to train *mujahedin* to fight the Soviets) from which Osama bin Laden apparently plotted the embassy bombings in Dar es Salaam and Nairobi.

One can debate whether such actions are necessary or arbitrary. Clearly, they are motivated by two sentiments that their promoters would argue constitute necessity. Part of the motivation is to punish transgressors so they will not or cannot repeat the actions. The attack on Qadhafi's compound signaled to him that if he did not cease his sponsorship of terrorism, he might well pay with his life. (Technically, of course, the United States did not intend for the air strikes to kill the Libyan dictator, since assassination of political figures is illegal. Qadhafi knew that had he been the victim of collateral damage, we would not have minded. He also knew that the only reason he was not a victim was that the bombs missed.) At the same time, retaliatory strikes are almost always intended to send the message to others who would commit similar acts that they will be the victim of similar retribution.

Employments of Choice

With the exception of crisis uses of force, the employments of necessity are unlikely in the foreseeable future, as they largely were in the past. Nuclear war is unlikely to occur because both sides understand the consequences and because, with the possible exception of some extremists in Russia, no one on either side has the motivation to start a conflict that might lead to nuclear war. The same is true of conventional war, in the sense of major cross-border invasions.

It is necessary to stress forcefully their unlikeliness, because the deterrence of nuclear war and the preparation for conventional war have been the primary purposes of the American military establishment for the past half century. And these scenarios, if they have not entirely disappeared, have certainly diminished on the menu of violence in the world. They remain a part of the mandate of the military, if not a part of its day-to-day "workload."

Put another way, we are warriors of necessity in a world that has more work for warriors of choice. The opportunities to employ force in the upcoming years will be where we choose them to be, not where they are thrust upon us. The probable opportunities for employments of choice will have many of the characteristics just ascribed to opportunities for crisis uses of force: they will present themselves in parts of the world that are unstable, where American interests are not clearly engaged, where we may have a deficient understanding of the nature of the problem and especially its long-range solution (if such solutions are in fact possible), and where the problem and its solution will have predominantly paramilitary and nonmilitary elements. Put bluntly, they are the kinds of problems for which the United States has not historically shown great talent.

Beyond the operational difficulties are conceptual problems. Employments of choice, by definition, do not fit neatly within the realist paradigm. The national interests at stake will not, by and large, meet the traditional standard of "vital," which means we do not *have* to respond. If we are to become involved, we will have to expand the criteria beyond traditional realism for reaching such a decision. That is the gist of the argument for realistic internationalism. The question is what the expanded list of criteria will include, which is a matter not yet decided.

The Kosovo experience demonstrates the torture of our conceptual path. By most traditional assessments, nothing that happens in Kosovo could affect American interests enough to justify involvement. Thus, to justify it, the criteria were subtly expanded without any articulation of the basis for changing the criteria. A stable Europe has always been important to Europeans, and since what is important to Europeans has also always been important to us, we are justified in acting. In the process, we transformed our conventional war concepts and the situation to meet the needs. We transformed NATO from a defensive military machine into an offensive one. Operationally, we transformed an internal war into a conventional conflict. This transformation allowed NATO to apply airpower to the situation and to structure the Kosovo Force (KFOR) along the lines of the World War II invasion of Sicily.

These transformations may not always be possible. Employments of choice may be malleable enough to be twisted into familiar scenarios some of the time, but not all of the time. This indeterminancy results in part from the nature of the problems that fall within the category and in part from the kinds of responses that are appropriate.

The three types of employments of choice discussed below are arranged in ascending order of likelihood and importance. I will begin by examining emerging threats or opportunities, which are chances to preempt a situation to our advantage. Next, the discussion will move to proliferation and terrorism. I will conclude with the most likely and most problematical instance: intervention (generally in the guise of peace or peace support operations) in the internal wars in the Second Tier.

Emerging Threats and Opportunities

There are occasions when military force can be employed or threatened, or when nonmilitary actions can be taken, to preempt harmful occurrences or to promote favorable situations that might not emerge in the absence of the action taken. Actively looking for these kinds of opportunities is particularly important in the contemporary environment, where many of the problems are at a fairly low level of visibility before they burst to the forefront but can be very dangerous and even gruesome when they do.

To what kind of anticipatory actions are we referring? As in the case of crisis uses of force, in the case of emerging threats there are no standard definitions or categories, given the rapidly changing international scene. In a way, actions taken in response to emerging threats or opportunities are the flip side of crisis uses: in the latter case, one responds to bad things that have happened; with emerging opportunities, one acts to prevent something unfavorable from happening or to ensure that favorable things happen.

An Opportunity Missed An opportunity to preempt genocide was missed in the Rwandan tragedy of 1994. Anyone conversant with the area knew there was a prospect for ethnically based violence in the country. Hutus and Tutsis had a long history of intergroup violence that dated back at least as far as the independence of Rwanda-Burundi in 1962. Tutsi were slaughtered after they attempted to seize power in 1963 and were slaughtered again in 1993. Yet, after a suspicious airplane crash killed the Hutu presidents of Rwanda and Burundi in April 1994, the international community stood by and seemed surprised when Hutu militia, blaming Tutsi insurgents for the crash, began the systematic slaughter of Rwandan Tutsi one month later. In the end, at least 500,000 died in the rampage, and another two million fled into exile in the surrounding countries, where they continue to be an unsettling factor in places like the Democratic Republic of Congo (formerly Zaire).

Should the international system have seen this coming and taken preventive action? Certainly, the history of the area suggested that developments should have been monitored, and there were press reports at the time that communications intercepted by Canadian and other sources foretold how events would unfold.

Why did the international community not act? To begin with, it happened in central Africa, where the major powers have few interests and to which they accordingly devote few intelligence resources. The clues may have been there and gone unnoticed, possibly because we were not looking for the right things. Moreover, we have a tendency to ignore the evidence of impending doom until it becomes too obvious to avoid, as when major violence breaks out. We may understand the problem but not be prepared to act early in the crisis. There is normally a cycle in these kinds of situations, including a period when the crisis is building but has not yet surfaced. During the pre-violence phase, it may be possible to dampen the situation and avoid major suffering; the problem is that no one is adequately focused at this point or prepared to take the appropriate actions, or the options available would create additional problems of their own.

The above are important considerations for dealing with future contingencies, especially if we make a couple of assumptions about how the international system will deal with these types of problems in the future. On the one hand, it is becoming clearer as Operation Joint Guardian unfolds in Kosovo that the international system has neither the resources nor the predilection to intervene in every internal war where atrocities are being committed. There are too many of these, and they are all expensive. Thus, some criteria are going to emerge for deciding where and where not to get involved. Dealing with emerging threats before they become system-wrenching is one way to simplify the problem. On the other hand, many of these crises will occur in Rwanda-like locales where the U.S. government has a shortage of regional experts. If we are to better anticipate the emergence of threats, and if we are to make intelligent decisions about whether to become involved if things blow up and how to conduct operations in those situations where we do become involved, then we need a better understanding of these countries (an assertion that anyone connected with missions like that to Somalia would readily concur).

An Opportunity Seized In contrast to Rwanda, the international community undertook preemptive action that may have prevented an attempt at the forceful return of Macedonia to Yugoslavia. The action was the commissioning of the recently dismantled United Nations Preventive Deployment (UN-PREDEP) to the Former Yugoslav Republic of Macedonia (FYROM) in March 1995.

When Yugoslavia began to disintegrate in 1991, the Macedonians joined the exodus, declaring their independence on September 8, 1991. The Serbian government of Yugoslavia did not attempt to force Macedonia (which had to adopt the formal name FYROM because Greece objected that "Macedonia" was a Greek province) to remain in the union, as it had other portions of the Yugoslav Federation. They reasoned that Macedonia was so destitute and disorganized that it would be unable to survive as an independent state and would come back, hat in hand, to rejoin Yugoslavia. They were wrong, and the FYROM was admitted to the UN in 1993.

Many in the international community feared that the FYROM was vulnerable to hostile Serbian action, either as part of the spreading violence centered in Bosnia or because of Serbian frustration when the FYROM did not collapse. The result was UNPREDEP, the first UN peacekeeping operation designed to prevent war from commencing, as opposed to resuming. To this end, the UN placed a small, multilateral force on the Macedonian side of the border with Serbia (including Kosovo) to monitor any possible Serb provocation and to force the Serbs to attack the United Nations before attempting reannexation. As of November 30, 1998, UNPREDEP consisted of 871 troops and police, the largest contingent of which was contributed by the United States (345), followed by Finland with 246, and Sweden with 106.

UNPREDEP was a "success" in that no Serbian incursion occurred while it was in place. Certainly, it cannot be proven that UNPREDEP prevented an attack, since no one could possibly know what would have happened had UNPREDEP not been in place. "Successful" or not, the mission was popular with the Macedonians. For one thing, the troops spent money in the local economy, which needed it.

UNPREDEP went out of business at the end of February 1999, but not because its mission was necessarily finished or because the Macedonians wanted it out. Rather, its renewal was vetoed in the UN Security Council by the People's Republic of China for a reason that had nothing to do with the situation in the Balkans: the Chinese decided to punish the Macedonians for accepting a loan from and recognizing the Republic of China (Taiwan). The lesson would seem to be that, regardless of the situation, politics is never very far beneath the surface and rears its head in strange ways.

Not all potential outbreaks of violence in which the United States may choose to become active will be amenable to action. However, it is likely that some will be amenable to early intermediation, and wherever possible, acting before disaster strikes will be financially cheaper and more humane than waiting until the situation explodes. The real problem in these cases may be getting leaders to act in situations that are not yet clear crises.

Terrorism and Proliferation

The placement of these two problems in the category of military employments of choice may seem problematical. I would argue, however, that the designation is appropriate. It is true that neither problem is amenable to military solution in the traditional sense: avoiding proliferation is almost entirely a diplomatic exercise whose only military implication is deterring proliferators after dissuasion fails; and reacting to terrorism (counterterror) is generally only paramilitary, with the exception of military retaliation after terrorist acts have occurred. One can also argue that the United States has little choice but to respond to provocations in either category, but that, too, is questionable: besides complaining, there was nothing we could do about the Indo-Pakistani acquisition and testing of nuclear weapons, since they were determined to possess them; and most terrorism affects us very little.

Having said all that, it is equally clear that ending proliferation and countering terrorism are major priorities of the U.S. government and that the government considers both to be national security problems for which the national security system has primary interest and, in some cases, jurisdiction. Moreover, the two phenomena are, in some ways, interactive. One of the reasons that the United States fears proliferation of weapons of mass destruction in the Second Tier is that such capabilities might be given to or stolen by terrorists who may use them on us. I would add that, despite political rhetoric to the contrary, both are fairly minor concerns for the United States, and the main reason why we devote as much energy to them as we do is because we have fewer serious national security problems than we did during the cold war. I recognize that my dismissal of these problems will not be popular with that segment of the national security community devoted to them, and I do not dismiss either problem as unworthy of concern. Compared to the avoidance of nuclear war during the cold war, however, terrorism and proliferation pale as problems.

My purpose is not to examine either issue systematically, since doing so would require a lengthy discussion of nonmilitary aspects as well. Rather, I will concentrate on those pieces of each problem for which military forces are relevant.

The Military Role in Counterterrorism Terrorism became an important part of the public agenda in the United States in the 1990s. Before a spate of domestic and international terrorist incidents during the decade, the problem was abstract for most Americans, consisting of acts committed by foreigners against other foreigners (for example, the attack by Palestine Liberation Organization guerrillas against the Israeli athlete compound in Munich during the 1972 Olympics). Occasionally, a terrorist act like the blowing up of Pan American Flight 103 over Lockerbie, Scotland, would catch the public eye, but such acts were infrequent and idiosyncratic enough that our concentration on the problem quickly dissipated. Neil Livingstone, an expert on terrorism, would routinely begin lectures on the topic with the observation that an American was more likely to be killed by lightning than by a terrorist act.

Events of the 1990s changed that perception. The attack on the New York World Trade Center by Middle Eastern terrorists in 1993 brought the subject home, and before our attention waned, that attack was followed by another on the Murrah Federal Building in Oklahoma City in 1995 and the arrest of the "Unabomber," Theodore Kaczynski, in 1996. Americans overseas were also the victims of terrorist attacks, as in the attack on American airmen at the Khobar Towers apartment complex in Dhahran, Saudi Arabia, in 1996, and the African embassy bombings of 1998.

Two distinctions can be made about terrorism and how to deal with it that help clarify the military component of the problem. The first distinction is that between domestic and international acts. The second distinction relates to how one responds to terrorism: through *antiterrorism* or *counterterrorism*. Antiterrorism refers to defensive measures taken to decrease the vulnerability of society or individuals to terrorist attacks. Installing metal detectors in airports is one example; putting barriers across access roads to complexes to slow the approach of bomb-laden trucks is another. Counterterrorism, on the other hand, refers to offensive actions taken to suppress terrorists by destroying their ability to act. The 1986 attack against Libya is one example; the cruise missile strikes against Osama bin Laden's camps in Afghanistan is another.

The two distinctions can be combined in matrix form to delineate the problem *(see Figure 3.1)*. The military role can be examined by looking at the matrix. Cells 1 and 2 refer to antiterrorist activities.

Domestically, there is very little role for military forces in antiterrorism, with two possible exceptions, both of which fall under the rubric of security. Within some military circles, there has been growing concern about the possibility of a terrorist attack against a U.S. military base or research facility (the security of which has been broadened and intensified since the allegations arose in 1999 of Chinese agents stealing U.S. nuclear secrets at Los

Figure 3.1 Two Dimensions of Terrorism

	Domestic	Foreign
Antiterror	Cell 1	Cell 2
Counterterror	Cell 3	Cell 4

Alamos Laboratory in New Mexico), or against a convoy carrying sensitive cargo. Where such a heightened concern has manifested itself (increased security is not universal), the major goal has been to make access to facilities more difficult.

Internationally, the military has taken security precautions to better protect Americans who live off military bases. In many cases, these precautions require extensive interaction and cooperation between American military and civilian authorities in the host country. The military also has partial responsibility for protecting other American installations overseas, such as embassies, by guaranteeing the physical protection of the grounds and planning and implementing plans to make facilities more bomb-proof and otherwise impenetrable.

The military's role in counterterror is similarly circumscribed. Domestically, counterterrorist activities such as infiltrating and monitoring terrorist groups fall within the jurisdiction of civilian agencies, notably the Federal Bureau of Investigation; military participation would be limited to investigating terrorist plots on military facilities or involving military personnel.

The major role for the military in the area of terrorism falls in foreign counterterrorism. The military instrument may be used to punish terrorists for acts they have committed and to diminish their ability to engage in future acts of terror. It is even possible to imagine elite military forces such as the Army's Delta Force being sent in to disrupt a suspected terrorist facility.

What this examination suggests is that the role of military force in dealing with terrorism is quite limited. One occasionally hears cries to "make war" on terrorists, but the analogy is overblown. Terrorism is the weapon of a small, weak group that cannot accomplish its political goals otherwise. Although terrorists often like to portray themselves as "freedom fighters" for one cause or another, their actions are, by and large, criminal acts that are treated as such by American and most other legal and political jurisdictions. In dealing with terrorists, paramilitary force may occasionally be considered, but it never goes beyond the discussion phase. If political forces outside the military establishment decide that the future of the American military lies in dealing with the problem of terrorism, then the military's future is bleak indeed.

The Military Role in Proliferation The same is largely true with proliferation. At one level, proliferation is more of a military problem than is terrorism, because the things we seek to prevent the proliferation of are weapons with military applications; and when antiproliferation efforts fail, it is the military that must come to grips with the consequences of new capabilities falling into hostile hands.

The proliferation problem is not a single problem, nor does the policy establishment deal with it as if it were. There is a distinction between the proliferation of actual weapons, so-called weapons of mass destruction, and of the means to deliver them to targets (the two problems are, of course, related; U.S. policy makers worry less about weapons that cannot be delivered than about those that can be). Weapons of mass destruction, in turn, is itself a rubric of issues rather than a singular issue. These are generally broken down into nuclear, biological, and chemical agents, and each has its own regimes that attempt to discourage nonpossessors from gaining the particular capability. In a parallel manner, the United States and the international community have attempted to restrict access to the most advanced delivery capabilities, notably missiles with strategic ranges.

Once again, the purpose here is not to examine the dynamics of the proliferation problem but to look at the role of the U.S. military in restraining potential and actual proliferators.

The goal is to dissuade countries that do not have a particular capability from getting it or, if that fails, convincing those countries not to use the capability. The goal, then, is deterrence. Deterring the proliferation of weapons of mass destruction and ballistic missiles can be thought of as having two distinct aspects: *acquisition deterrence* and *employment deterrence*. Acquisition deterrence refers to actions taken to convince a potential proliferator not to acquire the capability. It can take on positive forms, such as guaranteeing signatories to the Nuclear Nonproliferation Treaty access to nuclear fuel for their energy-producing reactors, or negative forms, such as threatening sanctions for noncompliance. *In extremis*, acquisition deterrence can take the form of attacking and destroying a nascent capability, which the Israelis did against an Iraqi nuclear reactor in 1981. Employment deterrence is traditional deterrence, wherein those who gain a capability are discouraged from using it by threats of retaliation.

The military contribution to these two aspects of deterrence varies considerably. Acquisition deterrence is a political and diplomatic process; the military's role is likely to be technical and advisory: making sure negotiators understand the technical nature of capabilities, analyzing data on the extent to which a capability has been attained, suggesting military components of sanctions, or assessing the military impact of proliferation on regional balances, for instance.

The military role is more direct in employment deterrence, since its primary dynamic is threatening a proliferator/attacker with a military response that would leave the attacker worse off than before the attack. This is the stuff of nuclear deterrence during the cold war, and it was a major part of our military effort. The role is more circumscribed with post–cold war proliferators, because most of the capabilities that are being developed cannot be used in a direct attack on the United States: India and Pakistan cannot attack the United States with their nuclear weapons, since they have no way to deliver them this far.

As a directly American problem, employment deterrence encompasses three scenarios, presented here in descending order of likelihood. The first is the use of weapons of mass destruction (for instance, chemical agents) against American facilities overseas. The second is the prospect of a regional conflict escalating to a use of weapons of mass destruction that might somehow engage the United States. For example, would we run the risk of being sucked into an Indo-Pakistani nuclear exchange or a chemical or biological weapons attack on Israel? The third is the use of exotic weapons, such as anthrax, in this country by a terrorist who released it in aerosol form or poisoned a big-city water supply (for example, Central Reservoir on Manhattan Island). These scenarios are of varying likelihood and probably deserve varying amounts of concern. Some of the concern, however, is appropriately military.

Peacekeeping in Internal Wars

The final use of force is outside involvement in internal wars, which are the most frequent manifestation of violence in the post–cold war world. To reiterate a general assertion made in Chapter 1, almost all of the violent conflicts in the contemporary world are internal wars, and hence they provide the most opportunities for involvement of American forces in violence in the world.

Kosovo is one example of what those involvements may be like. However, it would be misleading to think that all future actions will be similar to Kosovo. In a sense, getting involved in Kosovo was an easy choice to make, and accomplishing the task was comparatively easy—at least in the military phase of the "war." Kosovo is in Europe, making it easier for U.S. leaders to articulate a case to intervene there than in Africa and parts of Asia. The issues were reasonably well understood (at least on the surface), and the solution seemed attainable. But then, we are just starting the hard part, which is putting Kosovo back together.

We should not be lulled into believing that things will go so well in the future. The first post–cold war involvement in this kind of war by the United States was in Somalia, from which we retreated with a bloody nose and a bruised ego. The lesson from Somalia seemed to be "no more Somalias." It was too broad and sweeping a generalization at the time. Making the opposite assumption on the basis of Kosovo would be equally unfortunate.

Whether or when the United States should use armed forces in internal wars in the Second Tier is the primary policy question regarding the use of force for the next decade or more. It is both a policy and a strategy question. At the level of policy, I have already argued that we have no set of overarching political criteria to guide where and when to insert ourselves, and we will return to this question in Chapter 5.

We do not know how to deal with internal wars in a military sense, either. In Kosovo, we thought of the military part of the problem in conventional terms, and the answer was airpower. The conflict in Kosovo was not, of course, conventional, but Yugoslavia had enough physical infrastructure for the bombardiers to attack with effect, and NATO eventually exceeded the Serbs' cost-tolerance threshold. The mismatch between conceptualization and solution did not matter operationally. Applying the same concept to most African countries and adopting the same airpower solution would have quite different effects, since there is little infrastructure and there are fewer military targets to bomb in a Liberia or a Sierra Leone than in Kosovo.

These wars also do not fit the cold war model of internal war. It is ironic that in the wake of the Vietnam conflict, the U.S. military examined the kind of war we confronted there—Maoist-style guerrilla warfare—and learned how to counter it. But that model will not get you very far in understanding the new internal wars.

From Vietnam we learned about battling for "the hearts and minds of people" and centers of gravity (the political loyalty of the population) and all the other dynamics of internal wars fought between an established government and an insurgent group bent on gaining control of a country and ruling in accordance with some set of principles. In Kosovo, there was no battle for the hearts and minds of the Kosovar or Serbian populations; the idea was not to win over the opponent but to kill or displace the enemy population. There was no single center of gravity; there were two—the Kosovars and the Serbs—and they were mutually exclusive. To understand the politico-military dynamics of Kosovo and other new internal wars you must dismiss Mao and think instead of an interstate war that just happens to be occurring within the boundaries of a single state.

The dynamics of involvement in new internal wars, generally under the misleading designation of peacekeeping, are the subject of the next chapter. My purpose here is to place new internal wars on the menu of violence as the last menu "item" and to address four questions: Where do these wars occur? Why do they occur and what is their purpose? How do the primary combatants conduct them? And what are the politico-military dynamics of outside intrusion?

Most of these wars occur in those parts of Africa and central and southern Asia (including some of the Soviet successor states) that are poor, unstable, and outside the globalizing economy. The Balkans come as close as any place in Europe to matching that description. They occur at the periphery, where U.S. and other First Tier interests are least involved and where the outcomes will have the least effect on the rest of the world. As the Balkans demonstrate, these dynamics will not necessarily preclude action.

Demographically, the fact that most new internal wars occur in destitute countries modifies our understanding of the kinds of societies in which civil war occurs. The political development literature of the 1950s and 1960s suggested that citizens of countries already in the economic development process underwent a "revolution of rising expectations" and that revolution was most likely to occur when change was not happening as fast as many might want. The champions of revolution were those who espoused the most radical change, generally the communists. That dynamic is most relevant today in places like Indonesia, Thailand, and South Korea, where the "revolutionaries" wear three-piece suits, carry laptops and cellular phones, and champion radical ideas like capitalism and democracy.

The contemporary internal wars seem to occur in the most hopeless societies, where the "misery index" is at its highest and where there is little ennobling any combatant. Politically, their locus seems to be in the "failed states," a term devised to describe states like Somalia and suggesting an inability to achieve stable self-governance. Crushing poverty, of course, contributes to political instability. In some countries, such as diamond-rich Sierra Leone and Angola, the violence prevents exploitation of natural resources that could undergird prosperity.

The political purposes of these conflicts tend to be diverse and nontraditional. In some, like the criminal insurgencies of central Africa or the narco insurgencies of South America, the purpose is largely to sow anarchy: disrupting the political system to the point that political authority evaporates and there are no effective barriers to robbing and looting the country, or interrupting the political authority from exercising its jurisdiction in the drug-producing part of a country. In others, the goal may be reasonably traditional —the seizure of political power, as in Somalia—but the method is not: rather than the Maoist method of political conversion, the method is to terrorize, remove, or kill population segments, as in Somalia or Kosovo. In the latter, we may yet find that there was a subtler purpose to driving the ethnic Albanians out of Kosovo: gaining unambiguous control of the mineral wealth of the province.

That these conflicts go well beyond the Clausewitzian description of war as "politics conducted by other means" helps explain in part the savagery with which neighbor sets upon neighbor. In traditional insurgencies, the level of atrocity was moderated by the long-term goal of a single polity in which all would live, as well as by whatever restraint outside sponsors might impose. In new internal wars, there is little in the political goals to moderate the bestiality with which they are fought. There is no notion of restraint in the Rwandas, Bosnias, Somalias, or Kosovos of this world.

As noted, traditional models of warfare do not apply: these are neither conventional conflicts nor traditional insurgencies. Moreover, they lack a clean line between when peace turns to war and when war ends and peace returns (the "peace-war-peace" model of military employment).

In fact, they are rarely "wars" in any sense of that term that a military professional would recognize. There are no military "campaigns," in any conventional sense, and one can rarely find anything resembling battles between the competing "armies." In Kosovo, for instance, the KLA and the JLA bumped into one another and skirmished on occasion, but that was about it. Rather, what passes for military action in these conflicts tends to be acts of brutality by the armed elements of one side against the unarmed civilians of the other (not unlike Viet Cong actions in Vietnam aimed at suppressing political dissent). Given that context, the outcomes tend to be almost exclusively civilian deaths (estimates are that 90 percent or more of the casualties in conflicts since the Gulf War have been civilians) and the widespread displacement of civilian populations into internal or external exile.

The conduct of these conflicts gives rise to a concern with war crimes, as dramatically illustrated by the indictment in absentia of the president of Yugoslavia, Slobodan Milošević, on war crimes charges. As long as these kinds of conflicts continue, war crimes investigations and trials will be a growth industry. Their conduct also complicates national reconciliation following the conclusion of hostilities. During the cold war, the most vexing problem was in Lebanon, where intercommunal habitation patterns made it difficult to separate conflicting confessional groups and restore order. At that, the level of atrocity was nowhere near as high as in contemporary civil wars.

The problem of national reconciliation in places like Rwanda, Bosnia, and Kosovo is nothing less than monumental. Peoples who had lived in peace and as neighbors for a generation or more now are deeply divided by atrocities. There were reported instances in Rwanda where Hutu villagers would accompany the "militias" in order to identify neighbors as Tutsi for execution. There were similar reports about Serbs identifying Kosovar Muslims to Serbian police (we are also finding similar allegations against Kosovar Muslims).

The point is the effect the atrocities have on attempts to bring the country back to normal after the killing stops. The anguish of discovering killing fields and mass graves has to create enormous animosities, and it is hard to imagine they will disappear in even a generation. The wounds are too deep.

What is a potential intervenor to do in these kinds of situations? As the outcome in Kosovo and Bosnia shows, the end of the fighting is not the end of the problem. In Kosovo, the accumulation of atrocities meant a legacy of distrust and a fear of reprisal. One of the ironies of the withdrawal of Serb troops and their replacement by NATO troops was the massive migration of Kosovar Serbs, fearing KLA reprisals and uncertain the Western allies would protect them, to Serbia.

Kosovo also demonstrated that intervention in civil wars can be carried out for two separate and sequential purposes: stopping the killing and seeing that it does not recur (what I call conflict suppression, which entails peace imposition and peace enforcement), and building or rebuilding the state that has been devastated by war (state building). This two-part mission in Kosovo was by no means new; the same had been confronted more or less frontally in interventions in Somalia, Bosnia, and Haiti. In each of those cases, outside intervention was not the central factor in deciding the outcome of the hostilities. In Somalia, we intervened in an ongoing war, stopped the fighting so that food could get to the citizenry, stayed awhile, and left without seriously attempting to implement any comprehensive state-building plans. In Bosnia, we brokered a peace settlement and then went in to monitor compliance with it; SFOR has undertaken limited but probably inadequate state-building efforts. In Haiti, we intervened, took some steps to build a postinvasion peace (such as training a constabulary), and then left enough Americans in place to remind the Haitians that we might come back if they backslid.

Kosovo is different, however, in the massive and highly publicized nature of the air campaign. The emphasis we placed on the campaign and the stern statement of purpose with which we imbued it *created* a level of interest that was not evident before Operation Allied Power began and from which a retreat with only partial results would have been publicly and politically unacceptable. In the other instances, we could stop the fighting, stick around for awhile, and leave, hoping for the best after our departure. That option is not available in Kosovo.

The two purposes are separate, but they are also sequential. When we go into a shooting conflict, the first task is to end the fighting (*peace imposition*), which was accomplished in Kosovo when the Yugoslav government acceded to NATO's peace proposal. Once the fighting has stopped, the next step is to make sure that fighting does not recur (*peace enforcement*), which was the initial task of KFOR. The hope is that by creating security for all former combatants, the peace enforcers can allow the process of reconciliation to begin, at which time true *peacekeeping* can occur. If peacekeeping succeeds, then terminating the mission may be contemplated.

Moving from peace enforcement to peacekeeping, and then to creating a stable peace that will allow the withdrawal of the peacekeepers, is easier said than done, in part because of the war's legacy of hatred and distrust and the quite natural vindictiveness that poisons the local atmosphere. It is also true that the political situation must have been fractured, or there would have been no war in the first place. When crushing poverty is added to the mix, the situation only gets worse.

To create a situation where outside withdrawal will leave behind a stable polity requires state building. That means nurturing appropriate political leaders, creating a political system to which all or nearly all citizens are allegiant, and building a stable economy (including the prospect of growing prosperity) that all citizens are willing to support and that all prefer to the resumption of hostilities. That is the task we have cut out for ourselves in Kosovo. We have never done this before, we do not know how to engage in massive state building in an ethnically diverse and contentious country (although this problem is moderated by the large-scale exodus of the Serbs), and we are not sure if it is possible or how long it will take. But we will find out in Kosovo.

Conclusion

In this chapter I have surveyed the possible uses to which American forces may be put in the next decade or so. The conclusion is that, for the most part, American use of force will be an option which we will periodically exercise. It is possible that we will be forced to act in some cases: a conventional war on the Korean Peninsula or in the Persian Gulf is always a possibility, but not a high probability. Crisis uses are much more likely, but they will almost always and surely be limited in duration and size of commitment.

It is likely that we will use force in situations of our choosing, as we often have in the past. Certainly, other states will seek to influence our choices, as was the case in Kosovo, but whether we go and how we go will be our decisions. Some of the uses will be in response to emerging threats or opportunities, and in some instances, investing in emerging situations may be much cheaper than making a large commitment later.

Most of the opportunities will be in internal wars in the Second Tier, since that is where the fighting and violence are. We have been involved in several of these situations over the past decade, as we were during the cold war, but little pattern setting has occurred. If you try to derive commonalities from our experiences in Somalia, Iraq (the exclusion zones for Kurds and Shi'ites), Haiti, Bosnia, and Kosovo, the result will be meager. About the only common element is that once we get in, we find that the situation is more intractable than we had realized, that our involvement is more open ended than we had thought, and that long-term success is much more difficult to attain than we had calculated.

Kosovo may help clarify our thinking. We had found in Haiti and Bosnia that we can stop the fighting and keep it stopped as long as we remain (peace imposition and peace enforcement); in Somalia we found that if we leave, the chaos resumes. We suspect that reversion would occur in Bosnia, Iraq, and Kosovo as well.

What makes Kosovo different is our commitment to state building there. At the outset, the motivation was to rebuild the war-scarred country, some of the devastation having been created by allied bombing. Ironically, the first KFOR casualties resulted from the explosion of an allied bomb. Our commitment, however, goes well beyond physical rebuilding, to creating a peaceful and stable Kosovo.

Our level of commitment in Kosovo takes us into uncharted waters. Can we create a stable Kosovo (in whatever relationship to Yugoslavia)? We do not know, but the answer is important if state building is a goal. Whether we accomplish that goal should go a long way toward influencing whether we will engage in this kind of activity in the future. Since potential involvement in internal wars occupies such a large and prominent place on the menu of violence, involvement and its problems require detailed examination, which is the subject of the next chapter.

Bibliography

Builder, Carl. *The Masks of War: American Military Styles in Strategy and Analysis.* Santa Monica: RAND, 1989.

Friedman, Thomas L. "NATO or BATO?" *New York Times,* national edition, June 15, 1999, A31.

Scales, Maj. Gen. Robert H., Jr. *Future Warfare: Anthology.* Carlisle Barracks, Penn.: United States Army War College, 1999.

Snow, Donald M. *Distant Thunder: Patterns of Conflict in the Developing World.* 2d ed. Armonk: M. E. Sharpe, 1997.

———. *National Security: Defense Policy in a Changed International Order.* 4th ed. New York: St. Martin's Press, 1998.

———. *The Necessary Peace: Nuclear Weapons and Superpower Relations.* Lexington, Mass.: Lexington Books, 1987.

———. *UnCivil Wars: International Security and the New Internal Conflicts.* Boulder: Lynne Rienner Publishers, 1996.

4 | The Dilemmas of Involvement

IF WARS THAT RESEMBLE KOSOVO ARE THE ABIDING WAVE, providing most of the opportunities for the United States to supply major force, then understanding the dynamics of these conflicts is critical to deciding where this country will employ force in the future. Unfortunately, there is little consensus about what these wars are like, the extent to which they are unique, and, most important, what can and cannot be done through intervention with armed force to bring them to an equitable and stable end.

Reasons for the Lack of Consensus

A New Phenomenon

The first reason for the lack of consensus is that these kinds of wars, as a genre, are a relatively new phenomenon for American policy makers (with the possible exception of Vietnam). There were internal wars during the cold war, to be certain, but from an American perspective they were significantly different from today's variety. Our interest then was instrumental, not inherent. We became involved because we conceptualized the conflicts within the context of the competition with communism, not because we had any real interest in the outcomes per se. If one side, usually the insurgents, espoused some form of Marxist rhetoric (usually in order to get material support from the Soviets or the Chinese), then we were interested in countering whatever influence we assumed the communists might gain. If the conflict did not threaten to turn a part of the map red or blue, however, we had little interest. Today, the old criteria no longer hold, and if we are to become interested in a particular conflict or category of conflict, we will have to devise different criteria.

Our instrumental approach during the cold war, interestingly enough, led us to ignore the one internal war that resembles the new internal wars. That conflict was the "civil war" that raged in Cambodia between 1975 and 1978, when the Khmer Rouge regime systematically "cleansed" its population of intellectuals and people with any professional skills. Vietnam invaded Cambodia in December 1978 to end that "war"; in some ways, its intervention is similar to contemporary interventions. We remained uninvolved largely because it was an intramural contest between rival communist factions supported by the Chinese and Soviets. At one point, we indirectly supported the Khmer Rouge by backing their sponsors in Beijing during our courtship of China.

Insurgency warfare is one kind of conflict with which the American military is unfamiliar and is basically uninterested. As noted in the last chapter, the U.S. Army went to some lengths after Vietnam to understand insurgency as it was practiced during the cold war, but basic doctrine *(Field Manual 100-5)* continued to emphasize traditional European-style warfare. Although the military produced an impressive array of field manuals and the like, how much of their knowledge on insurgency seeped down to the ranks has always been questionable, as was the commitment from the top ranks, other than on paper. The typical attitude among the infantry was that guerrilla warfare was relatively uninteresting. That attitude is eerily similar to the modern mantra that any good soldier can do peacekeeping.

A New Form of Warfare

With the exception of Cambodia, new internal wars represent a relatively new form of warfare, at least as a variant of counterinsurgency warfare. Certainly, the level of savagery we witnessed in the second half of the twentieth century is not unknown in human history: during the Middle Ages Europe experienced savagery until powerful monarchs emerged to quell the anarchy, and the Mongol Hordes engaged in their own form of ethnic cleansing as they swept across Eurasia, killing whomever got in their way. We have become accustomed to comforting ourselves that gross savagery and brutality are behind us; it is not easy to admit that they are not.

Complexity of Modern Wars

A third reason for the consensual vacuum is the complexity of modern wars. These wars generally occur in places about which we know relatively little, so we do little to anticipate them or to head them off, and when they occur, we tend to be paralyzed by our lack of understanding. One practical result of our ignorance is that we often conceptualize the violence as the problem rather than as a symptom of deep underlying problems—political, economic, social, cultural. Europeans often reacted to colonial wars of independence in much the same way. When we intervene, we may do so for naive reasons. Conceptualizing the violence as the problem makes the imposition of peace the solution, but it may blind us to the impact we have on the situation on the ground. For example, NATO went into Kosovo to stop the ethnic cleansing and restore order; in effect, NATO also became champions of Kosovar independence in the process, a problem that the international community will almost certainly spend years trying to sort out.

Part of the complexity is also operational: How do political leaders deal with these situations after they have decided to become involved? The problem is multifaceted. After you have stopped the fighting, how do you keep it stopped? Whom, for instance, do you disarm, and whom do you not? What is the effect on the political and military balance when you disarm some but not all? Who is likely to resist such actions violently? Who actually controls the groups you seek to disarm? U.S. peacekeepers have encountered each of the conundrums and have responded with different approaches. In Somalia our effort to disarm the militias associated with Mohammad Farah Aidid was one of the factors that led to the ambush of U.S. Rangers in Mogadishu and ultimately to our withdrawal from the country. Aidid responded violently because he believed we were attempting to tip the politico-military balance against him. In Bosnia we attempted to disarm all organized groups, but we know that it is almost impossible to verify that a force has been completely disarmed. In Kosovo it was not immediately evident that the "representatives" of the Kosovar people, who miraculously popped up as NATO troops streamed in, actually had much control over KLA forces in the countryside or much support within the population.

Other operational problems include the number and variety of individuals, groups, and missions that must be coordinated and when coordination should begin. When the military force is a coalition, as will almost always be the case, and particularly when the coalition includes Russians, how do you establish and maintain chains of command? The chain of command, to be effective, needs to be determined ahead of time as part of an anticipatory process. Establishing such a chain in the NATO operation in Kosovo was relatively easy, except for accommodating the Russians, who jumped the gun and occupied the Pristina airport; it took a week's frantic negotiating to get the Russians to share responsibility with other countries in the mission. Then there is the matter of coordination between the military command and the numerous government officials, international organizations (such as the UN and the war crimes tribunal investigators), nongovernmental organizations (for example, Doctors without Borders), media representatives, and others. Each group will have its own independent agenda that it believes must prevail, and each group will think that its part of the operation is more important than other groups' parts. Establishing a command structure is not a modest task.

Inappropriate Analogies

Consensus over the U.S. response to new internal wars is elusive in part because when we were first thinking about these kinds of operations, we started from some marginally appropriate analogies. More to the point, the aura of importance that attached to the United Nations in the wake of its role in the Gulf War made that organization the agency of choice for a broad variety of roles envisaged in the UN Charter. It turned out be a bad choice on several counts.

The UN's prominence in the Gulf War meant that the Security Council would take the lead in conceptualizing what would be done in the future. In 1992, one year after the Gulf War, the Security Council commissioned then–secretary general Boutros Boutros-Ghali to define the problem of peacekeeping. His response, a 1992 document titled *An Agenda for Peace*, is a model of conceptual fuzzy headedness. Boutros-Ghali's recommendations contained the implicit assumption that post–cold war peacekeeping would be the same as it had been during the cold war—an idea that was simply wrong.

Turning the conceptualization over to the UN also meant that future operations would be "UN-sized." That means we were bound to think small, because the UN is perpetually strapped for money (thanks in no small measure to the fact that the United States is far in arrears in its contributions for, among other things, peacekeeping). The UN, implicitly, must think of problems as relatively small and easily (which is to say, cheaply) solved, since that is all that the members would provide the resources for it to do. Unfortunately, most contemporary situations are neither small nor cheaply resolved.

Moreover, the UN is almost uniquely ill-suited to run operations that have a military component. Many of the people who devote their careers to the UN do so because they want to promote peace and, conversely, because they hate war. Generally speaking their predilection makes them averse to the use of force and not terribly knowledgeable about or adept at directing the application of force. Canadian general Lew McKenzie, who was commander of the United Nations Protection Force (UNPROFOR) in Bosnia for awhile, explained that early in UNPROFOR's deployment, the forces could act only with specific permission from UN headquarters in New York. The office that could issue such approvals, however, was open only from 9 A.M. to 5 P.M., Monday through Friday. It did not take the Serbs and others harassing UNPROFOR long to figure this out and to take advantage of the situation.

For better or worse, we are in an era where peacekeeping operations will be the most common form of U.S. military activity. In order to understand them fully, the remainder of this chapter will address peacekeeping operations along two dimensions: their nature and the possible outcomes we can pursue through them; and the operational difficulties of obtaining different outcomes. On the basis of these determinations, U.S. political leaders will be better equipped to decide whether to become more involved or to look askance at such opportunities.

The Nature of Peacekeeping Operations and Possible Outcomes

The nature of peacekeeping operations and their possible outcomes are related. What you can do affects what you try to do, and what you try to do reflects your assessment of the situation.

Conceptualizing Intervention in Internal Wars

Some of the confusion that surrounds outside intervention in internal wars has to do with the unfortunate designation in the early 1990s of all missions as "peacekeeping" operations. It is unfortunate in part because it raises the false image that the current peacekeeping missions are like those developed and honed during the cold war, which they are not. The designation is also unfortunate because it conjures an image of tranquility that will almost certainly not match the reality when the "peacekeepers" hit the ground.

An attempt to clarify the conceptual problem must begin with a description of classic peacekeeping as it evolved during the cold war. Cold war peacekeeping operations were typically put in place at the *end* of an *interstate war*, where a *cease-fire* had been negotiated by the formerly warring parties. "End" means that hostilities had been completed; peacekeepers did not have to enter a war zone. "Interstate" means that the former combatants were sovereign countries, so that the two sides could reasonably be separated; continuing hostility of neighbor against neighbor was not a problem. "Cease-fire" means that the governments involved had agreed that they preferred a cessation of hostilities to their continuation. The United Nations Emergency Force (UNEF) placed between Israel and Egypt at the end of the Suez War of 1956 was the prototype for this kind of action.

Nearly all UN peacekeeping operations during the cold war were of the UNEF nature, but there were two important exceptions that actually reinforce the point. In 1960 the United Nations sent a force into the former Belgian Congo (later Zaire, currently the Democratic Republic of Congo) to deal with the civil war that broke out almost immediately after Belgium granted it independence. The United Nations Operations in the Congo (known by its French acronym, ONUC) remained involved until 1964 and became an active participant, even a partisan, in opposing the secession of Katanga (now Shaba) province. Almost all observers agree that the adventure was one of the UN's darkest hours. The other exception was in Cyprus, where the United Nations Force in Cyprus (UNFICYP) was placed between warring Greek and Turkish Cypriots in 1964, dividing the island along what would become known as the Green Line in 1974. The presence of the peacekeepers created security for everyone and made the solution of their differences optional. As a result, UNFICYP is still in place and will continue to be for the foreseeable future.

Contrast the cold-war era model of peacekeeping with the typical new internal war, using Kosovo as an example. Typically, the fighting has not ended, which means that some or all parties prefer the continuation of war to its conclusion and will oppose the imposition of outsiders whose goal is to end the violence. The reasons for the opposition may be that the outsiders will stop the winning side from making additional gains (the Serbs expelling all ethnic Albanians), or the losers from recouping their losses (the KLA as the Serbs withdrew), or one side from exacting revenge on the other side (some KLA units as the Serbs withdrew).

By definition, internal wars are wars not between states but between factions or peoples, making disengagement and a stable postwar environment in which peace can be nurtured harder to accomplish. Distrust, even hatred, among those who formerly lived side-by-side is more likely the case. Overcoming "hatred in close quarters" is much more difficult than sealing borders in a traditional peacekeeping operation. The panic and flight of Kosovar Serbs as "their" army left Kosovo and was replaced by peacekeepers who were coming to protect *everyone* illustrates the point: the Serbs were not sure they could trust NATO and fled into Serbia rather than take the chance.

The absence of a cease-fire agreement, much less a peace accord, that *all parties* have agreed to also marked early interventions in new internal wars. In Somalia, for instance, no one had signed anything when Operation Restore Hope arrived on the Somali doorstep. In Bosnia the Dayton Accords had been signed by the Bosnian Croats and Muslims and by the government of Yugoslavia (acting on behalf of the Bosnian Serbs). The leaders of the Bosnian Serbs were not present at Dayton, at least in part because most of them were under indictment for war crimes and would have been arrested upon leaving Bosnian Serb territory. Similarly, the Yugoslav government and NATO signed the cease-fire for Kosovo; neither Albanian nor Serbian Kosovars were directly represented (although the KLA and NATO signed a separate agreement).

When the conditions for classic peacekeeping can be met, the prospects for a successful operation are good unless the peacekeepers fail to do their job. They have everything going for them. They arrive at the invitation of *all* parties concerned, who view them as a way to reinforce a peace that they all prefer; the peacekeepers are viewed by all as welcome additions to the process.

The key to success in any peacekeeping operation is the neutrality of the peacekeepers. Peacekeepers almost always *want* to be neutral. However, since neutrality has different meaning and effects, *being* neutral is easier said than done. *Neutrality of intent* is the conscious desire and determination to treat everyone fairly and to avoid affecting the situation to the advantage of one side or the other. *Neutrality of effect* is the ability to conduct the peacekeeping operation in such a way that both sides feel the result is fair and that neither side feels the other benefits disproportionately from the presence or the actions of the peacekeepers. In a classic peacekeeping operation, the distinction between neutrality of intent and neutrality of effect is not important. The peacekeepers will enter as honest brokers seeking to reinforce the wishes of all concerned. As long as they do not act in such a way that one side or the other views them as partisan, their effect will be neutral as well. And as long as they continue to be viewed by the protagonists as neutral, they will be welcome and hold the trust of the parties.

The same cannot be said of peacekeeping in internal wars. Although peacekeepers can and usually do enter a situation with impartiality as their intent, they will never be able to achieve neutrality of effect. Inevitably, one side will benefit and the other will suffer, meaning some group or groups will never trust the peacekeepers. Because these places typically are war zones (although fighting may be temporarily suspended), there is no universal commitment to peace; the contingent that imposes and enforces a peace that one party or the other opposes is not a welcome addition to the mix. The mere act of intervention changes the status quo on the ground; since some favored the status quo and some disfavored it, some will be happier than others. Almost anything the peacekeepers do will advantage some and disadvantage others.

When outsiders intervene for what they believe to be noble causes, like ending the slaughter of innocents, they are acting nobly on behalf of humanity. Because their motives are lofty, they tend not to think of what they are doing in partisan political terms; neutrality of intent is implicit. Since those who are committing the atrocities are presumably doing so for political reasons (if not necessarily noble or defensible ones), they perceive the interruption as a hostile, partisan act that properly should be opposed. That is why NATO has come under isolated attacks and sniper fire in Kosovo; some of the people did not want us there to interrupt their mayhem (Albanian reprisals against Serbs and Gypsies, for instance).

Their desire to achieve neutrality of effect influences what the peacekeepers do. Once again, classic peacekeepers had it relatively easy. Their primary mission normally was to observe and monitor the implementation of an agreement to which all parties had agreed and which the parties trusted the monitors to uphold honestly and without prejudice. Classic peacekeepers did not get involved in violations unless they were fired upon, in which case they returned fire for their personal protection.

Neutrality of effect also influences how the missions are equipped, and it helps explain why the UN likes to think of all peacekeeping operations in classic terms. Classic peacekeepers are not combatants, they are more like the friendly cop on the block. As a result, they require less equipment than combat forces: they are armed with sidearms and rifles for self-protection, need binoculars to observe the neutral zone, and need noncombat vehicles to get them around. UN observer missions traditionally are unarmed and incapable even of self-defense. In fact, a number of the defenseless UN observers of the 1999 referendum in East Timor were attacked.

Operationally, classic peacekeeping operations are relatively inexpensive, and that is why the UN Secretariat likes them, even though it is not so naive as to believe that all peacekeeping operations fit the classic model. To repeat, the UN is perpetually in financial trouble (its critics argue that is so because the UN is grossly mismanaged) and can engage in peacekeeping operations only through assessments of its members, who may or may not pony up the cash. The United States, which is the largest contributor under the UN's assessment formula, is also the most likely to fall short of its quotas, which adds to the financial crisis of the world body.

Thinking of all interventions as classic peacekeeping operations may help the UN conserve its resources, but it does not conform to reality. Observation and monitoring are a part of what contemporary peacekeepers do, but they have to be prepared to do more: they *enforce* peace agreements in addition to seeing that they are carried out voluntarily. Classic peacekeepers passively observe and report violations of agreements; contemporary peacekeepers take corrective action when they see violations. They take a much more proactive approach. Because contemporary peacekeepers will inevitably suppress some actions, they will encounter opposition, sometimes violent opposition, to what they do.

Contemporary peacekeepers have a different mission and therefore have to be configured somewhat differently than their classic counterparts. Although the primary mission of contemporary peacekeepers is not to conduct combat operations, combat may be part of what they will do. As such, they are a hybrid between combat troops and classic peacekeepers. To accomplish their goals, they must be configured like combat units, as the forces in Kosovo are. Such a configuration is intended to intimidate those who might attack them, and thus it reinforces the ability of the peacekeepers to maintain order. Furthermore, in an atmosphere of "war without death," heavily armed peacekeepers are much less likely to incur the casualties that might turn public opinion against the mission and force its withdrawal. Clearly, however, quelling the violence by intimidating the combatants was the main driver of policy in Kosovo.

The UN's failure to recognize the difference between classic and contemporary peacekeeping was most clearly demonstrated by UNPROFOR in Bosnia between 1992 and 1995. UNPROFOR was the quintessential case of defining a place as in need of a peacekeeping force when in fact it was a war zone for which the classic peacekeepers were woefully ill-prepared and even more ill-equipped.

The original intent of UNPROFOR was to observe and monitor a cease-fire between Serbia and Croatia, a classic peacekeeping mission for which the lightly armed peacekeepers seemed appropriate. The problem, however, was that the cease-fire was fragile and proved to be temporary. If there was a role for UNPROFOR, it was peace enforcement, for which a more heavily armed force was needed, if only to defend itself adequately. Although the observing force remained in place effectively, Bosnia devolved into full-scale warfare, for which any international presence required peace imposers—fully armed combat forces.

There sat UNPROFOR, with its sidearms, rifles, and binoculars. It became a pawn of the various sides. At one point, UNPROFOR soldiers were manacled to Serb targets to keep NATO bombers from attacking them. The peacekeepers were batted back and forth by the combatants until the Dayton Accords came into force and UNPROFOR was mercifully dissolved and replaced by the heavily armed Implementation Force (IFOR), which later became the Stabilization Force (SFOR).

The United States has learned from UNPROFOR the folly of putting what amount to police officers into combat zones, and the UNPROFOR experience ensured that future missions would be manned by soldiers capable of imposing and enforcing order. Even as the Kosovo Force (KFOR) rumbled into Kosovo, looking more like combat troops than peacekeepers, we were still calling them peacekeepers, a testimony to our lack of conceptual sophistication. Fortunately, they were adequately equipped to deal with those Kosovar Serbs (and a few Albanians) who greeted them with sniper fire.

Peacekeeping, Peace Enforcement, or Peace Imposition?

Very few of the situations into which the United States or other powers are likely to be drawn resemble those for which classic peacekeeping is appropriate. Rather, in the contemporary world, a situation to which classic peacekeeping would be an appropriate international response will usually be a *goal* toward which the mission seeks to move, not a condition already in existence.

One can think of the range of operational situations as a continuum *(see Figure 4.1)*. The extremes are intuitive and represent discreet points on the continuum. A state of war means that there is violence among armed groups and that there is no clear indication that all sides wish it to cease, probably

Figure 4.1 The Conflict Continuum

War--/---------------------Unstable peace---------------------/--Stable peace

because they have goals they want to obtain through continued fighting. At the other end of the continuum is stable peace, where the fighting has ended and both sides prefer peace to renewed fighting and are willing to work to ensure the continuation of peace.

Unstable peace occupies the continuum between war and stable peace. Generically, unstable peace refers to the condition where peace (the absence of war) has been established but it is uncertain whether the peace would hold if the outsiders left. The continuum represents a changing likelihood of peace being self-sustaining, based on the feelings of the former combatants. Thus, at the war end of the continuum, it is likely that the unstable peace is the result of outside peace imposition and that some or all of the former combatants would take the field if the outsiders left. At the peace end of the continuum, almost all of the parties have been reconciled to the idea that peace is preferable, and the peace can probably be maintained with minimal force. The points in between represent combatants' varying preference for war or peace.

The continuum mirrors the distinction between classic and contemporary peacekeeping operations. As suggested, different situations require different conceptualizations of the military mission. The ideas of mission form, on the one hand, and situation on the ground, on the other, are combined in Figure 4.2.

We have witnessed all three of these situations in the Balkans over the past decade. The air campaign over Kosovo and Serbia was an act of peace imposition. Whether it intensified or ended the conflict may be debatable, but NATO conducted Operation Allied Force with the intent of forcing the Serbians to end their war on the Kosovars. The repeated statements by the NATO allies (especially the United States) that we would not put ground forces into Kosovo until a peace settlement was reached indicates that we viewed the task in peace imposition terms. When KFOR entered the country in late June 1999, the situation was one of unstable peace; the sporadic attacks on the peacekeepers and the acts of vengeance committed by each warring party against the others indicated that the unstable peace was much closer to the war end of the spectrum than to the peace end, and peace imposition remained the order of the day.

Figure 4.2 Situations and Missions

War--/---------------------Unstable peace---------------------/--Stable peace

| Peace imposition | Peace enforcement | Peacekeeping |

After the Dayton Accords were signed, Bosnia became a classic unstable peace/peace enforcement operation, closer to peace than to war on the continuum. Since not all parties to the war in Bosnia participated directly in the Dayton Accords, there was no question that peace would dissolve without the presence of IFOR/SFOR. However, since the outside forces were not attacked, the IFOR/SFOR mission entered Bosnia closer to the middle of the continuum than KFOR would enter Kosovo. The universal agreement that war would return if the outsiders left was evidence that Bosnia was not very close to achieving stable peace.

The United Nations Preventive Deployment (UNPREDEP) in the Former Yugoslav Republic of Macedonia (FYROM) represents a case of classic peacekeeping. There had been no fighting before the mission was approved and implemented; indeed, as its name implies, its purpose was to prevent the outbreak of violence. Although we can never know whether it was the existence of UNPREDEP or some other factor that led Serbia not to try to reannex the breakaway republic, we can say the two phenomena coincided.

Proper identification of a situation affects both the strategies and forces that are employed. At the peace imposition end of the spectrum, heavily equipped forces with the ability to engage in decisive offensive action are needed, both to quiet the situation on the ground and for self-protection. The heavily armed forces that rumbled into Kosovo as part of KFOR met that description. At the other end of the continuum, the small garrison of UNPREDEP soldiers was equipped and configured as classic peacekeepers, which was entirely appropriate given the garrison's status as observer and monitor.

The fascinating and under-investigated aspect of the continuum is the broad center: peace enforcement in conditions of unstable peace. In these situations, two distinct tasks must be undertaken. Conventional military action must be taken or threatened to keep the combatants apart and prevent them from resuming their mayhem. This goal is accomplished by traditional military tactics, such as patrolling, establishing checkpoints, and disarming individual citizens and groups. Yet the deployment of peace enforcers usually occurs amid some level of civil disorder, where individuals and groups seek revenge or take advantage of the lack of order to engage in acts of arson, looting, and even murder. Conventional military forces are not especially adept at dealing with civil disorder and may have to learn policing or constabulary functions on the spot (as in the early stages of KFOR).

Early in its deployment, KFOR recognized the dichotomy between conducting typical military operations and enforcing civil order. As the military command struggled to make sure that the peace that had been agreed upon held, it also saw the need for some other group to suppress the looters and other criminals. It thus called for the rapid insertion of an international police force to help restore domestic order.

If the purpose of intervention is more ambitious than simply stopping the killing for awhile, then the continuum suggests the strategy: try to move the situation from wherever it is on the continuum (war or unstable peace) toward peace. In Kosovo the international effort to end the war began with peace imposition, moved with KFOR to unstable peace at the war end of the spectrum, and has as a goal convincing the inhabitants progressively that they prefer peace to war (that is to say, has as a goal moving toward the stable peace end of the continuum). If an unstable peace becomes progressively more stable (more and more groups come to prefer peace to the alternatives), then peacekeepers can replace peace enforcers. If stable peace emerges, then the mission is accomplished and the peacekeepers can probably be withdrawn.

How do the intervening forces change as progress is made toward the peace end of the continuum? At the war end of unstable peace, the mission is pure conflict suppression, and the balance of forces must be weighted toward the military force portion of the overall package. As the situation moves toward the peace end, however, the danger of war presumably decreases to some extent, and the mission increasingly becomes maintaining an order from which the former combatants benefit and which they seek the peacekeepers to enforce. In other words, the policing features gradually become more prominent, and the military ones less so: the police officer's truncheon gradually replaces the armored personnel carrier as the symbol of outside intervention.

How does this transition from military to police power occur? No one knows, because until our involvement in Kosovo, we had never said that we would stay until we had solved the problem that we had come to solve. Having put ourselves on the line is what makes the Kosovar experience such an important precedent for the future. The question then becomes, what outcome will allow us to say that our job is done in Kosovo?

Realistic Actions: Conflict Suppression or State Building?

One shortcoming of interventions by the United States and other countries into the war-torn internal politics of dysfunctional states has been the absence of a clearly articulated and attainable goal. We raise the question of an "end game," the point at which we can declare the mission accomplished, only in general terms. Policy makers rarely offer a clear answer to the question.

Why is this so? In all of the places where the United States has become involved (with the partial exception of Haiti), our motivation was to end the great man-made human suffering that would get worse, even catastrophically so, without international action. Iraqi Kurds who had fled the vengeance of Saddam Hussein were starving and dying of disease on the Turkish mountain sides, Somalis were starving from the combination of a long drought and the withholding and theft of internationally supplied foodstuffs, Bosnians were suffering from the latest wave of Balkan ethnic cleansing, the Rwandans were being subjected to grotesque slaughter, and the Albanian Kosovars were the victims of yet another application of cleansing.

The images in each instance were stark and evocative, courtesy of global television, and especially Cable News Network. We became aware of the plight of the Kurds when CNN cameras focused on the wretched refugee camps in which they huddled. The distended bellies and reed-thin extremities of Somali children symbolized their suffering. Bone-thin Bosnian Muslims peering through the fences of detention camps reminded us starkly of World War II concentration camps. Although the images were somewhat delayed, the grotesque slaughter by machete in Rwanda turned our stomachs. The flight of panic-stricken Kosovars tugged at our heart strings.

The result was an understandable and generally laudable instinct to become involved, to make the suffering cease, something I call the *do-something syndrome*. When faced with great suffering and human misery, our first instinct is to rise to the occasion, to "do the right thing," in President Clinton's often used phrase.

There are two problems with the do-something syndrome. One is that it is a knee-jerk, though selective, response. The so-called *CNN effect* occurs: the images that we see on television create an urgency about the need to act that can blunt rational thinking and planning, including calm consideration of what we seek to accomplish. Moreover, television is inherently cursory in its coverage, obscuring important nuances and complications that fall outside a "sound bite." The other problem is that we are spurred to action only by those atrocities of which television makes us aware. There is no greater systematic barbarity occurring anywhere in the world than in the genocidal civil war in the Sudan, but most Americans are totally unaware of it. Why? Because the Sudanese government has told journalists that they enter the country at their own considerable personal risk. Hence, the TV cameras have not recorded the slaughter, and there are no demands to put a stop to the carnage. For the thugs and butchers, the lesson is quite clear: keep the Western cameras out and you can do pretty much whatever you want.

The do-something syndrome encourages reflexive responses that are not well thought out, and this tendency is reinforced by our peace-war-peace perception of conflict. The kinds of conflicts in which we are tempted to intervene are long, deeply rooted, and complicated. They are like volcanoes: they erupt periodically. You can act to moderate the effects of an individual eruption, but no matter what the surface conditions, the molten lava still lurks beneath, ready to return.

Thinking of peace as the normal condition and war as the aberration that is "solved" by the application of firepower distorts reality in the kinds of countries where the new internal wars occur. In one sense, the model is inverted: tension and conflict are the norms, periods of peace and stability are the exceptions. In Somalia, historically, order has existed only when a very strong clan leader or coalition of leaders has been able to assume authoritarian rule; when no such leader is present (which has been the case since 1991, when Maj. Gen. Mohammad Siad Barre was overthrown), the result is anarchy. The history of the Balkans is similar. Order has been the product of often brutal occupations by a succession of empires, and various groups have always collaborated to oppose whichever rulers were there. As a consequence, almost every group has long and deep resentments against nearly every other group. When the veil of suppression is lifted, those hatreds come to the surface. In Robert D. Kaplan's phrase, there are lots of "Balkan ghosts."

When these situations explode in front of us to our horror, we tend to see only the violence, and tend not to look below the surface as we craft our response. The problem can be likened to a medical emergency. When violence erupts, it represents the symptom of an underlying disease, which is the set of deeply held animosities that gave rise to the symptom. When we intervene with armed force to stop the fighting, we are treating the symptom, not the underlying cause of the wound. We are, in effect, putting a bandage over the wound and changing it to keep it clean for as long as we occupy the country under our care. That is fine if healing the wound also cures the disease. If keeping the people apart and stopping the killing create an atmosphere of reconciliation and cooperation that will result in stable peace, then the approach is adequate. If not, it is an expensive bandage.

Unfortunately, treating the symptom usually does not cure the disease. That takes a separate and much more arduous level of commitment, the outcome of which is very uncertain. We have chosen the latter course in Kosovo.

Framing these situations in this way allows us to distinguish realistic from unrealistic options for dealing with them. *Conflict suppression* and *state building* are the two possible routes the United States can follow. Although the processes are sequential (you have to suppress a conflict—impose peace—before you statebuild), they are very different and entail quite different problems, likelihoods of success, politico-military implications, and realistic outcomes. Knowing what the options are and what one can realistically expect to attain by doing one or the other are absolutely critical to forming a coherent policy and creating expectations that the public, which is the base on which policy must reside, is willing to support. Up to this point in the Kosovo deployment, U.S. political leaders have been less than clear and forthright about which goal we have been pursuing, what was involved, and what outcomes to expect. Our perception of post-Kosovo opportunities for involvement will be greatly affected by our ability to explain this distinction.

Conflict Suppression. The first goal that one can pursue is conflict suppression, which involves actions that either stop the fighting (peace imposition) or maintain a de facto cease-fire or negotiated, unstable peace (peace enforcement). The goal of forces engaged in conflict suppression is to ensure that fighting does not resume. They do so by taking actions that make it impossible for the former combatants to resume hostilities or make that resumption more costly than potential perpetrators are willing to accept. In pure conflict suppression, troops and accompanying gendarmerie are used almost exclusively to keep the lid on the violence; they may also do some rebuilding of infrastructure that has no political ramifications.

Conflict suppression has its advantages as a goal. We know how to do it in such a way as to minimize our costs, notably our human costs. Our learning curve began with Somalia, where we went into a war zone inadequately prepared mentally or physically for the situation. The U.S. and other national forces under UN auspices made friends with the natives, patrolled at less than full readiness, and did not have the heavy equipment to support combat operations. The result was a relatively large number of peacekeepers killed. According to UN statistics, 151 soldiers died in the two missions to the country (UNISOM I and II), of which 110 were killed as the result of "hostile action." In the Balkans, the casualty figures were 197 killed in UNPROFOR and three in UNPREDEP. The two Somali missions and UNPROFOR represent 25 percent of all UN soldiers killed (1,375) between 1948 and 1998.

We learned from the Somalia and Bosnia deployments. When the United States "intervaded" (part intervened, part invaded) Haiti, we sent in heavily armed troops who were instructed to view the population as potentially hostile. There was no fraternization with the Haitians; instead, the troops patrolled with their weapons constantly at the ready firing position. When we joined IFOR/SFOR, we went in armed to the teeth. That is also how we began in KFOR.

The purpose of peacekeeping in a hostile environment is straightforward: it is to intimidate the locals so that they will be afraid to engage in violence against one another and, of equal importance, against the peacekeeping force. This approach worked in Bosnia; there was not a single combat death among American forces from 1995 to 1999. In the first days of KFOR, the U.S. Marines spearheading the U.S. contingent came under sporadic sniper attacks, but they suppressed the snipers without American casualties, which, of course, the American people might have deemed unacceptable under the "doctrine" of war without death.

Conflict suppression is also the kind of mission with which the military can identify. The role is explicitly military: to take, consolidate, and pacify territory. Within those parameters, the military can reasonably protect its own personnel from serious harm. As a matter of predilection, the military generally objects to this form of duty under only two conditions: if it is asked to expand its role in such a way as to put the troops in harm's way (usually at the request of civilian authorities), or if the peacekeeping mission begins to create morale problems among the troops.

There is also a down side, however, to conflict suppression as a sole strategy: although the peacekeeping force can suppress the violence as long as it remains in place, conflict suppression does nothing to alter the underlying problems that gave rise to the fighting in the first place. Therefore, there is no end point at which the mission has been accomplished and the forces can go home. If the peacekeeping forces leave and the violence resumes—which it may well—then the question arises, "Was it worth the trouble?" Inevitably, some political and military leaders will answer in the negative and question the next proposed mission.

Once again, we have some experience in this regard. In Somalia, a mission designed as peacekeeping, or conflict suppression, flirted with peace imposition or peace enforcement when the UN forces attempted to disarm the militias, but they backed away from that expansion of purpose and left. Many of the elements of anarchy that were present when we arrived were still evident when we left and continue to the present. In Haiti, we went beyond conflict suppression (there was little conflict to suppress) to engage in acts like training an honest police force (a novelty in the Haitian experience). When we departed, however, we left behind a support group to assist with logistics and administration and a small contingent of combat forces for the support group's protection.

Bosnia is the relevant analogy for KFOR. The SFOR mission has been in Bosnia since the end of 1995, and it was two years before SFOR widened its activities beyond those associated with conflict suppression. Proactively searching out war crimes suspects was one of the tasks that SFOR undertook, and by 1999 almost all suspects (at least those outside the French zone) had been arrested. Conflict suppression alone, however, has not moved the situation toward any kind of resolution. It is difficult to find an observer who will predict anything other than a reversion to fighting if the mission is removed from Bosnia.

The same is true of Kosovo. By insisting that Serb military forces leave the province, we have tipped the balance of power to the KLA, which initially resisted being disbanded; is there any question in anyone's mind about what they would do should KFOR pull up stakes and leave?

Conflict suppression gives the United States comfort by its familiarity. Moreover, since the UN deputized NATO to act in the Balkan conflicts, the United States gained a healthy element of burden-sharing; in the KFOR operation, we have limited the need for coalition cooperation by assigning different geographic regions of Kosovo to different NATO countries and Russia. What is different about Kosovo is that we have promised to do far more than just stop the shooting for awhile. The longer we are there, the more we have committed ourselves to state building. As I argue, state building is difficult, and in some cases it may be impossible, especially when performed by outsiders. Moreover, it is an enterprise in which the military element is relatively minor; U.S. military force is reduced in weight and importance as conflict suppression makes the transition to state building.

State Building. The effort one makes to alter the political, economic, social, and psychological environment in a country that has experienced a new internal war is state building (or state rebuilding, depending on the situation). The rationale behind and need for these kinds of actions is straightforward: if political, economic, and social institutions had been working adequately before the war began, the conflict would not have occurred in the first place. Moreover, any structures that preexisted the conflict have probably been destroyed in the fighting. Thus, by definition there exists the need to build new structures that will facilitate the population's return to normal life. State building is the path to stable peace.

The United States has been reluctant to head down this path in the past and has done so only in fits and starts. We engaged in limited state building in Somalia when we tried to disarm the militias, starting with Aidid's in Mogadishu. Many observers both in and out of government called such efforts "mission creep" and derided them. We got our nose bloodied and retreated. In Bosnia we tried to return Muslims to homes from which they had been displaced. The Serbs who had occupied those houses resisted being turned out, in some cases violently, and by and large we relented.

Our reluctance to engage in state building has several bases. First, we are not quite sure how to do it. As mentioned in Chapter 3, we have some experience in rehabilitating prostrate enemies, as we did Germany and Japan after World War II, but the problems are not the same. Germany and Japan were defeated enemies that needed physical reconstruction and political education, but they were unified states without serious internal divisions and had well-educated populations that needed only the opportunity to get back to normal. That is not the case in the Balkans today. We also had some limited experience during our brief colonial rule over such places as Cuba and the Philippines, but the incentives were rarely there to develop our colonial holdings into stable, freestanding political entities (in fact, doing so would have violated the intent of most colonial policy, which focused on keeping colonies). There is simply no comprehensive set of guidelines, no instruction manual, for turning a war-torn, destitute, and deeply divided country and its peoples into a model of stability and prosperity.

Second, whatever efforts are necessary to rebuild a state are likely to be very costly and to have uncertain results. The early estimates for rebuilding the destroyed infrastructures of Kosovo and Yugoslavia were in the tens of billions of dollars, and such estimates are notoriously unreliable and usually low. Turning Kosovo into a model society, even if that is possible, will be a very expensive proposition. If success were a sure thing, the expense might be acceptable. But there are no assurances of success, because there is no precedent. If we knew rebuilding a bridge in Kosovo would facilitate peaceful commerce and prosperity, we would do it. Knowing that one faction of Kosovars might blow it up to spite their neighbors makes the proposition less attractive.

Third, when state building fosters change, the local population will not universally accept it. Changing the circumstances rearranges in some way who benefits and who does not. Those who benefit will embrace the changes; those who do not will not. The statebuilder will always enter a situation with the intent of being fair to all legitimate factions—neutrality of intent. However, neutrality of effect will likely be impossible to achieve. Sometimes, the expression of discontent will be violent, breaking the tranquillity and simplicity of pure conflict suppression and raising opposition to the effort even from within the state-building community itself. State building is a lot harder than conflict suppression.

The difficulties notwithstanding, we are committed to state building in Kosovo in all four of the dimensions identified in the opening paragraph of this section: political, economic, social, and psychological. Each requires a brief analysis before turning to the operational problems of state building.

Repair or replacement of the political structure begins with the realization that the old structure was dysfunctional or nonexistent. Who should propose a new structure that is acceptable to all parties concerned (assuming the legitimate representatives of all parties can be identified, which is no sure thing)? The alternatives are that the parties themselves do the drafting, with the help of the outsiders, or the outsiders do it. Both alternatives have advantages and disadvantages.

The advantages of outsiders proposing a system are that they have experience with stable political systems and can be relatively neutral in what they propose. The constitution that Gen. Douglas MacArthur wrote for Japan is a model of this kind of effort. At the same time, the disadvantages of such a process are that the population will likely construe the proposed system as being imposed and will reject it as alien. Furthermore, the outsiders may not know the political realities in the country well enough to produce a realistic document.

The other possibility is to bring the factions together in a constitutional convention to hammer out a document of their own, with the outsiders providing advice and guidance. That model sounds good but is likely to be more difficult to implement in practice than one might imagine. Given their war experiences, the various parties are going to be suspicious of the motives of other groups, to put it mildly. In a poisonous atmosphere of hatred and recrimination, producing a document that all parties feel is fair to them (protects their rights, gives them an adequate opportunity to participate) is likely to be very difficult. For better or worse, some form of democratic system is likely to be the outsiders' goal for people who probably have no experience with democracy.

Despite the difficulties, crafting a viable constitution and the supporting institutional infrastructure on which it rests is absolutely necessary for state building to be successful. Clearly, faith in the political system has been smashed by war, and unless faith in the legitimacy of the political system can be restored, very little else is possible. People must have faith that the judicial system is sound and fair, that the constabulary is impartial and not corrupt, and that the government bureaucracy provides services in a fair manner. The political system must, in other words, be made legitimate.

None of this is easy or fast, and we have seen what happens when democracy is declared without the institutional underpinning to support it. In that regard, Russia is the prime example of what can go wrong. Russia declared itself a democracy without having such basic institutions as a central bank to regulate the economy or laws on private ownership of property, and it has dissolved into near criminal anarchy, where there is almost no respect for government institutions. That is an outcome we do not want for Kosovo or for any other area in whose politics we become involved.

Not all of the actions taken by state builders will be dramatic. Some, in fact, will be mundane, as a real problem encountered early on in Kosovo illustrates. During the ethnic cleansing, the Serbs collected and destroyed the identification cards of Albanian Kosovars, who returned from internal or external exile with no identification. New forms of identification had to be distributed, but what kind? There were two alternatives, each with broad symbolic importance. One possibility was to issue Yugoslav IDs, since by the terms of the peace agreement between the government in Belgrade and NATO, Kosovo is still legally part of Yugoslavia. Many Kosovars, of course, wanted to shun everything Yugoslav and could be expected to oppose the issuance. Moreover, since there were very few Yugoslav officials in the province when NATO arrived, who would issue them? The other alternative was to issue temporary United Nations identification. UN officials were present to perform the task, but issuing non-Yugoslav identification may have suggested that Kosovar independence was really the UN's long-term goal. Thus, a seemingly minor problem became a major issue, the outcome of which was far more important than the specific problem.

Economically, the war-torn region is likely to be a shambles. In poor countries like Somalia and Haiti, there is little economic infrastructure to begin with and few physical or human assets from which to develop a growing prosperity to which the population might become allegiant. In Kosovo, the infrastructure that preexisted the conflict was destroyed by the war. Some institutions that dated from the period of Kosovar autonomy could be revived, but Kosovars with the experience to operate them were among those systematically murdered during the repression.

A stable, growing economy is absolutely necessary for reconciliation to occur. If the former warring parties are to put the often horrible past behind them and look toward a united future, then they must believe in a better, more prosperous life. In the beginning, providing the people with hope for the future may entail no more than providing assistance in rebuilding homes destroyed by war, providing interim housing and food while reconstruction occurs, rebuilding basic infrastructure such as power grids and potable water systems, repairing roads and bridges, and helping merchants and farmers get back into business.

All of these measures are time-consuming and expensive, but they are concrete and "doable." Simply restoring the economy to the status quo ante may not be enough, however; after all, economic wretchedness is one of the common characteristics of a violence-prone society. For state builders, creating a perception of increasing economic prosperity is part and parcel of legitimizing the postwar state. Without a sense of economic betterment in the future, formerly warring parties are less inclined to let bygones be bygones and to look toward the future.

There is a strong social dimension to state building as well. What do state builders do to improve the social condition in the country so that formerly warring parties can interact with one another in a reasonably civil manner? In the Balkans, partitioning was the means. In Bosnia the groups walled themselves off from one another and congregated in what amounted to ghettos; in Kosovo the losers fled the country in what amounted to reverse ethnic cleansing.

Partitioning may be the only solution where animosities have become so deep that reconciliation is psychologically impossible. However, it is neither a pretty alternative nor one that is universally available. Generally speaking, partitioning means uprooting people and relocating them within designated areas, as occurred in Bosnia. Those displaced are generally unhappy with their situations, because most of them are being forced out of homes and regions where they have lived all their lives. Moreover, the logistics are almost always painful and upsetting and only add to the alienation. And partitioning may reverse the roles of oppressed and oppressor, as the plight of the Kosovar Serbs and Gypsies demonstrate.

Partitioning may also be practically impossible. If intergroup mixing was great before hostilities began, then separating the parties geographically may not be possible. Lebanon is the prototype in this regard; much of the animus that surrounded the Lebanese civil war stemmed from the inability to separate Christians from Sunni Muslims and Shi'ite Muslims. There will be more Lebanons.

There is also a psychological dimension to state building, given the horror of war and the unique horrors of watching civilians, including loved ones, being victimized. War of any kind creates deep psychological scars on almost anyone touched by it; the uniquely nonmilitary manner in which the new internal wars are conducted multiplies the horrors. In Rwanda, whole villages were slaughtered, and the only survivors were those who fled or feigned death. In Kosovo, people were forced to watch the brutal execution of family members. When one adds the rape victims and those who were tortured or terrorized, the litany of psychological disorders becomes frightening.

The children are the hardest to help. The children of Somalia, Rwanda, and the Balkans have seen horrible things that would unbalance the strongest of adults; the acts of barbarity and savagery they have witnessed go beyond what any human should have to endure. Of the roughly one million Kosovars forced to flee their homes, many will bear the scars for a lifetime. Their number almost certainly outstrips the availability of adequately trained counselors and psychologists.

This list of obstacles to state building is daunting enough, and it does not even address the question of who ameliorates the problems. In the end, the people themselves will have to make most of the adjustments. Conferring legitimacy on a set of political institutions is not something that outsiders can do; the governed people themselves must do that. Social reconciliation cannot be mandated; psychological wounds have to heal. Only the short- to medium-term economic rehabilitation or development of a country can be conducted with outside financial resources and expertise; in the long run, the people themselves will have to learn to run their economic affairs. The question is how and when to teach them and whom to teach.

Outside intervention may be necessary to end the fighting and to hasten the recovery of countries torn by new internal wars. Peacekeepers can impose and enforce peace and assist in the other dimensions of national recovery. The above list of tasks is suggestive, not inclusive, of everything that needs to be done. One is struck by the daunting scale of even the partial list: its contents are difficult, complex, and time-consuming. To accomplish all of the goals of state building, and thus to leave behind a stable country capable of peaceful self-governance, requires a long-term commitment. We will not leave Kosovo any time soon; if we do not stay the course, we will leave behind the prospect of the war's resumption.

The Operational Level

In the preceding section, I tried to lay out in a realistic manner the kinds of situations that may present themselves to us in the future and point to options for becoming involved in them. I discussed the broad nature of the requirements for moving such a conflict in a favorable direction. The most demanding scenario is state building, and it is important to look at its operational aspects in detail.

State building is the task that we have signed on to perform in Kosovo. We are at the very beginning of the process. Many of the concerns raised in the last section have yet to be publicly addressed.

Policy makers need to understand the operational aspects of state building in order to determine whether we can or should engage in it. Kosovo is an ongoing laboratory in this regard, but it may give rise to general principles that can inform the decision-making process of when and how to become involved and allow more universal judgments to be made.

In this section, I address the things that have to occur to overcome the problems identified in the last section. Three questions are relevant: Where should we be willing to go to engage in conflict suppression and, especially, state building? What should we do in pursuit of conflict suppression and state building, and what are the predictable impediments to our constructive action? How will we go about doing the job?

Where to Go?

Where to go is a recurring question. Its answer will largely frame the American attitude toward involvement in peacekeeping operations around the world; since peacekeeping operations are the most frequent opportunities for the United States to use force, deciding in which ones to participate is a basic building block of employment policy.

The diesel fumes from the last retreating Yugoslav army vehicle had hardly cleared the air before observers began to speculate on where the United States would intervene next. The suggestions tended not to name locales in a direct way but to identify the properties of places that would make them eligible. Two sets of criteria that were suggested almost immediately represent the range of criteria.

On June 17, 1999, the *New York Times* began the debate with an editorial titled, arguably prematurely, "Lessons of the Balkans War." It proposed three qualifications for the future use of American force: extreme violence in the theater, danger of the violence spreading to neighboring countries, and "where democratic nations [*sic*] have the means to respond." A week and a half later, *U.S. News and World Report* suggested that presidential aides were proposing to the president that he issue a "Clinton Doctrine" comprising three criteria: a compelling American national interest, a moral imperative to save lives, and the potential to dramatically improve the situation.

The *New York Times* and *U.S. News and World Report* pieces were complemented by a cascade of other analyses that apparently were poised for presentation as soon as the fighting ceased in Kosovo. The July–August 1999 issue of *Foreign Affairs*, which reached subscribers on July 1, had no less than four analyses of the Kosovo situation. What can be said of the proposed criteria and analyses? I believe that all of them were premature attempts to reach generalizable conclusions from Kosovo. The heralds of airpower, for instance, had better wait for a final accounting of how many real, as opposed to dummy, targets they destroyed, and thus what can be expected of airpower in the future. Moreover, the success of intervention depends ultimately on achieving the political objective, which in Kosovo is a stable region that does not blow up in the world's face again. That goal is clearly contingent on the effectiveness of the state-building process, judgment on which is a long way off. UN Secretary General Kofi Annan's initial estimate of the length of the operation was ten years.

The *New York Times* criteria are surprisingly negative and, if adopted, would mean very little involvement. The editorial writers admitted as much, saying "the combination will be rare outside Europe." Since the Balkans is the part of Europe where the three criteria are likely to be met, the editorialists could have said southeast Europe. Moreover, the criterion of "extreme violence" is strange, negative, and defeatist; it implies that we will not act pre-emptively, as I suggest we should, but instead will wait for the carnage to become so great that we cannot ignore it. One would hope that policy and strategy would be more proactive than the *Times* proposes.

The proposed Clinton Doctrine criteria are simultaneously more expansive and more restrictive. In application, the first two are probably self-contradictory. "Compelling American national interests" will rarely if ever be involved in any of these situations. Yet a persuasive argument can be made for a "moral imperative to save lives" in many places where the United States has no compelling interests. The only instances where both criteria would apply would be where a democratic, First Tier government began to ethnically cleanse or violently suppress parts of its own population: Australia waging a war of genocide against the Aborigines, for instance.

In practice, there will be compelling interests *or* moral imperatives, not both. In that case, which criterion prevails? Strict adherence to the realist paradigm—the notion that force is used only where interests are vital or compelling—would preclude our engagement in these kinds of wars in the future.

Take a real example that had the potential to be the next Kosovo: East Timor. The island of Timor is part of the Indonesian archipelago, located northwest of Australia. Historically, Timor was divided by two colonial powers: the Netherlands and Portugal. When the Netherlands granted Indonesia its formal independence, West Timor became a part of the new Indonesian state, and East Timor remained a colony of Portugal. In the early 1970s an independence movement emerged in East Timor demanding an independent East Timorese state. In 1975, as part of its general retreat from empire, Portugal granted independence to East Timor. Independence did not last long. In December 1975 the Indonesian government of President Suharto declared East Timor a part of Indonesia and sent the Indonesian army into the territory to occupy it and, in a bloody campaign, to crush resistance to Indonesian rule. At the time, the international community expressed great outrage at the annexation but took little action.

The cause of East Timorese self-determination did not die down, and periodically East Timorese separatists and the Indonesian army would clash.

In 1994 the Asia-Pacific Economic Cooperation (APEC) met in Bogor, Indonesia (a suburb of Jakarta), and East Timorese nationalists demonstrated outside the halls where the eighteen leaders of APEC (including President Clinton) were conferring. The conferees ignored the demonstrators.

The fall of Suharto in 1998 and the subsequent relaxation of authoritarian rule in Indonesia revived the independence hopes of the East Timorese. The government of Indonesia showed no interest in allowing secession until 1999 because of the precedent it would set in other parts of this large, diverse, and dispersed country, but the East Timorese were determined to press their cause. When 78.5 percent of East Timorese voted for total independence in 1999 under the watchful eyes of UN observers and world television, it became more difficult for the government not to accede. Open calls for independence increased, and Indonesian militia (widely believed to be supported by the Indonesian military) ran wild, killing East Timorese and driving many into exile. With nearly one-quarter of the population refugees, an Australian-led peacekeeping force reestablished order and then turned command over to the UN to supervise state building. Its success remains to be seen.

How do the *New York Times* and proposed presidential criteria hold up in the East Timor situation? Their common criterion is the ability to conduct successful operations, which, in the East Timorese case, were easily met: Timor is a relatively small island (about eleven thousand square miles) that the U.S. and Australian navies could easily isolate. If the Indonesians tried to starve the East Timorese into submission (as they were accused of doing in the late 1970s) or to crush them, the criteria of extreme violence or moral imperative could arguably be made. However, there is no danger that the fighting would spread, except by inspiration to other separatists on other islands, and there are no compelling or even noncompelling American interests involved. So, if the problem arises again, do we go to East Timor? Hastily drawn criteria do not answer the question, and the willingness of the Australians, who were also interested in avoiding a flood of refugees, to jump into the breach made the question moot for the United States.

The foregoing assessment of the two sets of criteria and their possible application beyond Kosovo illustrate the issues that remain unresolved in deciding where we should intervene. The assessment reflects a shortage of serious contemplation. Take, for instance, the one criterion on which the two lists agree: the ability to act in a way that alleviates the situation. How can policy makers pronounce in advance that U.S. or other forces can solve a problem unless they know what the problem is? They can guess, but they might guess wrong. Is the criterion a rigid standard, or is it situation-based? The answer is not clear. Moreover, until we learn a great deal more about the effectiveness of state building in Kosovo, it is hard to imagine how we can assess the potential to dramatically improve a different situation through U.S. action. Furthermore, state building is ultimately an indigenous process that must spring from the people, who must find a way to marry their common will to a set of ideas applicable to their situation. Outsiders can, at best, help supply the ideas.

The foregoing assessment also shows that there are divisions among reasonable people on these issues that are not easily resolved, and it shows that the rush to judgment is premature. Within days of the end of the eleven-week bombing campaign about Kosovo, analysts were extolling the ascendancy of airpower and its ability to be decisive. The hyperbole was reminiscent of that over the air phase of Operation Desert Storm. The post-conflict study that assessed the effectiveness of aerial bombardment in the Persian Gulf dashed a great deal of that enthusiasm, and it is almost certain that the same thing will happen in Kosovo. The admonition of Maj. Gen. Robert H. Scales Jr. (USA) about firepower-negating strategies (see citation at the end of Chapter 3) will undoubtedly reduce our enthusiasm as we uncover the decoys that the Yugoslavs suckered us into destroying while their real equipment remained hidden and safe in caves and tunnels. The proper lesson from Kosovo may be to "rush" to judgment slowly.

What to Do?

The question of what a peacekeeping operation is to accomplish raises a dilemma of sorts, which the outcome of the Kosovo mission may help clarify. In the past, the American public has shown a willingness to support—or at least not oppose—missions that we have called "conflict suppression." SFOR in Bosnia and the mission to Haiti are the prime examples. The condition for public acceptance of these peacekeeping operations has apparently been the absence of American casualties—the preference for war without death. And the U.S. military has become quite adept at avoiding casualties by sending heavily armed forces to intimidate the population into not attacking the peacekeepers.

However, there is another way to avoid casualties that undermines the political goal of state building: avoid activities that are likely to produce violent resistance. Effective state building necessarily upsets the status quo, advantaging some groups and disadvantaging others. In Somalia there could be no stable order as long as the armed clans ruled segments of the country. Very reluctantly, the military allowed itself to be used to try to disarm those militias, starting with Aidid's militia in Mogadishu. Realizing his position would be weakened relative to the other clans if he submitted, he fought back, and the United States took casualties.

This example frames the dilemma. Engaging only in conflict suppression avoids casualties but it also precludes taking actions that might change the status quo in ways that promote stable peace. On the other hand, if we take actions that will nurture change, the result will likely be casualties that will erode public support for the mission. The dilemma, then, is the possibility that the public will support activities that do no real good in the long term (passive conflict suppression) but will oppose actions that may actually contribute to long-term success (state building).

There is some evidence that this is the conundrum we face. In Bosnia the participants clearly committed atrocities against civilians—most of those publicly identified were Bosnian Serbs, including the president of the Republic of Srpska (the Serbian portion of Bosnia), Radovan Karadžić, and his chief military leader, Ratko Mladić. A number of leaders have been indicted on war crimes charges, and it goes without saying that national reconciliation is not going to proceed smoothly as long as those guilty of heinous crimes go free. A major step in state building for Bosnia would seem to be an aggressive campaign to arrest those charged and bring them to trial. Nearly five years since the Dayton Accords were signed, many of the indicted officials remain free and are likely to remain so as long as they stay in their own designated zone of Bosnia (especially the French occupation zone). The "campaign" to apprehend them consists of wanted posters at checkpoints between zones; anyone on the list stupid enough to try to pass through a checkpoint might be arrested. Those who have stayed inside their own zone (even if they appear brazenly in public) have had little to fear, at least in the French zone.

Why? SFOR has concluded that aggressively pursuing Bosnians accused of war crimes would bring a violent reaction, including against those who do the pursuing. SFOR, in addition to avoiding casualties to its soldiers, also fears civilian casualties. If the purpose of SFOR is to enforce the peace in a manner that maximally protects SFOR members, this policy makes sense. If, on the other hand, the purpose is to build a solid Bosnian state that will remain peaceful after SFOR leaves, it makes considerably less sense.

The Bosnian example is relevant in Kosovo. As NATO and other parts of the peacekeeping operation entered Kosovo, one of the first things they found was evidence of mass executions and rampages against ethnic Albanian Kosovars in much larger numbers than had been estimated from overflights. Even before such discoveries had been made, there was adequate evidence for the war crimes tribunal in The Hague to issue indictments against a number of Serb officials, most prominently Slobodan Milošević, the president of Yugoslavia.

What will happen to the Kosovo set of accused war criminals? Hardly any have been arrested, and most are back in Serbia, where they are well protected from the not-so-long arm of international justice. Will we treat them the same way we have treated the accused war criminals in Bosnia, leaving them alone unless they prove guileless enough to wander across the border? Admittedly, Kosovo is not Bosnia, and KFOR has been more aggressive about apprehending war criminals within Kosovo. Unfortunately, many of those accused are in Yugoslavia, where KFOR has no jurisdiction.

The treatment of war criminals is a vital question for the long-term outcome in Kosovo. Albanian Kosovars, who prefer independence or union with Albania to remaining part of Yugoslavia, will find reunion even more distasteful if those who ordered their slaughter and displacement are still part of the governing structure. Reconciliation of the Albanian Kosovars and the Serbs has a chance (and no more than that) only if those guilty of the atrocities are brought to justice. A passive policy promotes Kosovar resistance to anything short of total independence and, in effect, champions Kosovar independence. We say we want Kosovo to remain part of Yugoslavia; however, if we do not aggressively pursue the war criminals, our policy is nothing short of schizophrenic.

The reason we have trouble answering the question "What to do?" is two-fold. First, the question is an extension of the international-neoisolationist and idealist-realist dichotomies. As suggested in Chapter 2, Americans are split on the question of activism in the world. Some argue that we have a moral obligation to come to the aid of mankind, especially when we are confronted by vicious inhumanities. Others say these things are none of our business and that we should worry primarily about ourselves. In the new world environment, where outside forces do not dictate what we will do and not do, it is more difficult to decide where and how we should interact with the rest of the world.

Second, these kinds of operations really are different from any we have tried doing before, and our uncertainty stems at least in part from our inability to see what the outcomes of different actions will be and the routes to those outcomes. We may want to "do the right thing," as President Clinton repeatedly has said of Bosnia and Kosovo, but what is the right thing? How do we get there? How will we know when we are there? As the old saying goes, if you do not know where you are going, you will never know when you have arrived.

I am going to assume that one of the endeavors we will attempt is state building. Kosovo is our initial venture in this direction, and the experience will go a long way toward determining our future attitudes toward this kind of activity. It is also largely uncharted ground; the most we may be able to do at this point is specify the parameters of the problem.

How to Do It?

U.S. policy makers and observers realized that the postfighting work in Kosovo would be incredibly more complex than had been the conduct of the aerial campaign. Despite the scale of Operation Allied Force, it was governed by doctrine that had been practiced for years. Granted, it did not go smoothly. It took a full month to deploy twenty-four Apache helicopters from their U.S. bases in Germany to the theater of operations, for instance, which seemed a rather long time, and assessments of the military impact of the campaign are gradually becoming more subdued. And, of course, it was a coalition effort, bringing with it all of the difficulties of coalition warfare—if on a small scale, since most of the effort was American.

Peacekeeping and state building in postwar Kosovo will be infinitely more complicated than was the war. There are many more tasks to be accomplished, and there will be many more groups and agencies involved in the operation, all with different agendas and priorities. Civilians with a variety of orientations and institutional perspectives and the militaries of several states will have to learn to interact in a manner whereby the Kosovars are the beneficiaries. And while all those who have come to help learn to live with one another, they will be figuring out which Kosovars they have to come to terms with and how they will work toward a common end. Since the Kosovars prefer independence and the peacekeepers have agreed that Kosovo should remain a part of Yugoslavia, the possibilities for working at cross purposes would seem to be at a maximum.

The roster of participants and their varying purposes are still evolving.

At this writing, the panoply of actors that will participate in the state-building process in Kosovo has not been assembled, and no equivalent mission has been mounted elsewhere to stand as a model for Kosovo or for other future involvements. Nonetheless, there has been enough experience from which to weave the broad tapestry of who will likely participate.

Before listing the groups and institutions that are likely to be on the scene, it is useful to provide a bit of context about what the mixture will be like. First, the participants will be diverse, ranging from professional soldiers to clinical psychologists and social workers. Second, they will be at cross-purposes at least some of the time, because what each seeks to accomplish will not always be compatible with what others seek. The press, for instance, will want to be on the scene, especially in times and places of trouble, and will want military protection. The military, which views protection of its soldiers as its primary priority, will be reluctant to accede to the media's requests, because doing so would put soldiers in harm's way. On the other hand, if journalists are injured or killed because of the failure to protect them, the military gets the blame, at least from the press (justly or not).

Third, there will be a certain amount of distrust among some of the groups, arising from divergent institutional perspectives and lack of understanding of one another. The greatest cleavage will likely be between the military command and the various civilian agencies engaged in the several aspects of state building. Disagreements will also arise among the civilian components, for instance, between UN officials who are charged with administering the territory and the often-aggressive nongovernmental organizations that provide care or monitor developments. Some of this disagreement is understandable: almost everyone thinks their task deserves a high priority, and not all can be accommodated equally. At the same time, misunderstandings are likely to arise from the fact that some of the groups have rarely if ever interacted with others, do not understand the others' perspectives or procedures, and have preconceptions and stereotypes that will, at least initially, get in the way of productive interaction.

With these problems in mind, we can look at the various groups and categories of groups that will have to interact to produce a stable peace. For the sake of convenience, I will divide them into three categories: the military, foreign civilian groups, and the citizens of the country involved (the target population). Each has different missions and reasons for being there. Harmonizing their mutual efforts is the key to success. As we will see, doing so will be difficult.

The Military. The outside military forces that enter the country are initially the most visible manifestation of an international presence. In most cases, they will enter the country after a cease-fire has been arranged, which means there is at least an unstable peace, and hence their job will be peace enforcement rather than peace imposition. At a minimum, their job is to ensure that the parties to the fighting do not regress, to create or restore a physical order that the former warring parties either respect or fear the consequences of challenging, and to act as a shield behind which the recovery and eventual state-building process can proceed. These were the first tasks for KFOR when it entered Kosovo and, with the exception of a few isolated attacks on arriving troops, they were achieved successfully.

These initial tasks are not all that the soldiers will be asked to do. In all likelihood, military engineers will be asked to assist in restoring basic services, such as electricity and water; building, provisioning, and to some extent supervising temporary housing, such as tent cities; assisting in infrastructure projects, such as repairing bridges or roads; and even assisting in the initial efforts to repair and rebuild homes and public buildings. All of these activities fall within the engineering capabilities of the military and are neither exceptional nor controversial. Included in this form of activity are more directly military actions, such as removing land mines, unexploded munitions, and other artifacts of the war that have to be removed to insure the physical safety of the citizenry. In Kosovo, much of the need for such activities is a direct result of the bombing campaign, thereby creating an even greater sense of obligation than we might otherwise feel.

A second extraordinary category of military involvement is so-called civic affairs. Beyond such actions as training local gendarmerie (after identifying candidates one can trust, which is often easier said than done), more direct activities include restoring or developing the justice system and aiding civilian authorities in building or rebuilding order in the country. In the U.S. military, a great deal of the resources to perform this function and other noncombat support functions, such as truck transport and medical care, come from the reserves, thereby necessitating activation of the reserves in support of missions. (As we shall see in Chapter 5, that may prove to be a problem in the future.)

The military may be asked to be more proactive in moving the state-building process forward, to which it may object. These actions may include capturing suspected war criminals, helping resettle people into abandoned homes, or disarming armed bands. These sorts of activities will be handed to the military because they might provoke a violent response, which the military is trained to deal with as no other group can. The military will, if Bosnia and Somalia are any indication, resist such assignments on the basis of "mission creep" (a term devised in Somalia to refer to the slow and incremental process of expanding the mission beyond the simple restoration of order). Mission creep, however, is a misnomer. When policy makers decide to engage in state building, the basic mission requirements of conflict suppression are superceded by a comprehensive program intended to create a stable peace. Everyone hopes that state building can be accomplished without military casualties, to which civilians object much more than does the military itself, but the decision to engage in state building includes such actions.

Beyond being asked to do things they would rather not do, the military is subject to other problems as well, two of which stand out. First, almost all of the outside interventions in civil wars are going to be coalition undertakings. The American public will not stand for unilateral interventions (except very small ones in places like Grenada) where other interested parties, including allies, stand idly on the sidelines. Burden sharing and the problem of *free riders*, beneficiaries of an action who do not take part in it, become matters of equity and perception.

Coalition activity is always difficult. In addition to having different formalities and protocols, coalition militaries will often have different missions, be controlled by political masters with differing agendas, have difficulty forming viable chains of international command, and encounter an array of other tactical and logistical difficulties (see Khaled bin Sultan's account of the politics of coalitions in *Desert Warrior*, his account of managing the coalition partners in the Gulf War).

The KFOR operation, since it is basically a NATO operation, minimizes these sorts of problems because the coalition partners have worked together for a long period to resolve them. Assigning discreet pieces of real estate to various national occupying forces helps minimize the degree or interaction and thus friction among them, but deployments outside of Europe, where NATO is unlikely to be the organizing device, will pose many more difficult problems. The early experience with the one non-NATO participant in KFOR, Russia, is testimony to the kinds of problems that can arise.

The coalition problem is particularly important to the United States. As the remaining superpower, the United States will be expected to participate, more often than not in a prominent leadership role, in most future missions. In Bosnia and Kosovo, American participation on the ground was the sine qua non for a successful cessation of hostilities; that is likely to be the case elsewhere. For instance, when East Timor became the site of a peacekeeping operation, it was hard to imagine that the United States would not be called upon as an impartial participant in the operation, although Australia stepped forward to assume the leadership role.

On the other hand, American participation is necessary because the United States is the only country in the world that has global reach. Any but the smallest future operation will require considerable airlift and sealift to get troops, materiel, and supplies to the theater of operation. Only the United States can provide such logistics support. Most such missions also require sophisticated intelligence collection and analysis on matters such as the movement of groups, and only America can provide the needed capability. If the United States decides to stay home, the international community will have difficulty sustaining a sizable mission. Although many foreign and domestic critics resent the United States for being too aggressive, we would be resented even more if our refusal to become involved resulted in a human tragedy opposed by the world. That tug between aggressive intervention and resentment of noninvolvement could be the salient question of the millennium. The new realism is somewhere between the extremes.

A second problem is that the longer a mission lasts, the more likely the foreign troops will be resented than appreciated for their efforts. Foreign troops will eventually be viewed as occupiers, even imperialists, by some or all groups in the occupied society. Moreover, when the intervention moves from conflict suppression toward state building, military participation will result in actions that are partisan in effect if not in intention. For instance, it was already obvious in the earliest stages of the KFOR operation that the way in which the occupying forces treated the KLA would be critical to the final shape of the outcome, especially in the eyes of the Serbian minority. As the perception of KLA fighters changed from one of liberators to one of communist thugs little better than their Serb counterparts, their treatment by KFOR became even more critical to the end game, a factor not wholly understood when the peace arrangement was being negotiated.

Foreign Civilians. All of the military problems pale in comparison with those of maintaining relations among the diverse foreign civilian institutions and groups that descend on a peacekeeping mission. Limited experience makes any generalizations about the civilian participants speculative. However, certain categories can be identified: representatives of international organizations and nongovernmental organizations; the media; contractors and other business executives; and the specialists, the people and groups with particularly needed expertise.

The representatives of international organizations, including the United Nations and its specialized agencies and other affiliated bodies, represent one interested civilian group of parties. If a peacekeeping operation is sponsored by the UN itself, these representatives will be prominent in organizing and coordinating the entire enterprise, as they were in Somalia. Organizing such an enterprise can prove to be controversial and tricky, as it was in Somalia and in the UNPROFOR phase in Bosnia. In Somalia the temporary lack of unity of command of U.S. and other forces under UN authority provoked such a political firestorm in the United States that American policy now is to insist on U.S. operational control of all U.S. troops in a peacekeeping operation. This requirement effectively means that the United States will have a lead role in any such allied effort.

The United States and NATO recognized the UN as the lead international organization in Kosovo. Security Council Resolution 1244 (the text of which is reproduced as Appendix A) establishes the UN Interim Administration in Kosovo (UNMIK) under Article 10 and, among other things, creates an oversight role for implementing what a June 15, 1999, press release refers to as the "four pillars" of the Kosovo operation, each of which is administered by a separate international organization. Humanitarian assistance is the responsibility of the United Nations High Commissioner for Refugees. Civil administration is administered by the UN Secretariat itself. The Organization for Security and Cooperation in Europe (OSCE), a fifty-five-member organization that includes all the states of Europe and North America, is to "concentrate on developing democratic institutions," and the European Union (EU) is on the scene to aid in the physical and economic recovery of the province. In order to coordinate these UN efforts, Secretary General Kofi Annan appointed a special representative, Bernard Kouchner, who assumed his post on July 15, 1999.

All of these international organizations and NATO have overlapping memberships. The United States is a member of all of them except the EU, and all of the European members of NATO (except Turkey) are members of all four organizations. The French emerged as early leaders in the arrangement: Dr. Kouchner, a former French cabinet member and founder of Doctors without Borders, became the chief civil administrator of the province with the title "special representative of the secretary general." He replaced the acting special representative, Sergio Vieira de Mello.

Will this pattern of UN involvement—where the organization participates in the state-building process but not the conflict suppression—set a precedent? In the early stages of the KFOR mission, for instance, the military and civilian components were highly compartmentalized, and the most prominent international organization representatives were members of the War Crimes Tribunal (a part of the UN by virtue of its affiliation with the International Court of Justice), who were searching for evidence of Serb atrocities. Resolution 1244, Annex 2.4, authorizes "the international security presence with substantial North Atlantic Treaty Organization participation"; however, it does not clearly state the working relationship between UNMIK and KFOR. Rather, a June 14, 1999, fact sheet describes as an UNMIK goal to "establish, on a priority basis, coordination mechanisms with the international security presence operating in the region (K-FOR)."

The centrality of the UN in future missions is a matter of some controversy. At one level, UN sponsorship (the authorization of actions and missions by the Security Council) adds legitimacy to operations, and because of the veto possibility, means that all of the major military powers at least do not oppose the mission. At the same time, the possibility that either China or Russia might use its veto over the military mission to Kosovo is one of the reasons that NATO, rather than the UN, was the legitimating agency of choice.

The other major source of controversy about UN imprimatur surrounds where or how the UN Charter limits what the UN can do in these kinds of situations. The charter was drafted more than fifty years ago with stopping interstate violence in mind; it is somewhat ambivalent on intervening in sovereign states. On one hand, Article 2 (7) suggests that involvement in "the domestic jurisdiction of any state" should not occur. On the other hand, Article 39 authorizes actions when threats to or breaches of the peace occur, and the article does not specify whether those actions are limited to cross-border incursions. A threat to the peace is whatever the Security Council says constitutes a threat (see the six articles cited at the end of the chapter from the May–June and July–August 1999 issues of *Foreign Affairs* as an introduction to the issue).

Kosovo is probably uniquely blessed (or cursed, depending on how final arrangements work out) in terms of international organization representation. As a part of Europe—and the region that causes Europe most of its security concerns—Kosovo has access to the wide range of international organizations and especially to Western funds. Other problem areas—Africa and South Asia, for instance—have no equivalent to the OSCE or the EU to which they can turn for assistance.

The second group of civilians comprises the representatives of nongovernmental organizations. These groups tend to be divisible into two subgroups, the caregivers and the monitors. They share two common characteristics: an overt desire to alleviate human suffering and an almost studied apoliticism that many other groups consider naivete. Their single-minded devotion to duty often places them at odds with other groups, either because they demand to be where the suffering is most acute (often in unstable areas) or because other groups perceive their actions to have untoward political consequences. Nongovernmental organizations and the military missions are likely to view one another with considerable suspicion and disdain initially.

The caregivers are likely to be the first on the scene when great human tragedy occurs. It is not at all unusual for representatives to be in-country while the fighting is going on and certainly well before an organized peacekeeping force enters the scene. In Somalia, for instance, organizations like Doctors without Borders preceded Operation Restore Hope, as did food providers such as CARE. They are also likely to remain after troops are withdrawn from missions that had conflict suppression as their goal. Their longevity and their devotion to alleviating suffering sometimes produce an aura of self-righteousness that annoys others. At least one author, Edward Luttwak, claims their presence is pernicious, blocking the parties from reaching decisive outcomes. Moreover, Luttwak states, "the defining characteristic of these entities is that they insert themselves in war situations while refusing to engage in combat" ("Give War a Chance," p. 38).

The other nongovernmental participants are the monitors. Since new internal wars have invariably been accompanied by atrocities, they are interesting to groups whose major purpose is to observe and report on human rights violations. Thus, representatives of organizations like Amnesty International and Human Rights Watch can be expected to be among the early arrivals in any peacekeeping operation. Where the countryside is secured, their often aggressive attempts to gain information at the sites of alleged atrocities are not particularly a problem. When they request armed guard to venture into unsecured areas in a situation of unstable peace not far removed from peace imposition, they are a source of some friction with the military.

Next, there is the media. Particularly in this modern era of worldwide, instantaneous reporting of events, the media is certain to be a major and influential part of any operation. In many instances (Somalia, Bosnia, and certainly Kosovo), the media first make the public aware of violence and atrocity, giving various publics an interest in what goes on later. During the Persian Gulf War and the war over Kosovo, the media reported from the "enemy" capital cities, Baghdad and Belgrade, while the fighting was under way. Given the high level of public interest, the media will always be present and active after the fighting is over.

Two comments should be made about the media's role. The first is the transitory role of the media. The media reflect the attention spans of readers and viewers. The media cover a story as drama until their audiences tire of it. The media are selective in order to maintain the drama. Allied bombers destroying a bridge over the Danube River in Belgrade may make the news; incremental progress in restoring that bridge probably will not. This selectivity means that media attention is likely to be intense at the beginning of a peacekeeping mission but will likely fade unless "newsworthy" events, like major violations of cease-fires, occur.

Although media publicity is necessary to alert the public to new internal war atrocities, it does not cover all such events. There has been essentially no outside coverage of the most genocidal of all civil wars of the 1990s: the war in Sudan. The reason is that the government takes no responsibility for the safety of journalists; in fact, the government is one source of the danger, which has effectively cowed coverage. The safety of media personnel is rarely guaranteed by the protagonists, of course, but the government's virtual threat of harm sets the Sudanese case apart. If the alleviation of human suffering in internal wars is to become a universal value, then some alternative mechanism to the open media must be found for identifying and publicizing these wars. The media is a less than adequate agenda setter.

A fourth group likely to enter a state-building process are the contractors and private business people. They are unlikely to be among the first arrivals, but for long-term state building to occur, both are necessary. The contractors add to the resources necessary for building or rebuilding the infrastructure, including sometimes the housing stock. The business people look for investment possibilities and will be encouraged in so doing by the sponsoring political authorities because prosperity breeds loyalty to the political system. The prototype in this regard is the mission led by the late Ron Brown, U.S. secretary of commerce, to Bosnia after the Dayton Accords were signed. Brown took with him an assortment of business people, who were being enticed to open operations in Bosnia and thus to create jobs and prosperity. The mission ended tragically when Brown's airplane slammed into a Croatian mountainside, killing all on board, but inducing private investor participation still stands as a useful idea for comprehensive state-building efforts.

The fifth and final group are the specialists, the individuals and groups that have needed expertise. One such group has already been identified—the psychologists, counselors, and social workers who help victims and their families adjust psychologically to the horrors of the wars. It is one thing to organize such efforts within the confines of relocation centers, as has been done in parts of the United States; it is quite another to put together and administer such an effort in a war-torn countryside.

Other experts likely to be in short supply are health providers (who are also caregivers). One of the first victims—by intent or happenstance—of these tragic wars is the health system. In many countries, these systems were underdeveloped before violence erupted, and the fighting only multiplied the problem. A potentially serious problem, for instance, is that of epidemics in refugee camps, especially in tropical climates. There is a possibility that some new disease, or old one that was thought long eradicated, for which inoculation is ineffective will break out and infect the caregivers. In the worst case, those infected may return to their native countries and spread the disease further. This has not transpired yet, but it could.

There are organizations that attempt to fill the need for medical care. Doctors without Borders will be there, and military medical personnel can step into the breach as well. Both, however, are limited resources and are insufficient to constitute a health system. Military medical personnel, most of whom (at least in the American contingents) are reservists, will likely not be around for long tours, will slowly dwindle in number, and will minister first to the needs of their respective national military contingents.

A final example of specialists might be planners. In Kosovo, for instance, it was clear when the fighting stopped that the major imperative facing UNMIK was to prepare the Kosovar population for the winter that would begin in less than five months. To prepare for the impending cold weather required a very large and complex effort that included repairing homes and providing alternative housing (all-weather tents, for instance). Since many refugees had left all of their belongings behind when they fled, many returned to find their dwellings looted of cookware and stoves, which UNMIK needed to provide, along with sources of heat and electricity to warm dwellings against the winter cold. The same was true of winter clothing.

The task proved daunting. A variety of agencies volunteered to help, but slow funding processes and resource unavailability resulted in shortfalls. By late summer 1999 it appeared that a sizable number of Kosovars would suffer through the winter months.

The foregoing description of the civilian organizations and individuals who must be part of a comprehensive state-building effort is almost certainly incomplete, because we have never mounted such an effort and thus lack the experience to anticipate all the problems and consequent needs that we might encounter. In Kosovo, we may be lucky. There is an infrastructure to be rebuilt; if we tried the same thing somewhere in central Africa, we would have to start near scratch. And the people and the locale of Kosovo are more familiar to us: Kosovo is a part of Europe. Other places might not be so inviting to those who would become part of the operation.

The mere listing of all these actors is daunting, perhaps even overwhelming, and I have been accused of being overly pessimistic. Yet the efforts are going to be extraordinarily complex and require coordination and cooperation among diverse groups and individuals with different orientations and perspectives on the problem of creating a stable society. I would assert that we currently have neither the expertise nor, to borrow a military term, the "doctrine" to mount a smooth operation to accomplish the goal. That does not mean, however, that doing so is impossible or that we cannot create the means to do so.

The Target Population. When all the outsiders are assembled and their various activities delineated and coordinated by some agency, the focus turns to the population of the country itself. State building can be facilitated by outsiders, acting as tutors and mentors, but ultimately the task of building or rebuilding a viable state must fall to the citizens themselves. Each state-building exercise will be a discreet enterprise, with special problems arising from idiosyncratic factors associated with the particular country in which it is mounted. However, some questions are probably pertinent to any peacekeeping operation. Although Kosovo is unique in that almost all of the hostile parties had left before the statebuilders arrived, I will use Kosovar examples to illustrate the answers.

The first basic question is: What is the situation? Clearly, some fundamental differences will have festered over a period of time that must be overcome before a viable peace can be achieved. The roots of the Kosovo conflict are long and deep, but its latest incarnation can be traced to the stripping of Kosovar autonomy within Serbia by then Serbian president Milošević in 1989. This action reignited the Albanian Kosovars' aspirations for independence, which eventuated in the formation of the KLA in 1996 *(see Appendix B for a chronology of Kosovo events)*. After Milošević became president of Yugoslavia in 1997, he began to tighten the noose around Kosovo, and some form of violence seemed inevitable.

The second question is: What do the parties want? The history of a conflict also defines what is acceptable to the parties. Repatriated after their forced exile, the Albanian Kosovars are being asked to accept a long-term solution wherein they remain a part of Yugoslavia (a sop to Milošević and the Serbs), which the Muslims oppose. The United States and the rest of KFOR/UNMIK clearly are hoping that Milošević is overthrown and replaced by a democratic government during the interim period, so that rejoining Yugoslavia will not seem so unpalatable to the Albanian Kosovars. But what if that does not happen? What if Milošević remains in power or is replaced by another Serbian strongman bent on authoritarian rule and the reestablishment of Serb control in Kosovo? Can UNMIK force the Albanian Kosovars to accept an outcome they oppose? If so, will that represent the victory or defeat of state building?

Part of what the parties want can be surmised from the answer to the third question: Who represents the legitimate aspirations of the people? In the chaotic aftermath of a conflict, there will be no shortage of volunteers for the mantle of legitimate leader of the country. Sorting out who that may be will be easier if we know in advance who the pretenders are. In Somalia we knew very little about them, and thus first courted then condemned possibly the only leader who might have been able to impose order on the country: Aidid. In Kosovo, by mid-July 1999 there was already an open and growing rivalry for the leadership role. Ibrahim Rugova, who led the peaceful and largely unsuccessful resistance to Serb domination after autonomy was rescinded in 1989, has presented himself as the logical and reasonable choice. His aspiration is opposed by the leader of the KLA, Hashim Thaci, who dominated the Albanian delegation at the Rambouillet peace talks, which produced a working document from which the eventual peace was fashioned. Nowhere in the early deliberations about the future of Kosovo was there representation from the remaining Serb minority.

The selection of someone whom the population trusts to represent their aspirations will go a long way toward determining the outcome of the state-building process. In the absence of such a person, the atmosphere may be one of retribution, further deepening wounds. De Mello, Annan's interim administrator, apparently thought that was the direction Kosovo was heading early in the mission: "Killings, kidnapping, forced expulsions, house burnings, and looting are a daily occurrence. These are criminal acts. They cannot be excused by the suffering that has been inflicted in the past. Kosovo's future must be built on justice, not vengeance" (quoted in the *New York Times,* July 16, 1999). Finding leaders who represent the legitimate aspirations of most people will go a long way toward determining if retribution or reconciliation is the norm.

Finally, there is the question: How much can outsiders accomplish? During the cold war, U.S. policy makers and observers tended to believe that outside intervention could be more effective than it turned out to be. The prototypes for the failure of intervention during this period, of course, were the American adventure in Vietnam and the Soviet fiasco in Afghanistan. In the post–cold war period, UN participation in the Somali civil war stands as the same kind of experience.

Whether intervention in the form of state building as it is now being implemented in Kosovo will succeed or fail is an open question. The difficulty is moderated somewhat by the fact that the Kosovars are European; the kind of reconstruction that we are attempting is not totally alien to them. It is possible that they will embrace the UN-led effort to democratize and economically uplift their society, because what we are trying to do matches their own aspirations. But maybe not.

The other possibility is that the longer we stay and the harder we try to graft the Western democratic system upon them, the more they will come to resent our presence. It has happened before; much of the American disillusionment over Vietnam stemmed from the fact that the Vietnamese did not appreciate what we were trying to do for them. Foreigners may liberate a people and set things right in the short run; if they overstay their welcome, however, they may be viewed as little more than imperialists.

Is there potential for that to happen in Kosovo? Unfortunately, the answer is yes. There is one sticking point in the UNMIK operation that could drive the outsiders and the Kosovars apart in an unreconcilable manner and torpedo the whole enterprise. That issue is Kosovar independence. In the Rambouillet accords, independence was mentioned as a possibility at the end of the transitional period. The provision was embraced by the Kosovars and rejected by the Serbs. In the final agreement, sanctioned by Resolution 1244, that prospect was diluted.

Kosovar aspirations for independence will simmer for a time as the rebuilding and recovery unfold, but they will never be far from boiling over. Unless a free, democratic, and nonthreatening Yugoslavia blossoms in the next few years, there is no way the Albanian Kosovars will accept less than an independent state (which might or might not be incorporated into Albania). What if UNMIK/KFOR insists on reconciliation and reunion with the Serbs? Will the outside liberators then become the enemy? And will the entire effort unravel in the process?

For that matter, what if an apparently free and friendly Yugoslavia emerges? Milošević might be overthrown (we are working hard to make that happen), democracy might bloom, and the Yugoslav economy might turn prosperous, fertilized by outside investment. Would the Albanian Kosovars, who have had about as much to do with Serbs as they care to, say they want out anyway? Or would they opt to be remarried to Yugoslavia? Can two cultures in which animosity to one another is integral be transformed quickly?

Conclusion

After this lengthy recitation of the conceptual and operational problems of interfering in the internal conflicts of other countries, the reader might reasonably ask, what has this to do with the future use of American military force in the world? It is not a bad question, and I do have an answer.

My rationale for dwelling on the complexities of peacekeeping operations is that they will present the primary opportunities for the United States to exercise its optional use of force in the next decade or so. We know from our experiences over the past decade or so that we can engage in successful conflict suppression in these situations. We have done so in Bosnia, Haiti, and now Kosovo.

I think Americans—policy makers and citizens alike—will find that simply prying the combatants apart and keeping them from one another's throats for a period of time will not be satisfying. If all we do is provide a nonviolent interlude between killing and other forms of atrocity, we will feel as though we have not done very much. That is all we accomplished in Somalia, and despite apologias from people like Chester Crocker (the assistant secretary of state for African affairs at the time) that we did keep some people from starving, it is not the kind of uplifting outcome that Americans will embrace.

Although some people will disagree, I believe that Americans always have and always will expect more when their forces are placed in harm's way. Americans will judge the Bosnias and Kosovos of this world based on whether we leave those places better than when we arrived. "Better" means more peaceful, more stable politically (preferably democratic), and more prosperous. *Stable peace* is something the American people will find adequate to justify sacrifice. That is just the way we are. And that is why the discussion of state building is relevant to the questions of where and when to use force in the future.

Involvement in new internal wars is justifiable if the outcome is popularly sustainable stability; whether that outcome can be predicted is really a question of whether state building can work. If it cannot succeed, then the conflict suppression (peace imposition and enforcement) that precedes and coincides with state building is not worth our effort in the contemporary breed of new internal wars. If state building is not possible, we should conclude that intervention in other people's civil wars, whether mandated by the UN or anyone else, is not a legitimate use of American military force. Of course, such a determination would mean that we have little use for our military, but it is better not to use it than to use it foolishly.

Can state building work? We do not really know. The mission to Kosovo is a major extension of our past experience at intervening in and attempting to reshape countries, an experience that has been mostly unsuccessful, especially in Latin America. Kosovo is the first place where the UN has been institutionally unengaged in the conflict-suppression stage yet remained central to the state-building stage. At the same time, the use of UNMIK to lead the efforts of other international organizations as well as nongovernmental organizations is a new exercise, and it is one that will undoubtedly be affected by the unique perspective of Special Representative Kouchner. Also, the evolving relationship between UNMIK and KFOR represents a new approach to the problem.

The bottom line for the U.S. evaluation of its intervention in Kosovo is whether the state-building effort works, in the sense that Kosovo emerges after UNMIK's withdrawal as a sustainable, nonviolent country or province. If the effort succeeds, then there is a reasonable likelihood that it will serve as a positive precedent for future interventions by the international community generally and by the United States specifically. Simply put, success in Kosovo will likely legitimize the future use of American military force in these kinds of operations.

Failure, or possibly worse, an inconclusive ending, is another matter. We have already trapped ourselves into two open-ended, post–cold war military situations from which extraction would be difficult. Our commitment to protect the Kurds and Shi'ites of Iraq from their government's reprisals (Operations Northern and Southern Watch) is approaching a decade in duration; calling off the operations would likely subject those groups to great privation. The SFOR operation is nearly five years old, and although the UN raised the possibility of troop reductions in 1999, no one believes that the removal of SFOR would result in continued peace. The great danger in Kosovo is that it will be Bosnia all over again.

Bibliography

Boutros-Ghali, Boutros. *An Agenda for Peace: Preventive Diplomacy, Peacemaking, and Peace-Keeping.* New York: United Nations, 1992. (A supplement was issued in 1995.)

"The Clinton Doctrine." *U.S. News and World Report,* June 28, 1999, 9.

Crocker, Chester. "The Lessons of Somalia: Not Everything Went Wrong." *Foreign Affairs* 74 (May–June 1995): 2–8.

Durch, William, ed. *The Evolution of UN Peacekeeping: Case Studies and Comparative Analysis.* New York: St. Martin's Press, 1993.

Franck, Thomas M., et al. "Sidelined in Kosovo?" *Foreign Affairs* 78 (July–August 1999): 116–122.

Glennon, Michael J. "The New Interventionism." *Foreign Affairs* 78 (May–June 1999): 2–7.

Hagen, William W. "The Balkans' Lethal Nationalism." *Foreign Affairs* 78 (July–August 1999): 52–64.

Kaplan, Robert D. *Balkan Ghosts: A Journey through History.* New York: St. Martin's Press, 1993.

Kifner, John. "Laying Claims to Govern in the Ruins of Kosovo." *New York Times,* national edition, July 16, 1999, A8.

"Editorial: Lessons of the Balkans War." *New York Times,* national edition, June 17, 1999, A30.

Luttwak, Edward N. "Give War a Chance." *Foreign Affairs* 78 (July–August 1999): 36–44.

Nye, Joseph S., Jr. "Redefining the National Interest." *Foreign Affairs* 78 (July–August 1999): 22–35.

Rodman, Peter W. "The Fallout from Kosovo." *Foreign Affairs* 78 (July–August 1999): 45–51.

Snow, Donald M. *Distant Thunder: Patterns of Conflict in the Developing World.* 2d ed. Armonk: M. E. Sharpe, 1997.

———. *UnCivil Wars: International Security and the New Internal Conflicts.* Boulder: Lynne Rienner Publishers, 1996.

bin Sultan, Khaled. *Desert Warrior: A Personal View of the Gulf War by the Joint Forces Commander.* New York: HarperCollins, 1995.

United Nations Home Page: *www.un.org.*

5 | Peace Games?

WE RETURN TO THE QUESTION POSED AT THE OUTSET: WHERE should the United States be willing to deploy and employ armed force? There is no agreed upon answer, and our experience in Kosovo, which I have argued throughout will be terribly important in framing an answer, is too fresh and too incomplete to be of much help right now.

Our difficulty in determining where and when to intervene begins with the absence of a well-defined grand national strategy. In trying to form a strategy, we are plagued by the allegedly amorphous nature of the post–cold war environment, one so shapeless that in a decade we have not decided what to call it. It is not the cold war, but we do not know what it is.

University of Chicago political scientist John Mearsheimer was correct when he speculated on why we will miss the cold war. The cold war was concrete and structured. Where we should be prepared to fight was where we had to be ready; wars of necessity, not of choice, dominated our concerns. Occasionally we suffered overextended notions of what we had to do and forayed into small (the Dominican Republic) and large (Vietnam) situations where a more dispassionate appraisal might have counseled more caution than we exercised. Still, the framework for when and where we should be prepared to fight was clear.

It is not at all clear any longer. The implosion of communism as an operating political philosophy and as an opponent of Western-style political democracy and economic capitalism has removed a large, malignant tumor from the international system's dynamics. Where there once was a formidable opponent and obstacle, there now is a geopolitical void. Much is different, and much is the same. It is not easy to grasp.

How can we describe the salient characteristics of the new arrangement? We can begin with the observation that the new system has been in place so long that describing it as unpredictable, chaotic, or overly fluid is a cop-out for constructing a grand strategy. If we do not know what the system is like, it is because we are not looking very hard or very well.

Contemporary Influences on Grand Strategy

I suggest that five interrelated characteristics of the contemporary environment cumulatively define the situation around which a grand strategy should be fashioned. None are revolutionary or particularly surprising.

Great Economic Divide

The world is no longer divided among political ideologies. It is divided, as it always has been, economically between the haves and the have nots. With the demise of communism as an operating philosophy and competitor for political loyalties, there is no longer a meaningful debate about political and economic systems. Political democracy and market economics represent the values or aspirations of almost the whole world. Certainly, democracy and capitalism are not universally practiced: North Korea and Cuba still maintain themselves to be communist; the People's Republic of China and Vietnam are still ruled by communist parties, even though they cannot be said to preach Marxist economics; Islamic fundamentalists hold sway in places like Afghanistan and Iran; and governmental thuggery prevails in parts of Asia (Burma, for instance) and most of Africa.

What is different, however, is that nowhere is authoritarian rule extolled the way it was in the past. The Chinese are not attempting to export communism; they *are* exporting great masses of consumer goods. If anything, the list of thugs in power is slowly growing shorter. Despite the potential for national disintegration after he was forced to resign, Suharto left office in Indonesia amid relative calm, and even in places like Iran, demands for political and economic liberalization reverberate with increased frequency. The Western values of democracy and market economics are the aspirations of the overwhelming majority of people; since much of the substance of these values is American, they help define our place in the world.

Lone Superpower

The United States has moved from being one of the central players in the system to being *the* central player, a position that has increased both U.S. leadership and international resentment of that leadership. When the cold war ended, it became fashionable to talk about the United States as the remaining superpower and about a unipolar system with the U.S. as the pole. In the early days, there was a sense of exhilaration, even exuberance, about this new state of affairs; we had prevailed, and now the world aspired to be like us.

We no longer talk in such expansive tones, even though the United States is still the central state in the system and is more dominant now than it was a decade ago. The international community reacted to U.S. dominance with a combination of envy for U.S. power and disdain for what is commonly referred to as American "arrogance."

Two events of the past several years, one economic and one geopolitical, illustrate America's split image in the world. The reaction of the U.S. economy to the economic crisis that began in Thailand in 1997 and spread throughout east Asia evoked both awe and anger. When the crisis broke, many observers speculated that the Asian "economic flu" would spread to the United States, causing massive dislocation in the U.S. economy and thus showing the extent of economic globalization. Although the U.S. market reacted negatively, it quickly righted itself. The U.S. economy was so strong that it could withstand even a major assault. That was good news in that it stopped the slump from spreading globally; it was not such good news in that it showed how far above the rest of the pack the United States stood economically.

Further stoking international ire, the United States was perceived by many in the international community as responsible for the austerity measures dealt out by the International Monetary Fund (IMF) as a condition for bailing out the affected economies. The measures imposed were clearly drawn from the U.S. model of economics, not the Asian model. A number of states openly resented the rules of "transparency" that the IMF imposed on Asian financial institutions, believing them to be reminiscent of rules imposed by the U.S. government on American savings and loan institutions in response to the scandals of the 1980s. Whether the requirements were sound or not, many people resented their imposition.

The international reaction to the U.S.-dominated Operation Allied Force may have similar characteristics. While holding in awe the quantitative and qualitative scope of the U.S. military effort, the international community fretted about U.S. dominance of the war effort. The primary rule of engagement was the avoidance of U.S. combat casualties. That ruled out sending ground combatants into the fray and necessitated, among other things, bombing from high altitudes, outside the range of Yugoslav antiaircraft fire. The goal of zero casualties was achieved, but observers wonder if that achievement did not come at the cost of greater Kosovar suffering than would have been the case had soldiers been on the ground to protect them and had the bombers been flying low enough to minimize collateral damage to civilian property. The international community chastised us for waging what Edward Luttwak has called "disinterested war," where we prize our own skins above all else. American journalist William Pfaff went even further, saying, "It is anti-heroic war, and has been called a coward's war." These are strong words and ominous conclusions, with which we will have to come to grips when contemplating future Kosovos.

While resenting how the United States dominated the operational planning and execution of the war, the international community could not help but be awestruck at its magnitude. That a gap existed in lethal capabilities between the United States and the rest of the world had been strongly suggested by the Persian Gulf War, but it was clear during Allied Force that the gap had become a chasm. During the 1990s the United States had downsized but modernized its military, while others had simply downsized theirs. The huge differential in military capability is no threat to the major players, but it hurts their pride.

International Agreement

There is a level of major power agreement that has not been witnessed since the eighteenth century. In the years leading up to the French Revolution, there was remarkable ideological agreement among the leading states of Europe, which constituted the international order of the time. Monarchism was the prevailing political expression, although political democracy was on the horizon and would shatter the uniformity of political systems. Mercantilism was the economic philosophy of a Europe just entering the industrial revolution. The leading powers fought minor wars on the continent, and some spilled over into the colonies as the British, French, and Spanish battled one another in North America, but most of the wars were over territorial adjustments with little geopolitical import. The major powers had little other than imperial ambition to fight about.

With the fall of communism, a similar uniformity exists today. Political democracy is the universal credo of the First Tier, and this ideology is spreading rapidly worldwide. Freedom House, which annually rates every country in the world for its adherence to freedom, proclaims that there were 117 electoral democracies in 1999, compared with 69 in 1989, when the cold war ended. It says 88 countries were free and another 53 were partly free in 1999; the respective figures for 1989 were 61 and 39. The only large areas that are not free today are the heart of Africa and a good deal of central and eastern Asia. That these are also the most violence-prone and unstable areas (see the figures in Chapter 1) is not coincidental.

The dominant economic philosophy of today is, of course, capitalism, and it is expressed most strongly in the application to international free trade of the Ricardian theory of comparative advantage. The gradual globalization of the economy has the major political democracies at its core but also encompasses major nondemocracies like the People's Republic of China, about which we would worry a lot more if it were not so entwined in global economic activity.

International agreement on the political and economic fundamentals is not only widespread but also well institutionalized. The political and military concord is institutionalized principally in the NATO alliance, in which all of the major military powers participate. When, as in Bosnia and Kosovo, Russia collaborates, it further expands the operational unanimity. The G-8, which includes Russia, coordinates the international economy and is linked with other major economic associations like the European Union, North American Free Trade Agreement, and Asia-Pacific Economic Cooperation. Although these regional associations sometimes squabble with one another, their fundamental values are the same. At the apex of this web of institutional arrangements is the UN, and Security Council resolutions have become valuable tools for expressing international concern and justifying international action when circumstances seem to require it.

This structure and process provide the philosophical and institutional basis for international consensus building on a number of issues, including when and where to use force. Nonetheless, it will not be as easy to gain consensus and marshal forces outside of Europe as it was in Kosovo, and more somber, objective analysis of Operation Allied Force is likely to reveal that the international collaboration was not as smooth as it appeared to be. The idea of bloodless war is also likely to strain international consensus and come under more scrutiny as the international community contemplates future interventions in "humanitarian wars." The world powers may also question the wisdom of pummeling an adversary in the name of humanitarian concerns. Regardless of these difficulties, the institutional base for building consensus is available to an extent that would not be possible in a more ideologically competitive environment.

Opportunities in the Second Tier

Most of the "opportunities" to assist countries in the throes of humanitarian and other disasters will be in the poorer countries of the Second Tier, not in areas within or adjacent to the major powers. This point is worth reiterating because it contrasts with the locations of the two largest peacekeeping operations: Bosnia and Kosovo. Although one can debate the extent to which we are interested in Balkan tranquillity (an oxymoron, given history), the locations are closer and more familiar to us, both geographically and psychically, than those where violence and instability are most likely to occur. Indeed, with the exception of the Balkans, nowhere do First Tier states border countries where internal explosions may occur (excepting perhaps North Korea and Japan).

Recognizing this geographic fact is important as we assess the criteria for intervening and for determining the extent of involvement (conflict suppression versus state building, for instance). To make the decision to go the distance and statebuild in Kosovo was comparatively easy: most Westerners agreed that the parties were worthy, and our ignorance about what would be involved meant we were uninhibited by the ardor of the enterprise. Even at that, it was a tough call for decision makers. The decision will not be so facile when the location is neither so near nor so compelling. Nearly a year after the international force ended the chaos in East Timor, on the other hand, evidence of promised state building is sparse indeed.

If we are to avoid making bad decisions due to ignorance, we need greater public awareness and education on the nature of these situations and the global environment in which they occur. The failure to make a compelling case for involvement in these internal situations will inevitably embolden and cede the field to the neoisolationist tribunes among us.

Paralysis by Paradigm

The major dynamic paralyzing military force remains strict adherence to the cold war realist paradigm and its major post–cold war artifact, the interest-threat mismatch. The key term is *interest:* What issues in the world are sufficiently important to us that we would use military force to ensure that they are resolved to our satisfaction? The major guidepost that we have utilized in the past to decide where force is and is not appropriate is that of vital interest: an interest whose violation would be intolerable to us and which we will use all forms of power to protect.

Few of our most important interests are now threatened, and the interest-threat mismatch means there will be few if any wars of necessity in the next few years. The only possible exceptions are a major flare-up in the Persian Gulf region that threatens our addiction to Middle Eastern crude oil or a last-ditch, desperate attempt by the North Koreans to break out of their misery by going south. The Korean scenario, while conceivable, seems less likely all the time, despite occasional provocations. It is not clear who would effectively threaten our access to the oil.

Each of these five characteristics of the contemporary world influences the strategic choices of the United States and its First Tier allies as we look toward the future. The absence of an ideological divide and the presence of conceptual comity among the major powers in the system facilitate major-power cooperation and coordination on an approach to the problem of internal, humanitarian war. Such was not possible during the cold war or before. As part of any coordinated strategy, the international community will have to address the economic divide between the haves and have-nots. Our incentive to do so mixes economic self-interest (the more countries incorporated into the global economy, the better) and security concerns (prosperous states and, especially, democratic states are much less likely to be tumultuous).

The realist paradigm inhibits the development of a strategy relevant to current world conditions. However, we cannot abandon it entirely as long as the international system comprises sovereign states that perceive the world in terms of their important interests. We are no closer to world harmony and governance today than we were in the 1940s and 1950s, when such notions were first put forward. The state system will endure, and so must realism.

That does not mean we need to take the realist paradigm to excess, which we did even before the onset of the cold war and continue to do on occasion. Our fear of diluted sovereignty caused us to refuse to ratify the Convention on Genocide for four decades (a position that left us isolated with a cast of generally unsavory fellow nonsignatories). U.S. national sovereignty is not now threatened by compliance with the mandatory jurisdiction of the international war crimes tribunal unless Americans commit war crimes. A less obstructionist stance on land mines might have brought us in from the international cold on that issue as well.

To argue that we should abandon realism in order to avoid paralysis would risk being labeled a Pollyanna and naive. There are legitimate reasons why we should not jeopardize our sovereignty, and there are legitimate places where vital interests should continue to guide our policy decisions. Should we adhere strictly to cold war realism, however, we run the risk of irrelevance in the world. We do not need to abandon realism; we need to extend it to match a changed environment.

A Strategy of Realistic Internationalism

The classic realist paradigm is too narrow; it restricts the role that the United States perceives it should play in the world, and application of the correlates of the paradigm distorts reality and paralyzes policy. The realist's world has not gone away so much as the horizons of the necessary use of force have broadened.

We need a broader definition of where we will use force in order to unite geopolitical reality with policy and strategy. The core of a strategy of realistic internationalism is the realist's directive: We should be prepared to use force in defense of traditional vital interests, in those employments of necessity identified in Chapter 3. The rejoinder, of course, is that such employments will be very infrequent in the foreseeable future, with the exception of reactions to isolated crises.

We must expand the concept of employments of choice, those places and situations where we are not compelled to arms by basic threats to our existence or well-being but find the use or threat of force necessary for other reasons. One attractive example might be preemptive actions—whether they be political, economic, or military—to defuse situations that, if left alone, might fester into bloody conflict. The problem is that neither the public nor policy makers are inclined to support action when there is no demonstrable disaster. Policy makers, in particular, are too busy with today's problems to concentrate on problems months or years in the future.

New internal wars are one area where an expansion of the use of force is dictated by the changed international environment. The use of force in these situations will form the operational core of U.S. force strategy and doctrine for the next five to ten years. To some extent, we have already expanded our use-of-force doctrine, if not very loudly. The Weinberger Doctrine of 1985 laid out criteria for U.S. involvement in Third World conflicts; it was a very restrictive policy in light of the Vietnam experience. Chairman of the Joint Chiefs of Staff Colin Powell added his doctrine of overwhelming force to the Weinberger Doctrine. (Powell reportedly was the author of the Weinberger Doctrine.) The Clinton administration added criteria for U.S. involvement in UN peacekeeping operations through Presidential Decision Directive (PDD) 25 in 1994 and also PDD 56 in 1997, which authorizes politico-military contingency planning for potential trouble spots around the world.

The groundwork, therefore, has been laid to specify when the United States will and will not involve itself in new internal wars. What we need to do now is elevate our concern for these situations to a higher position in grand national strategy. The definition of realistic internationalism is the following: In addition to protecting traditional vital interests, the United States is willing to act, with force when necessary, in situations that pose a threat to international peace and tranquillity and that, if ignored, will result in significant humanitarian disaster for the population of a country or countries. This addition, which has to some extent already been articulated by the Bush and Clinton administrations, moves the bar that separates when we will employ force and when we will not so as to place in the former category what have been called "humanitarian wars," "wars of values," and a host of other names.

Why should we do this? From a cold and calculating view, I would argue that it is in our enlightened self-interest to do so, for two reasons. On the one hand, the United States has a real interest in a world that is peaceful and stable. Such a world is likely to become more democratic and more prosperous, and thus is likely to provide better opportunities for the United States to interact positively in economic and political senses. If, for instance, the Burmese people were to rise against the government that their oppressors call Myanmar, would it be in our interest to cheer their success? Or, if their leaders acted atrociously, to oppose their actions? Put another way, would we be better off with a democratizing, capitalist Burma in which we and others could invest? How much national treasure are we willing to spend to achieve a favorable outcome?

The answers to such questions are not cut and dried. While no one would seriously argue that an autocratic, destitute Myanmar is preferable to a democratic and prosperous Burma, a lot of people would argue about whether the United States is interested enough in what goes on there to intervene. The same was true of U.S. involvement in the East Timorese conflict. Even knowledgeable people, with a comprehensive understanding of the situation, could reasonably disagree on whether to intervene there or in other specific circumstances. The decision is even further complicated because these wars will routinely occur in places about which the American people and their leaders are less than fully knowledgeable.

The second reason for taking account of these kinds of actions in our military planning arises from the unique place of the United States in the world, to which the discussion often returns. If the United States is the central player in the international system, the only country with global interests and global reach, then we will have some level of interest almost everywhere. Moreover, given our military and economic predominance, we will have to participate at some level in any international response. We are too much in the spotlight to sit in the wings; and whereas others may disagree with the judgments we reach, they will expect us to reach them.

People who hold worldviews that are more neoisolationist or traditional realist may disagree with this assessment. Moreover, it is possible to argue that the application of realistic internationalism will lead to an endless string of U.S. interventions in the most obscure parts of the globe that will eventually overstretch and exhaust U.S. capability and will. The criticism is valid if the policy is implemented indiscriminately to all outbreaks of violence everywhere in the world, but that is not what I propose. Rather, I suggest fifteen guidelines for determining what the U.S. response should be to any humanitarian disaster. If implemented, the guidelines would not only help policy makers determine where to respond but would provide mechanisms for heading the problems off before they become disasters.

Guidelines for Intervening in Internal Wars

The criteria I propose for determining U.S. policy toward internal wars and humanitarian disasters are not unique. Eleven of the fifteen are rooted in official U.S. government documents like Presidential Decision Directives 25 and 56 and the Weinberger Doctrine, which created what amount to checklists and provide guidance. The remaining four criteria stem from my early reactions to the Kosovo campaign.

The following proposed guidelines differ from those of existing government documents in their extent and their emphasis. They are sequential, in terms of both the order of their consideration within the U.S. government and the stage of a crisis. Moreover, they can be thought of as a procedural and substantive checklist on the advisability of U.S. involvement in a particular situation. The more of these guidelines we have followed, the more likely policy is to be informed and proper. For an orderly progression, I have divided them into four sequential categories: preinvolvement criteria, precipitating causes, conditions for approving intervention, and conditions for a successful operation.

Preinvolvement Criteria

One unsettling characteristic of international, including U.S., responses to humanitarian disasters is how poorly they seem to have been anticipated and how little was done to prevent or moderate the situations by prior actions. This lack of anticipation is curious because in almost every case that has brought an international response, experts, if not the general public, understood the potential for disaster. The starvation in Somalia did not start overnight; there were warnings of impending disaster in Rwanda; the ethnic composition of Bosnia made it ripe for trouble; and the potential for ethnic cleansing or some similar tragedy in Kosovo had been known almost since Slobodan Milošević became president of Serbia in 1989 and rescinded the autonomous status of Kosovo. Anyone who could not see the storm clouds forming over East Timor and the Democratic Republic of Congo was not looking very closely.

Why is the record of preinvolvement so dismal? Certainly it is not for lack of bright people within the national security and foreign policy bureaucracies. There are any number of contributory factors: the failure of parts of the bureaucracy to communicate with one another, turf battles that inhibit cooperation across bureaucratic lines, the pressure of day-to-day problems, the natural tendency to set aside problems until they reach critical status.

The best way to deal with the ethnic cleansing, genocide, and other humanitarian disasters associated with new internal wars is to prevent them from happening in the first place. Preventive actions of one sort or another, if they succeed, are far cheaper in human and other terms than peace imposition or peace enforcement. Thus, the first three guidelines specify actions that should be taken before a new internal war flares to the point that the international community ponders intervention. Most of them are stunningly obvious; however, their combination is useful.

1. Understand and Assess the Situations in Advance. Given the intellectual resources available both inside and outside the government, there is no reason why the potential "hot spots" around the globe cannot be identified and analyzed in detail. We could analyze the history of the country as it relates to violent potential, cultural and ethnic differences that may contribute to violence, socioeconomic and political bases of differences, the leaders and followers of various political and military or paramilitary factions, and sources and supplies of arms.

Collecting and analyzing this kind of information is not exactly rocket science. Ted Gurr of the University of Maryland, for instance, maintains a detailed database on 275 ethnic minorities at risk (see the bibliography at the end of the chapter), and all of the information suggested above is readily available from public and classified sources. Indeed, through PDD 56 the White House has already directed the executive branch to engage in contingency planning, although it is not clear how active the process is. Regardless, knowing the turf in some detail will facilitate the monitoring of trends that might lead to violence, suggest strategies that might prevent violence, and, if that fails, provide a detailed "map" of the situation for forces that might be called upon after violence erupts.

2. Anticipate and Attempt to Prevent Violence. After thoroughly assessing the situation in a given country, analysts should be able to anticipate when situations are destabilizing and to foresee opportunities for resolving problems short of violence. Being on the scene and feeling the "pulse" of the body politic is a major function of the U.S. intelligence apparatus. However, in most of the countries where new internal war is likely, U.S. assets, which for years have been geared toward the Soviet threat, are deficient. The intelligence assets of other countries, particularly former colonizers who spent decades or centuries on the scene and thus have a detailed understanding of local situations, may be superior to ours and should be the basis on which we act.

Attempting to head off and settle differences before they boil over is preferable to cleaning up after disaster has struck. The terrible carnage in Rwanda might have been prevented if a relatively small peace enforcement (rather than a lightly armed and impotent peacekeeping) force had been dispatched soon after the presidents of Rwanda and Burundi had perished in a suspicious airplane crash. The Dayton meeting on Bosnia could have been convened in late 1991 instead of 1995. Negotiations on Kosovo could have been conducted—or for that matter, imposed—between 1990, when Yugoslavia sent troops into the province, and 1996, when the KLA began its campaign. The Democratic Republic of Congo might may well go up in flames again if ways are not found to promote the wealth and stability that its natural resources should endow. The international community attempted to prevent disaster in East Timor by placing UN observers and the media into the region for the referendum voting of August 30, 1999. However, those observers were inadequate to prevent pro-Indonesian "militias" from forcing many East Timorese to flee for their lives. Earlier intervention by the international force might have prevented the suffering.

Raising these possibilities is more than an exercise in "Monday morning quarterbacking." There were opportunities and signals that could have allowed governments to act in ways that *might* have prevented or moderated all of these disasters, but no government explored them with the vigor necessary to intervene successfully. It is not entirely clear why none did so, and unraveling that problem is the legitimate topic of a further study. Some leaders recognize that lack of foresight is a problem. President Clinton, for instance, has confided that one of his greatest foreign policy failures was not anticipating and intervening in Rwanda, a deficiency that influenced PDD 56.

On the other hand, perhaps none of the aforementioned crises could have been avoided even through early international intervention. Luttwak may be correct that solutions are possible only through the "transformative effects of both decisive victory and exhaustion" ("Give War a Chance," p. 44). A mindset that looks at particular potential problems as things to be preempted may reduce the need for peace enforcers.

3. Exhaust Other Remedies. This suggestion, which flows from anticipation of crises and attempts to prevent them, has roots in the Weinberger Doctrine and in general American beliefs about the use of force. One of the six criteria for employing American forces under the Weinberger Doctrine was that the use of force be a last resort, undertaken only after all other methods have failed.

A reluctance to use force is only natural, and it is a viable policy option if attention is focused on a problem area before the problem degenerates into violence. The international community has tended to focus on disasters only after the killing and suffering have begun, when the only options are inattention or military action. Most Americans would feel more comfortable intervening with military force in the internal affairs of states if they felt that we had done all we could to solve the problem short of force. Americans do not want to remain in the shadows of a crisis until the last moment before our troops are deployed. Americans do not want or like surprises. Policy makers must cultivate popular support for involvement as they lead us into a situation. A collective sense of understanding can contribute meaning to a mission and help policy makers adjust the course if need be.

Precipitating Factors

If it proves impossible to head off an internal war before atrocities are committed, what will cause the United States to consider becoming involved in one way or another? I suggest two guidelines that will activate the search for a policy response: the existence or looming prospect of a humanitarian disaster, and an international consensus that some form of response is appropriate and necessary.

4. Humanitarian Disaster. We are all aware of the horrendous actions that have triggered peacekeeping operations in the past decade, and some of the images have been invoked here. A consensus has emerged in the international community that world powers should become involved in the worst of these tragedies: genocidal campaigns such as that waged by the Hutu against the Tutsi in Rwanda, for instance. The slaughter of Armenians by the Ottoman Turks early in the twentieth century would also have met the standard for international involvement, as would the Holocaust.

What criteria short of genocide should activate a response? Some people express the criteria expressed quantitatively, in terms of the number of people killed or displaced. American analysts Stephen Solarz and Michael O'Hanlon, for instance, set the standard at "tens of thousands" killed per year; others suggest levels of internal or external displacement of peoples, such as the herding of Albanian Kosovars from their homes into internal and external exile.

Quantitative criteria will always be suspect in these situations. Even in hindsight the numbers are tenuous. No one will ever know with any precision how many people were slaughtered in Rwanda because no one counted at the time, and there were no outsiders present to keep tabs. When wars occur in remote parts of the world, reportage will always be incomplete, anecdotal, and biased toward one side or the other. It may be that the existence of atrocity is as much as one can confidently chronicle. In that case, the assessment of the extent of disaster and the appropriate response will remain subjective and matters of individual judgment. The existence of a humanitarian disaster is necessary to activate an international response, but it may not be sufficient.

5. International Consensus. A humanitarian disaster will be sufficient to activate an international response only in those places where a substantial number of global powers agree that action is necessary *and* are willing to participate in such an action. There is no universal agreement on how consensus can be ascertained, although Security Council resolutions are as good a barometer as there is. In some cases, regional organizations may reach the decision, as NATO did in Kosovo. In others, one organization may make the military decision (as NATO did in forming KFOR), while another legitimizes and manages the state-building activity (as the United Nations did through UNMIK).

Consensus is vital. The United States will rarely act unilaterally, except in very small actions in its backyard (Grenada, for example). International agreement, and especially multilateral participation, will generally be the sine qua non for American public acceptance and for foreign leaders to avoid U.S. charges of free riding. Moreover, multilateral participation is already a part of U.S. policy: PDD 25 requires as a prerequisite for U.S. participation both an international response and the necessity of U.S. participation for the success of the mission.

Minimum Conditions for Approving Intervention

If a situation seems to merit action, and if there is international consensus that something should be done, the question then turns to the advisability of becoming involved. Existing policy is more complete at this level than at the previous levels: of five conditions that will be discussed, four are a part of existing policy directives.

6. Definable National Interest. It should go without saying that the United States will not contemplate intervening in any situation where it has no interests. The question is what level of interest is necessary for the United States to act. The answer flows from the definition of realistic internationalism: less than traditional vital interests will be adequate to activate us. PDD 25 specifies the circumstances under which the United States will vote for UN peacekeeping operations: international aggression; urgent humanitarian disaster combined with violence; and sudden interruption of established democracy or gross human rights violations, combined with violence or the threat of violence. (For a detailed discussion, see Cimbala, "Clinton and U.S. Peacekeeping.")

This determination of interest and assessment of the precipitating causes should be considered as permitting rather than commanding U.S. action. The interests that the PDD describes have the effect of extending the realist paradigm to include less than vital situations where the United States might, rather than necessarily will, use force. The PDD, for instance, specifies that participation in a peace operation "advances U.S. interests, and both the unique and general risks to U.S. personnel have been estimated and are considered acceptable." If one cannot find *anything* of importance to the United States in a given situation, that should preclude U.S. action. The need to go to the trouble of finding interests at least requires that the question be asked and answered and that policy makers have an opportunity to agree or disagree with the resulting assessment.

7. Clearly Defined Objectives. That we should know exactly why we are intervening in a particular conflict and what we expect to achieve sounds obvious. As a formal policy requirement, however, it became necessary only in the wake of the Vietnam war. Rightly or wrongly, the military drew from that conflict the lesson that we need clear objectives that can be translated into military strategies. In the Clausewitzian language of the Weinberger Doctrine, the need for an objective translated into the need for an "end point," a point where we could declare that our objectives had been met and hence we could disengage. PDD 25 requires that "clear objectives exist, and it is clearly understood where the mission fits on the spectrum from traditional peacekeeping to peace enforcement."

Defining an end point sounds easier than it really is. First, identifying unambiguous and measurable objectives is often difficult in the new internal conflicts. For instance, if conflict suppression is the objective, is it achieved when the fighting stops or only when the enforcers can leave without a high likelihood of hostilities resuming? If state building is the goal, to what extent must governmental, administrative, and other structures be in place and functioning before we can declare the objective met? Second, the idea of clear-cut objectives is reflective of the peace-war-peace model of conflict, which does not describe the highly fluid contemporary conflicts. The types of conflicts in which we are likely to contemplate involvement will usually lack these sharp distinctions. Third, explicit political objectives traditionally guide the military as it devises strategies and tactics to accomplish the political goals from which the military mission gains its meaning (essentially the Clausewitzian dictum that "war is the continuation of politics by other means"). The problem in the contemporary environment is that the political and military objectives become entwined and both have to be adjusted as the situation evolves. The sharp distinction between the political and military realms is an illusion.

As the specification of interests serves multiple purposes, so too does the specification of objectives. First, it forces policy makers to specify what they hope to accomplish. Does the United States suppress conflict or statebuild? Deciding that in advance may help us avoid the mission creep that occurred in Operation Restore Hope in Somalia, where we allegedly wandered into some forms of state building without realizing that was what we were doing. Second, specifying objectives forces policy makers to analyze whether their political goals can be achieved by military means and, if so, how. In Vietnam, for instance, was the problem a lack of political and military objectives (as many military apologists suggested), or the inability to translate known objectives into methods for their attainment (as I have asserted)?

8. Public and Congressional Support. Like the requirements that interests and objectives be analyzed and stated explicitly, the requirement for popular and congressional support arises from the Vietnam experience. Congressional authorization of our participation in Southeast Asia (beyond appropriating funds for the troops once they were committed, which could hardly be avoided) rested entirely on the Gulf of Tonkin resolution of 1964, which authorized reprisals for reported attacks on U.S. naval vessels. There was no public referendum at all, and many in the military attributed their loss of public support to the absence of a prior commitment by the public. The need for explicit support is reflected in both the Weinberger Doctrine and PDD 25.

The military, and especially the Army, devised and implemented a remedy of sorts for this problem. Gen. Creighton Abrams, army chief of staff during the 1980s, purposely reassigned a number of vital army functions to the reserves. As a result, the reserves must be called to active duty in the event of any major deployment. By assenting to having their friends and neighbors pulled from their homes and put on active duty, the public makes at least an indirect statement of support for military action. The nation felt the impact of reserve call-ups first in Operations Desert Shield and Desert Storm, and most recently in Allied Force.

Public and congressional support for peacekeeping operations will always be difficult to develop and sustain. Because they arise in places that are invariably foreign, most people and many of their representatives have very little knowledge of them and hence any basis to support them (other possibly than some gory pictures on CNN). If past deployments are an indication, support will increase if a mission appears to be succeeding. For instance, the public initially opposed the U.S. deployment in Bosnia, but the public now supports it. The perverse, some would say cynical, cost of sustained public support, however, seems to be the absence of U.S. combat fatalities. The policy makers sense that public opinion would turn against the mission if the body bags started coming home, and that assessment was certainly a factor in determining how our air forces would attack targets in Kosovo and Serbia. One of the interesting things to watch in the future is whether the public changes its attitude toward casualty avoidance overseas and whether policy makers follow suit, even while recognizing that such a change would mean U.S. soldiers will die in a future deployment.

9. Appropriate Forces and Resources Available for Proportional Response. This guideline is stated explicitly in the Weinberger Doctrine and in PDD 25. In the language of the presidential directive, U.S. troops would be deployed only if "the necessary means to accomplish the task are available, including forces, financing for the operation, and an appropriate mandate for the operation."

However, the notion of *appropriate* forces is not fully developed in U.S. policy circles. Peacekeeping, at one end of the continuum, is largely a policing activity (making sure the parties do not break agreements), whereas peace imposition, at the other end, is a military, combat function. But what about the middle of the continuum—peace enforcement—which mixes combat readiness and constabulary duty in varying proportions? Peace enforcement requires a combination of special skills that neither combat troops nor observers are likely to possess. There should be special military training, possibly even a separate military operational specialty (MOS), for peace enforcers. The military itself disagrees.

10. State-Building Mechanism. We have neither a master plan nor an operational or procedural capability for rebuilding a society, but we will need to develop them if we are going to remain in the state-building business. Kosovo, our laboratory for state-building experimentation, will almost certainly suffer from our need to learn on the job how to construct or reconstruct a civil society.

Specifying such a plan goes beyond our scope, but we can generalize. First, policy makers need to define the tasks, for example, according legitimacy to a regime and promoting a prosperous economy. Then they need to define the end conditions that would mark a successful state-building process and devise a way to measure progress toward the end conditions. We have already learned in Kosovo that a major requirement is rebuilding the criminal justice system—police, courts, prisons, and so on—but we need to identify the other institutions that require overhaul and whom should overhaul them. Policy makers also must decide if the Kosovar model of operational control—UN overlordship of the state-building enterprise (UNMIK) and NATO command of the military mission (KFOR), with no hierarchical relationship between the two—should be maintained in future peacekeeping deployments. We also need a means of determining whom among a population to trust and bring into the process so as to legitimize it in the eyes of the people. The plan also must include provisions for turning an operation over to the target population without risk of reversion.

The early experience in Kosovo demonstrated the need to have a complete package of services and expertise available that can be put in place rapidly. The most striking failure in the UNMIK package was a shortage of international police who could be brought rapidly to the scene to restore public order and end Albanian Kosovar reprisals against Serbs and Gypsies and vice versa. The UN and NATO traded recriminations over this problem; NATO maintained it had neither the troops nor the expertise to assume the policing role, and the UN pleaded for military intercession while it recruited a police force and transported it to the scene. Regardless, it is questionable whether three thousand or so police could have prevented the violence that twenty thousand troops could not. The tragedy of the situation was revealed when fourteen Serb farmers were murdered while trying to harvest their crops in late July 1999.

Conditions for a Successful Operation

If the minimum prerequisites for joining peacekeeping operation have been met, the question becomes whether to participate. Once again, some of the following guidelines for making that determination have been anticipated in previous policy documents, but since they were designed to cover operations less ambitious than state building, they must be reassessed in that light.

11. Honest Assessment of the Prospects for Success. Developing and maintaining the bonds between the government, the public, and those forces that are dispatched as peacekeepers hinge on a clear definition of the mission's goals and an honest assessment of whether attainment of those goals is likely. The relationship is that of Clausewitz's trinity, and the message is the same: If the armed forces are to carry the mission to conclusion, then the public must come to understand and accept that the course is proper. Both PDD 25 and the Weinberger Doctrine specify this kind of assessment.

Performing such an assessment is no easy task, for the simple reason that we have very little precedent for defining or conducting a state-building exercise. (The operations in Germany and Japan after World War II, for instance, were quite different, since they involved rebuilding developed societies.) It is one thing to describe the preferred end state in the abstract: a stable and prosperous polity that can continue peacefully after the withdrawal of international forces. Specifying in detail how this will come about and how we can confidently measure success is more difficult, and the last thing that the international community would want to do is proclaim success, leave, and have the situation revert.

Ironically, in conflict suppression we can easily specify the means (combat troops), but the end (likely reversion once we leave) is unappealing and probably unworthy of the effort and sacrifice. In state building, the end (stable peace) is certainly worthy, but we are largely unable to specify the means. UNMIK is responsible for providing the means to the end in Kosovo, and its success or failure will have enormous precedential value.

12. Commitment to Stay the Course. The Weinberger Doctrine and PDD 25 require that the United States make a commitment to stay the course once engaged. However, the likely duration of a successful, full-blown state-building mission probably exceeds that envisioned by Caspar Weinberger and the authors of PDD 25. Secretary General Kofi Annan estimated at the beginning of the Kosovo mission that the UN commitment there would span at least a decade, and some wonder if that is long enough. The U.S. missions to protect the Iraqi Kurds and Shi'ites are approaching a decade, and no end is in sight. The occupation of Bosnia has no end in sight, either.

How many of these missions will the American public accept at any one time, and how long will they support any one of them? How many of them can U.S. troops (including reserves, who will increasingly be called up in state-building operations) conduct without wearing down and losing morale? Will the American people tire of missions where the end is unforeseen and American blood and treasure are fed down apparently bottomless pits? Each of these is a serious question that has not been asked publicly. Because peacekeeping operations will consume an increasing part of the foreign and national security agenda, a broader debate is appropriate.

13. **Willingness to Incur Costs.** This requisite contains two separate dimensions: human costs and financial costs. Is the United States willing to expend the lives of its young men and women in uniform in the name of missions where there are no important American interests at stake? This question is at the heart of realistic internationalism's expanded definition of "national interests." If Operation Allied Force is an indication, the current conventional wisdom is that Americans will not accept loss of life, but is that assessment correct?

The assessment is important for at least two reasons. If conventional wisdom is correct, then the foes of U.S. peace enforcers will undoubtedly conclude that the way to evict us is to kill a few Americans. Blood has not yet been shed in Kosovo, but it is just a matter of time until it is. And, if conventional wisdom is incorrect, the result will be American casualties. If "war without death" is essential for American public and political support, the logical solution is to avoid these situations altogether.

The other dimension of costs is the actual expense of the deployments. Long deployments wear out equipment and use stores that must be replaced, and that affects readiness in two ways: it diminishes resources on hand that might be needed to handle emergencies, and it drains money from readiness accounts that fund training, prepositioning, and other activities related to combat readiness. How long can the military "rob Peter to pay Paul" without negative effects? The political system must be willing to provide the resources necessary to support state-building efforts, and the American people must be willing to provide unstinting support.

14. Flexibility and Adjustability of Force. This requirement comes from the so-called Powell Doctrine of overwhelming force and is included in PDD 25's criteria for engagement in peace enforcement actions. Powell's logic is simple and straightforward: since operational requirements can change as a mission unfolds, political authorities must allow military commanders to adjust the kinds of forces that they deploy and how they will be employed. This may seem unassailable, but there has been a widespread feeling in the military that civilian authorities "micromanage" military operations, especially in pursuit of casualty minimization. The charges of micromanagement were greatest in Vietnam and were only partially mollified in the Persian Gulf War. In peacekeeping operations with shaky political support, military commanders can be expected to chafe at overscrutiny of military operations.

15. U.S. Operational Command and Control of U.S. Forces. This requirement, included in PDD 25, arose from the Somali experience. During one phase of that adventure, U.S. military units were placed under the technical command of the United Nations, although they remained operationally under U.S. command. Unfortunately, the UN's failure to coordinate the actions of U.S. troops with those of other national forces contributed to the ambush of the Rangers. The fiasco created a political firestorm in Washington; the sine qua non for U.S. participation is that no American will be under the command of a non-American.

While this requirement is understandable from a domestic political standpoint, it has consequences. If the United States participates in even a small way, it will always have to assume leadership of the military aspect of any peacekeeping operation. The only alternative would be to turn leadership over to a foreign national but assure substantial autonomy for the Americans in the operation. Dividing responsibility among national militaries by geographic zones, as was done in Bosnia and Kosovo, is one way to finesse this problem. In Kosovo, KFOR is commanded by a British lieutenant general, but all Americans are directly commanded by the U.S. military.

Institutional Adjustments

Our experience to this point suggests that the U.S. government and military are not adequately prepared to play a large role in peacekeeping operations. The deficiencies from which we suffer can be placed in three different but overlapping categories: inadequate assessment of societies that may become the subject of operations; lack of a state-building plan that includes both conceptual and operational bases; and a lack of clearly designated and prepared forces adequate for the volume and complexity of potential requirements. Each problem has substantive and procedural implications.

These problems and their solutions have not entirely evaded the U.S. government. PDD 56, promulgated in May 1997, addresses the need for better coordination of efforts within the government. As American researcher Tonya Langford catalogues in "Orchestrating Peace Operations," an article on the implementation of PDD 56, the directive covers the establishment of an executive committee, development of political-military implementation plans, interagency rehearsal, interagency after-action review, and interagency training.

These initiatives are noble and helpful, but Langford points out their limits. The first and most important is that they are U.S.-centered, whereas the operations we have described are highly international, going well beyond the U.S. government's interagency planning parameters. The process has been implemented only at fairly low levels within the government, and it is unclear how much senior officials know about the process or are committed to it. Because the process has been conducted by a small group of people inside the Clinton administration, there is also concern that it might not survive a change of administrations, as new personnel not dedicated to the success of PDD 56 enter the process.

Adequate Assessments

This problem is largely a holdover from our cold war experience. During the cold war, the government resources dedicated to gathering information on foreign countries were concentrated on the communist world, not the Second Tier countries that are ripe for peacekeeping operations. The concern that we did evince for them was in the cold war context: Who are the communists and what can we do to counter them? Thus, our pool of expertise in many of the places where the international community might need to consider peace operations is almost certainly not what it might be. Moreover, such experts as exist are stretched thin and have insufficient time to engage in the kind of detailed analysis I have suggested is necessary. According to Langford, PDD 56 has produced political-military plans for Bosnia, eastern Slavonia, Kosovo, central Africa, and "elsewhere." She does not comment on the thoroughness or quality of any of them.

If we are to avoid bumbling inappropriately into complex situations, this state of affairs must be rectified. Bridging the gap between the current state of knowledge and a more desirable level should not be insurmountable. There is a great deal of knowledge and expertise outside the U.S. government, and this would seem to be an ideal situation in which to privatize the collection and analysis of information. It would not be all that difficult to cobble together a team of academic and nonacademic experts—at minimal cost—to produce a thorough assessment of, say, East Timor. The assessment would be subject, of course, to review and modification by appropriate implementing and advisory agencies such as the CIA. An organization such as the United States Institute of Peace, which has no vested interest in the outcome, could provide the framework for a large-scale but not overwhelmingly expensive effort that might save us embarrassment in the future.

Adequate State-Building Mechanism

The PDD-56 process addresses the lack of an adequate state-building mechanism but is too narrow in scope to provide a complete answer. The steps mandated in that process bear upon the problem but fall short on at least two grounds. First, they do not specify a comprehensive *plan* for implementation—a list of the things that must be done and in what order. Second, since the effort is a parochial one within the U.S. government, it is unlikely to work out in detail the procedures that will be needed in a real-world, multilateral effort such as that described in Chapter 4.

Both shortcomings can be addressed. Devising a comprehensive, general plan that can be modified to suit a state-building program in any given situation has to be a major priority if state building is to be an important enterprise. Devising such a plan will be controversial, time consuming, intellectually abstract and contentious (since there is so little experience), and hard. It must also be highly creative. These are not conditions in which government bureaucracies tend to thrive. They *are* conditions that the academic marketplace deals with all the time. Commissioning an international team of top-notch, nongovernmental experts from academia, business, communications, health, public safety, agriculture, and so forth could be useful. This is not a particularly radical idea; numerous academics enter and leave government service, and the "think tanks" are stocked with academics. My suggestion is to harness this resource more systematically to policy purposes.

Procedurally, the process of preparing for peacekeeping operations needs to move beyond the purview of the U.S. government interagency process to include the various groups identified in Chapter 4. Some coordination already occurs at the small-group level (panels at conferences and the like), but it is probably not enough.

What we need is something like *peace games,* analogous to the more familiar war games. The idea would be to bring together under some auspices representatives from all of the agencies and groups that have responsibility for peace operations and put them through a series of realistic simulations and exercises. The purpose would be two-fold. First, it would provide an opportunity to participate in a process in the abstract, where real lives are unaffected, from which to learn what to do and what not to do. More realistic procedures should be the result. Second, it would allow interaction among groups and individuals who otherwise would probably have little interaction. At the bureaucratic level, the result might be a better understanding of bureaucratic cultures, priorities, work patterns, and the like (which are the results of the interagency process within the U.S. government). At the interpersonal level, some people who might be called upon to work together in the future might get to know one another. Involving academics in the peace games would benefit faculty, students, and curricula at U.S. and foreign universities, which in turn would promote citizen education and thereby contribute to greater understanding of peacekeeping operations.

Designated and Prepared Forces

Whether regular forces should be trained and predisposed to engage in peace enforcement is a controversial matter within the United States armed forces and especially the U.S. Army, which shares the primary responsibility for such operations with the Marine Corps. Although the Army leadership recognizes that peace enforcement differs from peacekeeping and from combat operations, it holds the semi-official position that any well trained soldier can perform MOOTW (military operations other than war), including the kinds of peace enforcement ongoing in Kosovo.

This is not the appropriate forum for a detailed analysis of this issue, but it is appropriate to raise issues. Clearly, peace enforcement differs from the basically constabulary nature of peacekeeping and the basically combatant nature of peace imposition. It is a hybrid in which the skills of both may have to be exercised and where the balance between the two kinds of activities may shift in individual situations and across time. Moreover, the interaction between peace enforcers and the population on which peace is imposed will always be uncertain and potentially adversarial, and the act of an individual soldier may have broader political ramifications than that soldier may realize at the time. In some ways, peace enforcement may require the kinds of decision-making skills that are more closely associated with the training of special forces; just as the situations that special forces face are idiosyncratic and not capturable through doctrinal training, so too are the problems faced by peace enforcers.

Peace enforcement is thus different. If the U.S. armed forces are to play a major role in peace enforcement in the future, it should be a discernible military operating specialty (MOS), with its own specialized training, procedures, and even career tracks. Moreover, we should devote resources to preparing future peace enforcers within one of the military commands (the U.S. Special Operations Command comes to mind). For that matter, we should be training some soldiers in the art of negotiation.

Conclusion

The U.S. uses of force are not as clear for the future as they were in the past. In those conceptually simpler days, we had real, enduring opponents whose malevolence was well known. We knew, or thought we knew, what those enemies would do if we were not diligent in preparing for the wars that we hoped would not come. In retrospect, the cold war period was a "golden age" for thinking about the uses of U.S. military force. But it was also a unique age and something of an aberration.

Defense planning in the cold war era, the motor of which was the realist paradigm, had as a central reality the Damoclean sword of nuclear war. Occasionally, the paradigm led to warped policy. It contributed to the most divisive military event in U.S. history of the twentieth century: the conflict in Vietnam.

If those were the good old days, we may have reason to be glad they are behind us. Since the end of the cold war, U.S. military forces have been buffeted by the contradictory effects of downsizing and increased deployments in small, nettlesome conflicts in remote corners of the globe. The environment has not always been easy for those in uniform, but the dangers are less than they were before. And this fact supports my argument that we need to take the time to develop insights and plan for future deployments in this changed national security environment.

The tasks before the U.S. armed forces over the next decade or so are going to resemble those of the 1990s much more closely than they will those of the four decades that preceded the 1990s. Ralph Peters, novelist and former U.S. Air Force intelligence officer, describes them with particular force:

> The model of war with well-ordered army pitted against well-ordered army is largely gone. Today's—and tomorrow's—enemies are half-trained killers in uniform, tribesmen, mercenaries, criminals, children with rusty Kalashnikovs, shabby despots, and gory men of faith. The most dangerous enemy will be the warrior who ignores, or does not know, the rules by which our soldiers fight, and has a gun in one hand, a cell phone in the other, and hatred scorching his heart.

Big wars of necessity will always remain a possibility, however remote, but they will not dominate the scene. Rather, small, savage internal wars typical of the 1990s, in which we are tempted to intervene as a matter of choice, are the problems we have standing before us. The world wars, Korea, and Vietnam are our past; the Kosovos of this world are our immediate future.

Bibliography

Bacevich, A. C., et al. *American Military Policy in Small Wars: The Case of El Salvador.* Cambridge, Mass.: Institute for Foreign Policy Analysis, 1989.

Cimbala, Stephen J. "Clinton and U.S. Peacekeeping." In *Clinton and Post-Cold War Defense,* ed. Stephen J. Cimbala, 153–168. Westport: Praeger, 1996.

Freedom House. *The Map of Freedom, 1999.* Washington, D.C.: Freedom House, 1999.

Gurr, Ted Robert. *Minorities at Risk: A Global View of Ethnopolitical Conflicts.* Washington, D.C.: United States Institute of Peace Press, 1993.

Langford, Tonya. "Orchestrating Peace Operations: The PDD-56 Process." *Security Dialogue* 30 (June 1999): 137–149.

Luttwak, Edward N. "Give War a Chance." *Foreign Affairs* 78 (July–August 1999): 36–44.

Mearsheimer, John J. "Why We Will Soon Miss the Cold War." *Atlantic Monthly* 266 (August 1990): 35–50.

Peters, Ralph. "The Future of Warfare." *World Press Review* 46 (August 1999): 38–39 (reprinted from *McLean's,* April 26, 1999).

Pfaff, William. "War for Kosovo Probably Last of its Kind for NATO." *Albuquerque Journal,* July 7, 1999, A10.

Snow, Donald M., and Eugene Brown. *Beyond the Water's Edge: An Introduction to U.S. Foreign Policy.* New York: St. Martin's Press, 1997.

Snow, Donald M., and Dennis M. Drew. *From Lexington to Desert Storm and Beyond: War and Politics in the American Experience.* 2d ed. Armonk: M. E. Sharpe, forthcoming 2001.

Solarz, Stephen, and Michael O'Hanlon. "Humanitarian Intervention: When Is Force Justified?" *Washington Quarterly* 20 (autumn 1997): 3–14.

U.S. Government. *Clinton Administration's Policy on Managing Complex Contingency Operations, Presidential Decision Directive-56.* Washington, D.C.: U.S. Government White Paper, 1997.

———. *Clinton Administration's Policy on Reforming Multilateral Peace Operations, Presidential Decision Directive-25.* Washington, D.C.: The White House, 1994.

Appendixes

Appendix A | Resolution 1244 (1999)

Adopted by the Security Council at its 4011th meeting, on 10 June 1999

The Security Council,

Bearing in mind the purposes and principles of the Charter of the United Nations, and the primary responsibility of the Security Council for the maintenance of international peace and security,

Recalling its resolutions 1160 (1998) of 31 March 1998, 1199 (1998) of 23 September 1998, 1203 (1998) of 24 October 1998 and 1239 (1999) of 14 May 1999,

Regretting that there has not been full compliance with the requirements of these resolutions,

Determined to resolve the grave humanitarian situation in Kosovo, Federal Republic of Yugoslavia, and to provide for the safe and free return of all refugees and displaced persons to their homes,

Condemning all acts of violence against the Kosovo population as well as all terrorist acts by any party,

Recalling the statement made by the Secretary-General on 9 April 1999, expressing concern at the humanitarian tragedy taking place in Kosovo,

Reaffirming the right of all refugees and displaced persons to return to their homes in safety,

Recalling the jurisdiction and the mandate of the International Tribunal for the Former Yugoslavia,

Welcoming the general principles on a political solution to the Kosovo crisis adopted on 6 May 1999 (S/1999/516, annex 1 to this resolution) and welcoming also the acceptance by the Federal Republic of Yugoslavia of the principles set forth in points 1 to 9 of the paper presented in Belgrade on 2 June 1999

(S/1999/649, annex 2 to this resolution), and the Federal Republic of Yugo-slavia's agreement to that paper,

Reaffirming the commitment of all Member States to the sovereignty and ter-ritorial integrity of the Federal Republic of Yugoslavia and the other States of the region, as set out in the Helsinki Final Act and annex 2,

Reaffirming the call in previous resolutions for substantial autonomy and meaningful self-administration for Kosovo,

Determining that the situation in the region continues to constitute a threat to international peace and security,

Determined to ensure the safety and security of international personnel and the implementation by all concerned of their responsibilities under the pre-sent resolution, and *acting* for these purposes under Chapter VII of the Char-ter of the United Nations,

1. *Decides* that a political solution to the Kosovo crisis shall be based on the general principles in annex 1 and as further elaborated in the principles and other required elements in annex 2;

2. *Welcomes* the acceptance by the Federal Republic of Yugoslavia of the principles and other required elements referred to in paragraph 1 above, and *demands* the full cooperation of the Federal Republic of Yugoslavia in their rapid implementation;

3. *Demands* in particular that the Federal Republic of Yugoslavia put an im-mediate and verifiable end to violence and repression in Kosovo, and begin and complete verifiable phased withdrawal from Kosovo of all mil-itary, police and paramilitary forces according to a rapid timetable, with which the deployment of the international security presence in Kosovo will be synchronized;

4. *Confirms* that after the withdrawal an agreed number of Yugoslav and Serb military and police personnel will be permitted to return to Kosovo to perform the functions in accordance with annex 2;

5. *Decides* on the deployment in Kosovo, under United Nations auspices, of international civil and security presences, with appropriate equipment and personnel as required, and welcomes the agreement of the Federal Republic of Yugoslavia to such presences;

6. *Requests* the Secretary-General to appoint, in consultation with the Security Council, a Special Representative to control the implementation of the international civil presence, and *further requests* the Secretary-General to instruct his Special Representative to coordinate closely with the international security presence to ensure that both presences operate towards the same goals and in a mutually supportive manner;

7. *Authorizes* Member States and relevant international organizations to establish the international security presence in Kosovo as set out in point 4 of annex 2 with all necessary means to fulfil its responsibilities under paragraph 9 below;

8. *Affirms* the need for the rapid early deployment of effective international civil and security presences to Kosovo, and *demands* that the parties cooperate fully in their deployment;

9. *Decides* that the responsibilities of the international security presence to be deployed and acting in Kosovo will include:

   (a) Deterring renewed hostilities, maintaining and where necessary enforcing a ceasefire, and ensuring the withdrawal and preventing the return into Kosovo of Federal and Republic military, police and paramilitary forces, except as provided in point 6 of annex 2;

   (b) Demilitarizing the Kosovo Liberation Army (KLA) and other armed Kosovo Albanian groups as required in paragraph 15 below;

   (c) Establishing a secure environment in which refugees and displaced persons can return home in safety, the international civil presence can operate, a transitional administration can be established, and humanitarian aid can be delivered;

   (d) Ensuring public safety and order until the international civil presence can take responsibility for this task;

   (e) Supervising demining until the international civil presence can, as appropriate, take over responsibility for this task;

   (f) Supporting, as appropriate, and coordinating closely with the work of the international civil presence;

   (g) Conducting border monitoring duties as required;

(h) Ensuring the protection and freedom of movement of itself, the international civil presence, and other international organizations;

10. *Authorizes* the Secretary-General, with the assistance of relevant international organizations, to establish an international civil presence in Kosovo in order to provide an interim administration for Kosovo under which the people of Kosovo can enjoy substantial autonomy within the Federal Republic of Yugoslavia, and which will provide transitional administration while establishing and overseeing the development of provisional democratic self-governing institutions to ensure conditions for a peaceful and normal life for all inhabitants of Kosovo;

11. *Decides* that the main responsibilities of the international civil presence will include:

(a) Promoting the establishment, pending a final settlement, of substantial autonomy and self-government in Kosovo, taking full account of annex 2 and of the Rambouillet accords (S/1999/648);

(b) Performing basic civilian administrative functions where and as long as required;

(c) Organizing and overseeing the development of provisional institutions for democratic and autonomous self-government pending a political settlement, including the holding of elections;

(d) Transferring, as these institutions are established, its administrative responsibilities while overseeing and supporting the consolidation of Kosovo's local provisional institutions and other peace-building activities;

(e) Facilitating a political process designed to determine Kosovo's future status, taking into account the Rambouillet accords (S/1999/648);

(f) In a final stage, overseeing the transfer of authority from Kosovo's provisional institutions to institutions established under a political settlement;

(g) Supporting the reconstruction of key infrastructure and other economic reconstruction;

(h) Supporting, in coordination with international humanitarian organizations, humanitarian and disaster relief aid;

(i) Maintaining civil law and order, including establishing local police forces and meanwhile through the deployment of international police personnel to serve in Kosovo;

(j) Protecting and promoting human rights;

(k) Assuring the safe and unimpeded return of all refugees and displaced persons to their homes in Kosovo;

12. *Emphasizes* the need for coordinated humanitarian relief operations, and for the Federal Republic of Yugoslavia to allow unimpeded access to Kosovo by humanitarian aid organizations and to cooperate with such organizations so as to ensure the fast and effective delivery of international aid;

13. *Encourages* all Member States and international organizations to contribute to economic and social reconstruction as well as to the safe return of refugees and displaced persons, and *emphasizes* in this context the importance of convening an international donors' conference, particularly for the purposes set out in paragraph 11 (g) above, at the earliest possible date;

14. *Demands* full cooperation by all concerned, including the international security presence, with the International Tribunal for the Former Yugoslavia;

15. *Demands* that the KLA and other armed Kosovo Albanian groups end immediately all offensive actions and comply with the requirements for demilitarization as laid down by the head of the international security presence in consultation with the Special Representative of the Secretary-General;

16. *Decides* that the prohibitions imposed by paragraph 8 of resolution 1160 (1998) shall not apply to arms and related *matériel* for the use of the international civil and security presences;

17. *Welcomes* the work in hand in the European Union and other international organizations to develop a comprehensive approach to the economic development and stabilization of the region affected by the Kosovo crisis, including the implementation of a Stability Pact for South Eastern Europe with broad international participation in order to further the promotion of democracy, economic prosperity, stability and regional cooperation;

18. *Demands* that all States in the region cooperate fully in the implementation of all aspects of this resolution;

19. *Decides* that the international civil and security presences are established for an initial period of 12 months, to continue thereafter unless the Security Council decides otherwise;

20. *Requests* the Secretary-General to report to the Council at regular intervals on the implementation of this resolution, including reports from the leaderships of the international civil and security presences, the first reports to be submitted within 30 days of the adoption of this resolution;

21. *Decides* to remain actively seized of the matter.

Annex 1

Statement by the Chairman on the conclusion of the meeting of the G-8 Foreign Ministers held at the Petersberg Centre on 6 May 1999

The G-8 Foreign Ministers adopted the following general principles on the political solution to the Kosovo crisis:

- Immediate and verifiable end of violence and repression in Kosovo;

- Withdrawal from Kosovo of military, police and paramilitary forces;

- Deployment in Kosovo of effective international civil and security presences, endorsed and adopted by the United Nations, capable of guaranteeing the achievement of the common objectives;

- Establishment of an interim administration for Kosovo to be decided by the Security Council of the United Nations to ensure conditions for a peaceful and normal life for all inhabitants in Kosovo;

- The safe and free return of all refugees and displaced persons and unimpeded access to Kosovo by humanitarian aid organizations;

- A political process towards the establishment of an interim political framework agreement providing for a substantial self-government for Kosovo, taking full account of the Rambouillet accords and the principles of sovereignty and territorial integrity of the Federal Republic of Yugoslavia and the other countries of the region, and the demilitarization of the KLA;

- Comprehensive approach to the economic development and stabilization of the crisis region.

Annex 2

Agreement should be reached on the following principles to move towards a resolution of the Kosovo crisis:

1. An immediate and verifiable end of violence and repression in Kosovo.

2. Verifiable withdrawal from Kosovo of all military, police and paramilitary forces according to a rapid timetable.

3. Deployment in Kosovo under United Nations auspices of effective international civil and security presences, acting as may be decided under Chapter VII of the Charter, capable of guaranteeing the achievement of common objectives.

4. The international security presence with substantial North Atlantic Treaty Organization participation must be deployed under unified command and control and authorized to establish a safe environment for all people in Kosovo and to facilitate the safe return to their homes of all displaced persons and refugees.

5. Establishment of an interim administration for Kosovo as a part of the international civil presence under which the people of Kosovo can enjoy substantial autonomy within the Federal Republic of Yugoslavia, to be decided by the Security Council of the United Nations. The interim administration to provide transitional administration while establishing and overseeing the development of provisional democratic self-governing institutions to ensure conditions for a peaceful and normal life for all inhabitants in Kosovo.

6. After withdrawal, an agreed number of Yugoslav and Serbian personnel will be permitted to return to perform the following functions:

- Liaison with the international civil mission and the international security presence;

- Marking/clearing minefields;

- Maintaining a presence at Serb patrimonial sites;

- Maintaining a presence at key border crossings.

7. Safe and free return of all refugees and displaced persons under the supervision of the Office of the United Nations High Commissioner for Refugees and unimpeded access to Kosovo by humanitarian aid organizations.

8. A political process towards the establishment of an interim political framework agreement providing for substantial self-government for Kosovo, taking full account of the Rambouillet accords and the principles of sovereignty and territorial integrity of the Federal Republic of Yugoslavia and the other countries of the region, and the demilitarization of UCK. Negotiations between the parties for a settlement should not delay or disrupt the establishment of democratic self-governing institutions.

9. A comprehensive approach to the economic development and stabilization of the crisis region. This will include the implementation of a stability pact for South-Eastern Europe with broad international participation in order to further promotion of democracy, economic prosperity, stability and regional cooperation.

10. Suspension of military activity will require acceptance of the principles set forth above in addition to agreement to other, previously identified, required elements, which are specified in the footnote below.[1] A military-technical agreement will then be rapidly concluded that would, among other things, specify additional modalities, including the roles and functions of Yugoslav/Serb personnel in Kosovo:

Withdrawal

- Procedures for withdrawals, including the phased, detailed schedule and delineation of a buffer area in Serbia beyond which forces will be withdrawn;

Returning personnel

- Equipment associated with returning personnel;
- Terms of reference for their functional responsibilities;
- Timetable for their return;

- Delineation of their geographical areas of operation;

- Rules governing their relationship to the international security presence and the international civil mission.

Notes

1. Other required elements:

   - A rapid and precise timetable for withdrawals, meaning, e.g., seven days to complete withdrawal and air defence weapons withdrawn outside a 25 kilometre mutual safety zone within 48 hours;

   - Return of personnel for the four functions specified above will be under the supervision of the international security presence and will be limited to a small agreed number (hundreds, not thousands);

   - Suspension of military activity will occur after the beginning of verifiable withdrawals;

   - The discussion and achievement of a military-technical agreement shall not extend the previously determined time for completion of withdrawals.

Appendix B | Kosovo Chronology

Time line of events relating to the crisis in Kosovo, 1989–April 2000
(Major milestones are set in bold face.)

EU—European Union
ICTY—International Criminal Tribunal for the Former Yugoslavia
KFOR—Kosovo Force
KLA—Kosovo Liberation Army
NATO—North Atlantic Treaty Organization
OSCE—Organization for Security and Cooperation in Europe
UNHCR—United Nations High Commissioner for Refugees
UNMIK—United Nations Interim Administration Mission in Kosovo

1989

Pressured by Serbian president Slobodan Milošević, the Kosovo Assembly abolishes the province's autonomous status. Legislation is passed that denies ownership and work to Albanian Kosovars. Tens of thousands of ethnic Albanians in Kosovo lose their jobs. Serbia suppresses Albanian cultural institutions in Kosovo.

1990

Serbia dissolves the Kosovo Assembly. In response, ethnic Albanian legislators in the province declare a republic.

1991

A secret referendum is held in which the Republic of Kosovo is created. Only Albania's parliament recognizes the self-declared republic.

1991–1992

The Socialist Federal Republic of Yugoslavia breaks up. Wars break out in the former republics of Slovenia, Croatia, and Bosnia-Herzegovina; Serbs ethnically cleanse and seize control of significant parts of the latter two. In response, the international community imposes sanctions on Yugoslavia. Serbia and Montenegro proclaim the Federal Republic of Yugoslavia. The United States recognizes the independence of the former Yugoslav republics.

In defiance of the Serbian authorities, ethnic Albanians elect writer Ibrahim Rugova as president of the self-proclaimed Republic of Kosovo and set up a provincial assembly. Serbia declares the election to be illegal. The Kosovo Albanians begin nonviolent resistance to the oppressive rule from Belgrade.

Slobodan Milošević is reelected president of Serbia.

1995

Bosnian peace talks conclude at Wright Patterson Air Force Base in Dayton, Ohio. Despite the Dayton Accords, many international sanctions on Yugoslavia remain in place due to Serbian actions in Kosovo.

1996

In response to continued suppression by Belgrade and attacks from the Serbian police, the Kosovo Liberation Army (KLA) begins reprisals, claiming responsibility for a number of bombings and attacks against Serbian police and state officials.

1997

Slobodan Milošević, barred by the constitution from running for a third term as president of Serbia, runs for and wins the presidency of the Federal Republic of Yugoslavia in July. As president of the Federal Republic, he continues to exploit and manipulate Serbian nationalism.

In October, Serbian police crush Albanian Kosovar student demonstrations. The KLA responds with additional attacks against the Serbian police.

1998

MARCH 31: The UN Security Council adopts Resolution 1160, condemning the excessive use of force by Serbian police against civilians in Kosovo; it also establishes an embargo of arms and materiel against the Federal Republic of Yugoslavia.

JULY 6: The U.S. charge d'affaires in Belgrade, Richard Miles, and his Russian counterpart launch the Kosovo Diplomatic Observer Mission, which begins to patrol Kosovo in armored vehicles and to report on freedom of movement and security conditions throughout the region.

SEPTEMBER 24: NATO takes the first formal steps toward military intervention in Kosovo, approving two contingency plans—one for air strikes and the second for monitoring and maintaining a cease-fire agreement if one is reached.

SEPTEMBER 29: The UN high commissioner for refugees (UNHCR) announces that as many as 200,000 civilians have been displaced within Kosovo since fighting began in February. Sixty thousand of them are now living in the open without shelter. The situation threatens to worsen with the onset of winter.

NOVEMBER: The Kosovo Verification Mission, headed by an American, Ambassador William Walker, begins to arrive and function. Its mission quickly expands beyond verification to trying to head off armed conflict through negotiations and mediation.

1999

JANUARY 30: The North Atlantic Council agrees that Secretary General Javier Solana may authorize air strikes against targets on Yugoslav territory.

FEBRUARY 6: Talks begin in Château Rambouillet, in France, under the auspices of the Contact Group (France, Germany, Great Britain, Italy, Russia, and the United States).

MARCH 15: Talks resume at the Kleber Center in Paris. The ethnic Albanian delegation signs the interim agreement proposed at the February meetings in Rambouillet. President Clinton encourages President Milošević to agree to the terms as well in order to avoid further conflict and bloodshed.

MARCH 18: The Paris peace talks are suspended, as the Serbian delegation refuses to budge and, in fact, walks back from its earlier positions at Rambouillet. In the meantime, one-third of Yugoslavia's armed forces have massed in and around Kosovo.

MARCH 19: Kosovo Verification Mission withdraws.

MARCH 20: Yugoslav armed units launch an offensive, driving thousands of ethnic Albanians out of their homes and villages, summarily executing some, displacing many others, and setting fire to many houses.

MARCH 24: NATO air strikes begin. Tens of thousands of Kosovars have already fled the heavy fighting throughout Kosovo.

MARCH 26–30: The North Atlantic Council decides to escalate the air campaign to phase II and then phase II-plus.

APRIL 1: Three U.S. soldiers are captured near the Macedonia-Yugoslav border and shown, bruised, on Serb television.

APRIL 3: NATO missiles strike central Belgrade for the first time and destroy the Yugoslav and Serbian interior ministries.

APRIL 12: NATO hits a passenger train south of Belgrade, killing thirty, according to the Yugoslav government. NATO apologizes for the accident.

APRIL 14: NATO air strikes hit a Kosovar civilian convoy in Kosovo. Yugoslavia reports sixty-four dead.

APRIL 18: UN High Commissioner for Refugees Sadako Ogata estimates that well over half a million Kosovars have fled to other countries since the bombing started.

APRIL 20: NATO secretary general Javier Solana directs update of ground force plans.

APRIL 22: NATO announces intensification of air campaign.

APRIL 23: NATO destroys the Serbian state television building in central Belgrade, killing at least ten people.

MAY 1: Reverend Jesse Jackson secures the release of the captured U.S. servicemen following a three-hour meeting with President Milošević.

MAY 5: Two U.S. Army pilots are killed when their Apache helicopter crashes on a training mission in Albania, the first allied deaths in the NATO actions against Yugoslavia.

MAY 7: **NATO planes accidentally bomb the Chinese embassy in Belgrade, killing three and wounding twenty.**

MAY 14: About eighty-seven Kosovar Albanians are killed in the village of Korisa by NATO bombing. NATO says that it hit a military target and suggests that Serbian troops were using civilians as human shields.

MAY 22: NATO bombs army barracks at Kosare, unaware it was captured by Kosovo Liberation Army guerrillas a month earlier.

MAY 27: **President Milošević and four other Serbian leaders are indicted by the UN war crimes tribunal for crimes against humanity.**

JUNE 3: Yugoslavia accepts terms brought to Belgrade by European Union envoy and Finnish president Martti Ahtisaari and Russian envoy Viktor Chernomyrdin. NATO announces that its raids have killed more than 5,000 members of Yugoslav security forces and wounded more than 10,000.

JUNE 7: NATO and Yugoslav commanders fail to agree to terms of pullout from Kosovo and suspend talks. NATO intensifies bombing. A B-52 bomber catches two Yugoslav army battalions in the open near the Kosovo-Albanian border, possibly killing many hundreds of them.

JUNE 9: Senior NATO and Yugoslav officers sign a military technical agreement.

JUNE 10: **After receiving definite evidence that Serbian forces are withdrawing from northern Kosovo, NATO secretary general Solana suspends NATO air strikes.** UN Security Council adopts Resolution 1244 on Kosovo, entrusting to the secretary general establishment of an international civilian administration in Kosovo, under which the people of Kosovo can enjoy substantial autonomy. The resolution sets up an unprecedented UN operation —the UN Interim Administration Mission in Kosovo (UNMIK)—encompassing the activities of three non-UN organizations under the UN's overall jurisdiction. It consists of four substantive components, or pillars: interim civil administration (UN-led), humanitarian affairs (UNHCR-led), reconstruction (EU-led), and institution building (OSCE-led). A NATO-led force (KFOR) is to provide an international security presence.

June 12: Russian troops enter Pristina three and one-half hours before NATO troops enter Kosovo and take up position at the airport.

June 18: Secretary of State Madeleine Albright and Defense Secretary William S. Cohen reach agreement with their Russian counterparts in Helsinki about Russian participation in Kosovo. They decide that Russia will not have a separate sector in Kosovo, that unity of command of the international security force will be preserved, that Kosovo will not be partitioned, that Russian troops will serve in U.S., French, and German sectors, and that all KFOR forces will operate under common rules of engagement.

June 20: **In accordance with the June 9 military technical agreement, Serbian forces completely withdraw from Kosovo, leading NATO secretary general Solana to officially end NATO's bombing campaign in Yugoslavia.**

July 18: Two U.S. KFOR soldiers die in an accident near Domorovce when their armored personnel carrier overturns.

July 28: Donors pledge $2.082 billion in aid for Kosovo at the Donor's Conference in Brussels. The U.S. pledges $556 million in additional humanitarian aid and urgent nonhumanitarian aid for Kosovo, from the budget supplemental passed by Congress and signed by the president on May 21, 1999. The $500 million promised by the United States is going toward food aid, health care, clean water, emergency shelter, winterization supplies, landmine clearance, and agricultural assistance. All U.S. pledges are subject to a clear assessment of overall needs, congressional concurrence, and confirmation that U.S. aid will form one part of a robust international effort.

July 30: World leaders meet in Sarajevo at the Stability Pact Summit. President Clinton announces during the summit that he will work with Congress to provide $10 million this year and more over the next two years to strengthen the independent media, nongovernmental organizations, independent trade unions, and the democratic opposition in Serbia.

August 4: The UNHCR estimates that nearly 90 percent of the more than 850,000 ethnic Albanians who fled Kosovo during the war have returned to the Serbian province.

November 10: ICTY prosecutor Carla del Ponte informs the Security Council that investigators have exhumed 2,108 bodies from gravesites in Kosovo. She warns that this figure does not necessarily reflect the total number of victims. Also, of 529 gravesites identified, only 195 have been examined to date.

NOVEMBER 17: Donors at the Second Donors Conference for Kosovo, meeting in Brussels, pledge over $1 billion to start the first phase of the reconstruction of Kosovo, which covers recovery needs until December 2000.

2000

FEBRUARY 13: Violence breaks out in Mitrovica, during which at least one Kosovar is killed and two French peacekeepers are wounded by snipers.

MARCH 2: **A Russian KFOR soldier dies of gunshot wounds he sustained on February 29. He is the first peacekeeper to die as a result of a deliberate attack by the local people.**

MARCH 6: Briefing a private meeting of the Security Council, UNMIK head Bernard Kouchner of France says the United Nations work in Kosovo lacks clear political objectives and sufficient resources.

Appendix C | Select UN and NATO
Peacekeeping Deployments

Deployments in the Balkans

Bosnia-Herzegovina

United Nations Protection Force (UNPROFOR)
March 1992 through December 24, 1995

Operation Joint Endeavor (also known as the Implementation Force, or IFOR)
December 20, 1995, through December 20, 1996

Operation Joint Guard (also known as the Stabilization Force, or SFOR)
December 21, 1996, through June 19, 1998

Operation Joint Forge (continuation of SFOR)
June 20, 1998–

Macedonia

United Nations Preventive Deployment to the Former Yugoslav Republic of Macedonia (UNPREDEP)
March 1995 through February 1999

Kosovo

United Nations Interim Administration Mission in Kosovo (UNMIK)
June 1999–

Kosovo Force (KFOR)
Entered Kosovo June 12, 1999

Other Deployments

East Timor

United Nations Mission in East Timor (UNAMET)
June 11, 1999 through October 25, 1999

United Nations Transitional Administration in East Timor (UNTAET)
October 25, 1999–

International Force in East Timor (INTERFET)
September 1999 through February 28, 2000

Haiti

United Nations Mission in Haiti (UNMIH)
September 1993 through June 1996

United Nations Support Mission in Haiti (UNSMIH)
July 1996 through July 1997

United Nations Transition Mission in Haiti (UNTMIH)
August through November 1997

United Nations Civilian Police Mission in Haiti (MIPONUH)
December 1997 through March 2000

Somalia

United Nations Operation in Somalia I (UNOSOM I)
April 1992 through March 1993

United Nations Operation in Somalia II (UNOSOM II)
March 1993 through March 1995

INDEX

Index